SKETCHES FROM MEMORY

A RUGBY MEMOIR

STUART BARNES

POLARIS
PUBLISHING

First published in 2019 by

POLARIS PUBLISHING LTD
c/o Turcan Connell
Princes Exchange
1 Earl Grey Street
Edinburgh
EH3 9EE

Distributed by

ARENA SPORT
An imprint of Birlinn Limited

www.polarispublishing.com
www.arenasportbooks.co.uk

British Library Cataloguing-in-Publication Data
A catalogue record for this book is available on request from the British Library.

Designed and typeset by Polaris Publishing, Edinburgh

Printed in Great Britain by Clays ltd, Elcograf S.p.A.

CONTENTS

ACKNOWLEDGEMENTS	v
A MEANDERING MADNESS	vi
ALL BLACKS	1
BASSALEG SCHOOL	14
CHILCOTT	26
DROP GOALS	38
ENGLAND	50
THE FRENCH	63
GUSCOTT	75
HALF BACKS	85
INJURIES	96
JUDAS	107
KICKING	118
LIONS	128
MUNSTER	140
NEWSPAPERS	152
OXFORD UNIVERSITY	163
PROFESSIONALISM	173
QUITTENTON	185
THE RECREATION GROUND, BATH	197
SCOTLAND, 1993	209
TELEVISION	221
UP AND UNDER	232
VILLAINS	243
WORLD CUP, 1995	254
XAVIER GARBAJOSA	266
DUKE OF YORK	275
ZIRAKASHVILI	286

To Florică Murariu (1955–1989)
and rugby's unremembered heroes

ACKNOWLEDGEMENTS

THIS BOOK doesn't happen without the presence of my wife, Lesley. Apart from the earliest chapters, she has shared a sometimes selfish life of a sportsman living in constant fear of failure – the third person in the marriage, if you like, if not for the presence of my wonderful step kids, Kate and Matthew. They and their four children bring me and the world great joy. Also a brief dedication to John, my late father, who I proudly carried, like Anchises, through a few decades of rugby.

On the rugby front, Jack Rowell towers above all, a mentor, a mastermind, a man of great intellect and no little wickedness. To all my generation of Bath players – love and loyalty is about time not location.

Finally to David Luxton, my agent, who believed in this book when I was despairing of a publisher. That publisher was Peter Burns. Any man who keeps in a jet-lagged Lions section which mulls over dark, deranged deeds in Washington – written while in Whangarei – and the nature of a parallel world, will do for me. Oh, and Roger Jones for naming a beer after me, no greater honour and all that. Thank you.

A MEANDERING MADNESS

THERE'S A labyrinth in Sydney's Centennial Park, at the northern end of Willow Pond. Quiet, calm, a good place for introspection – the perfect place for a break after the hyperbole of the 2017 Lions tour of New Zealand. Or for plotting a few chapters of a book. One without a beginning or end. Or certainly any sense of chronology.

There's only one way of entering the labyrinth, only one path towards the centre. It takes you in unexpected directions. Away from where your senses insist. But keep going. It is a continuous path. You will get to the designated end of the journey. Eventually. As an analogy for what I have been writing . . . well, it is absolutely hopeless. A labyrinth may be brilliant for training the right side of the brain but it has no relevance to the reality of life. Or so it seems to me in the writing of this book. Or rugby. If there is one thing I have learned in an obsessive rugby life that spans from either 1972 or 1973, who knows, to 2019, it is that nothing is inevitable. Not in the way the labyrinthine pathway is. Just keeping on isn't sufficient. You have to change, chameleon-like, in the face of the evolving challenges encountered. A labyrinth fools you in its very simplicity. A lot of sports books are similar. Labyrinthine. They start at the beginning of the subject's life, as he picks his one and seemingly only pathway towards fame and the big fat book deal and, if he's famous enough, a few minutes on the couch with Graham Norton. So we follow the hero through his or her sporting life – the facts and the fights, making mistakes but rarely tilting at windmills; briefly deviating off track but not too far, or for too long. There will be a middle and an end that neatly ties the tale, signifying . . . not a great deal, for all the sound and fury found within. Facts and figures help find the way through the life, the labyrinth. You will make it to the end and possibly find the feeling hollow. Something is missing.

That something is the fragmentation which is a person's imagination. An imagination which shapes our inner existence. Yes, we are all born, we live, we die. But what makes for the interesting life are the fragments that flood our memories in no particular order. In the deep of the night, who amongst us thinks their life through chronologically? Our life, all life, is random. Unordered. Quixotic. The story with a start, a middle and end is no more than a skeletal framework. There is more truth to be found in the meandering madness of the maze.

This book is more maze than labyrinth. There is a page one and a final page but there's no chronology. Dates. Statistics. Facts. Truths. Not an abundance of these traditional tools of the trade. Doubt, not certainty, resides here. From the first page onwards, this is a book of feelings, not a factual journey. If there is a bookish chronology in the opening few chapters it stems from nothing but the purest coincidence. The book's design, as we may loosely call it, is that of an alphabetical soup. The first chapter and the second do kick off with my rugby beginnings but only because the All Blacks and 'Baize-leg' school start the alphabet. Thereafter time is inconsequential. As is order. This is an anarchic book. There is recognition that there are multiple ways to live a life and multiple personalities crop up; no single path is set to take you where you want to be. These pages have their share of false starts, dead ends, traps – too many of my own making. In a labyrinth it is impossible to get lost. In a maze it is pretty damned hard not to. The same applies to rugby union. From the breakaway of the Northern Union in the nineteenth century to the professionalisation of union a hundred years or so later, rugby has made its muddled way through the ages. To analyse a sport from its inception onwards is to kill it with the false gods of fact. Rugby is a rugged experience, not a fact.

Facts must make way for memory. But memory, to paraphrase Colm Toibin, 'lives in a shadowy ambiguous place . . . comforted by soft eroding edges . . . that is enough for now'. Yes, memory can comfort or crush you. Love it, loathe it. Don't trust it. Memory plays games with us. Here, it has been let off the leash. Allowed to wander where it will. Snapping and snarling, swerving as if playing the sevens of my distant youth. It smiles too. I don't pretend to know whether these memories are 'right' or 'wrong', don't pretend to know whether such definitive terms have any place on this planet. I just let this pack of memories trample unstoppably through my mind and saw where they took me. The answer's all over. Bruised and battered in places, grinning at the good old days in others. I'm still not sure whether I am searching for a way in or out of this maze.

Men and monsters, friends and enemies, referees and much else rumbustious are bundled into this alphabetic soup which I hope will leave you with a warm, spicy, lingering taste. From Kiwi greats to a squat Georgian prop who made his name in the heart of the Auvergne, here is my A-Z of rugby union. I will wander and wonder with you, ever content to be a tiny, often puzzled part of this ever-changing landscape. I am delighted for you to join me. It begins back in the 1970s, in Cardiff and with the All Blacks . . .

ALL BLACKS

THE ALL Blacks are in town, in the capital city, Cardiff. The Principality pitting its finest against New Zealand. All of Wales waiting, waiting, waiting for the miracle to come. At the time of writing they still are. There's a cold wind blowing through the back of my memory, coming off the Taff. I am transported back in time to 1973, to an afternoon of indelible stamps. The first time I ever saw the All Blacks. A midweek match, a half day off school. A Tuesday . . . perhaps? I am not certain of that. There was much more to the day than escaping the misery of metalwork. No Vulcan was I. I enjoyed my comprehensive education, loved games lessons, English, books. A bit of blood and gore with the Tudors; I had more of a way with words than numbers. But there wasn't a potential Einstein in Bassaleg Comprehensive who would opt for double maths or physics over an opportunity to purchase a Wales versus New Zealand programme. Proof that 'I was there'. Max Boyce and his giant leak. This is Wales in the 1970s. The mines are yet to be closed, the steel is still being forged by future Welsh forwards in Port

Talbot. Wales is alive. Never more so than when the All Blacks cross the Severn Bridge.

I stand on tiptoes and see them steam out of the old National Stadium changing room. The Welsh team, first to emerge from the tunnel, are waiting, forwards snorting fire, lots of huge hair and headbands. Eager, ever-desperate for the glory of beating 'The Blacks' for the first time since 1954. An impossible distance in time to one hungry for a taste of his teens. Wales, the great power of the Old World with Gareth and Gerald and JPR – doctor death with his sideburns and shoulder charges a shuddering speciality. Warrior poets, that's what these long-haired Celtic demigods were: poets. But poetry is superfluous, frilly nonsense to the uncomplicated prose of the men from near the Antarctic, who have come north from the bottom of the world.

The All Black captain was Ian Kirkpatrick. A big man, seventies sideburns, a flanker. He ran hard, ran straight, through the Welsh defence. A try under the posts. The only try in a game New Zealand won 12–3. I carry the memory with me through the years, from 1973 to this time of writing. Yet another witness to Welsh woe while less fortunate friends pondered algebraic formulations. But I was privileged, a schoolboy rugby star who could not wait to get on that bus. I was the English infiltrator from Essex, my dad having followed work deep into the valleys of Gwent to become a sales manager who sold cardboard packaging for a company called Thames Case, part of Unilever – long gone now.

I was the contrary kid, even then, refusing the easy option to weave into the Welsh horde, yet simultaneously incapable of cheering on the countrymen of my blood – except against Wales, of course. I hated having to express my support for ugly old England with their lugubrious approach, which was clod-hopping compared to those circles Wales ran around most teams in the seventies. England's plodding pack, their servile half backs under orders to kick in order to placate the ponderous ogres who lumbered half-wittedly from one lineout to the next. Whereas Wales flashed around the field, romantic, slashing, cavaliers. But they were Wales and I was born in Thurrock, not Port Talbot. Luck of the dice. I sought a team to support, to shout about and here they were . . . the All Blacks. Rugby's fallen angels. So much more interesting than God and his gang of do-gooders. These sinewy farmers who metamorphosed from God-fearing farming men to feckless thugs the moment they pulled on that dark and delicious black jersey. Deepest black except for the silver fern over the heart. It was love at first sight.

I haven't the faintest idea where to find my Bath, England or Lions shirts, but my All Black number ten shirt? It is folded in a decaying kit bag, not on display, but I find it in the proverbial flash. The one Wayne Smith – who would go on to become one of the world's leading coaches – wore against England in 1985. When I played the All Blacks. Black against White. Good versus Bad (as far as the rugby went). Just playing against them was something back then. We didn't have the assistance of sports psychologists getting into the English ego, convincing us we could cut through the black. The very thought of beating New Zealand in their home land was no more than a pre-match meeting pretence.

Sixty years have been and gone since Wales last won against the men in black. It wasn't twenty years way back then, when I was first blinded by the black of New Zealand. And that seemed an eternity to a rugby nation which made a mythology of its own rugby men. Those were days when the perfect black wasn't tarnished with the names of sponsors. The All Blacks wouldn't sell their soul to Mammon. Not then. Damned if they had souls. These were rugby's dissolute days. There was only tenuous television coverage, few cameras, even fewer replays . . . turkey shoots for the thugs. The allure of aluminium-studded evil attached to these men in black so seductive, decades before they rebranded their game for the glittery age of entertainment.

The occasion is ingrained in my mind. The match passed in a moment. Other than Ian Kirkpatrick scoring between the posts all I recall is a splash of urine bouncing off the terrace onto the tailored calves of my grey school trousers. In the schoolboy enclosure too. The corner of the south stand. The Taff End, open to the elements. An afternoon when it literally pissed down on me. No man forgets the first time he is pissed upon. But could he make it up . . . fantasise all of it – not simply the splash and hissing steam of some drunkard's urine? The idea is to write this book with the aid of nothing but memories. My inner Virgil to guide me through the yellowing and treacherous years. Yet here we are in the first stage of the journey and I revert to journalistic type. Check my facts. Facts of which I am sure. A little like checking the back door at night when you know you have locked it. Just in case . . . I can guarantee the game took place in 1973, confident the scorer was Kirkpatrick. Would have one of those excitable Cheltenham Festival-sized punts to which I am occasionally prone on the scoreline, 12–3. It would only take a few seconds. Nothing wrong with due diligence. 'No one need know.'

. . . The horror, the horror.

I have been living in the wrong year. For over forty years. Wrong year, wrong scorer, wrong scoreline. It wasn't 12–3 to New Zealand. It was 19–16. The skipper didn't score, Keith Murdoch did. The same man involved in an 'incident' with a Cardiff bouncer the night of the game. One day he was celebrating a rare Test try, the next he was on his way home, disgraced. Didn't he jump off his New Zealand-bound plane in Australia? Went walkabout. Many years later I saw a play about Keith Murdoch. In New Zealand, where else? There was me confusing the All Blacks' upright skipper with one of their more sulphurous sorts. Forty fucking years. Murdoch died in Australia while my agent was searching for a publisher. 2018, the year of fact expulsion, barging into the narrative.

The facts fell away, as unreliable as Falstaff's troop. The match took place in 1972, not '73. So much for the school trip, the half day, the wonderful escape from metalwork. Was I even there, hearing those Welsh hosannas of hope sung in a way in which only working men bursting with eight pints of Brains Bitter can harmonise? I was ten, attending a prep school. Making a name for myself in the egg and spoon races. First prize was not a spot in the schoolboy enclosure. Yet still I can close my eyes and see the All Blacks emerge through the murky mists of time. I hear the Welsh national anthem belted out in all its Celtic passion, can smell the piss on those pressed grey trousers. What I initially wrote remains real – for me – whatever the facts. It isn't just Donald Trump and his alternative facts. Facts and the imagination inextricably opposed, facts hacking away at the poetry that is an elemental part of rugby union. As any reader of autobiography is aware, there are various versions of fact. Here are some more of mine, based in black, maybe disguised as memory, maybe not.*

It is 1978. Cardiff, again. No doubt. As Max Boyce, Wales' rugby bard, once said, 'I was there'. There's nothing alternative about this memory. Wales lose, again, to their black nemesis. In this instance the margin is an agonising one point. 12–13. The

---

* As I sit in my office on a crisp October morning, the book is with my publisher; I am reading an exchange on Twitter: whether Wales versus Scotland played outside the 2018 international window deserves to be a 'full' international. Peter Jackson, once of the *Daily Mail*, is regaling former Welsh international, Tom Shanklin, with the stunning fact that in 1974 Wales played the All Blacks, midweek, a Welsh XV. No caps awarded. New Zealand won 12–3. Maybe their skipper scored. I can barely believe what I am reading. The Cheltenham bet would have paid off. I WAS right. But a Welsh win, technically, would not have broken the spell. No caps, just clarity where there was complete confusion. It was all in the term, 'XV'. Once again I smell the piss on my schoolboy trousers and I see those Ian Kirkpatrick sideburns. My mind is not lost to me, but it has meandered in many strange directions as I groped my way through these back pages, sketching my memories.

black angels dive and dip to an all-time low. Sitting on some splintered wooden seat next to my father, tensed among chapel-goers disguised as drinkers. The desperate pray and pour. It is a crumbling section of the now rearranged national stadium. Far from the best seats in the house but it's here it all happens – fifty yards at most from where I sit on the edge of my seat. Wales are leading, the clock ticks towards the final whistle. The lifting of the Kiwi curse, the breaking of the black spell . . . 'WAY-ELS, WAY-ELS, WAY-ELS'. Then the strangest thing. Andy Haden, a second-row forward Hurricane Katrina would not have budged, catapults out of what will be the last lineout. To call it ham acting would have been an insult to pigs. No one saw any Welsh arm shove Haden. There was no illegal Welsh arm. But there was a referee. An alternative fact before we knew such things existed. Roger Quittenton, the referee, blew the whistle and raised the arm to signal a penalty for New Zealand. A kick to win, to kill a national dream. Brian McKechnie, international cricketer, average All Black, steps forward and boots the ball through the posts. A dagger into 50,000 or so hearts. Silently, I cheer. One of the many small treacheries I have fleetingly regretted with age. There are few, if any, bounds to what an All Black would and will do to win. I met McKechnie in the Langham Hotel, Auckland, two nights before the first Test of the 2017 Lions tour. I told him about the Englishman who silently willed the kick over. Good things come to those who wait. Brian was the typical plain-spoken honest Kiwi guy. As for Hades Haden, in the forty or so years since his controversial display of diving, he has often been asked about that moment. Never have I even heard the rumour of remorse.

From the pantomime villain to arguably the most revered of All Blacks, Richie McCaw. The twice World Cup-winning captain didn't so much break the laws of rugby union as bend them to his implacable will. None had such an encyclopaedic understanding of the game's laws or such an assertive control over referees. He was an All Black when many future international referees were rising through the ranks. They were awed to be on the same field as the great man, the master of manipulation – it could be argued, with the tongue not so firmly in the cheek, that he has effectively – *extremely* effectively – refereed more Test matches than any official. In one of the colossal rugby careers he represented New Zealand on 148 occasions. He was sin-binned three times. This represents the most remarkable statistic in the history of the game. A red-faced embarrassment for referees, an irritation to opposition, hilarious to the point of surreal for those with both eyes opened wide. I sat in the press box at Wembley Stadium when he was sin-binned against Argentina. A pool match in the 2015 World Cup. Argentina were playing at pace. The All Blacks were rattled. A quick tap penalty from the Pumas, chaos in the black ranks. The All Blacks skipper is prostrate on the turf, so rapid is the Argentine tempo. Out flashes the captain's foot, as cynical and instinctive an act as is imaginable. But that's not how Richie saw it. 'A dumb mistake,' said he. From some callow kid, maybe, from the captain of the All Blacks . . . how dumb did you think we were, Richie? This guy is one of the best open sides of them all. Open sides understand when and when not to cheat, like no other position. He didn't dither in the mere mortal world of dumb mistakes. He always knew what he was doing. Always in control. Always with blood cold as the Antarctic that thrashes around not so far from his home region of Canterbury on the South Island. Always knew the temperature of a match. He took the match thermometer onto the pitch with him.

In New Zealand any criticism of McCaw is regarded as fiction – make that magic realism. An unjust assertion, an act of something found halfway between jealousy and heresy. But I'll stand by my opinion. So precise was McCaw's timing at the breakdown, referees found it impossible to work out the difference between the legality and illegality of his entrance, the real thing and a fake. Aura usually swayed the decision the flanker's way. He symbolised the

All Blacks – no rugby nation escapes the attention of referees like New Zealand. In the 2017 Lions series, Romain Poite's mistaken last-minute decision to reverse the full penalty against the visitors in the third Test, downgrading it to an All Black scrum and saving the Lions, was the stunning exception to the rule. The All Blacks play the most positive rugby on the planet and as a reward they tend to receive the benefit of the doubt from the whistle-blowers of world rugby. Should the world north of North Island resent the likes of McCaw? Not at all. You do what you can. Push the laws as far and, if possible, a little further. Don't take seriously the ex-international television pundit when he shakes his head in sorrow and criticises a team for cynicism. He's either employed to play the part of the one-eyed patriot or he's another of the many members of rugby's battered fraternity whose mashed up memory has a habit of deceiving him . . . the All Blacks can cheat until the cows come home. It's not their problem.

Fast-forward seven years from Wales' terminal encounter with Hades Haden and I am out of the stands and on the field, playing for England against the All Blacks. We were touring New Zealand. We were no more than an average side, but I was playing some of my best rugby in an England shirt. Brian Ashton, who would play such an influential role as Bath's attack guru, not to mention leading England to a World Cup final in 2007, was a sympathetic backs coach. He brought out the best in me. Brian's lateral thinking was a challenge. Not one of the more common English rugby traits. Assured of the fly half spot, I was relaxed, revelling in one of my very few spells within an England set up. Had I been able to kick through the mud in Christchurch as effectively as the All Blacks' Kieran Crowley had, we would have won the first Test. Was it the sticky underfoot conditions or the inconceivable notion of beating the All Blacks that made the boots claggy with cack? In an England shirt we were not used to winning. Not expected to win. Not mentally ready to win.

The native press pummelled their boys. The disgrace of even entertaining the notion of defeat at the hands of England. Some of us read the press, saw the bait, knew New Zealand would take it. We went to bed on the Friday night ahead of the second Test preparing for war, not rugby. To stick with the martial metaphor, we expected the All Blacks to come out firing in Wellington. We read that one wrong. It was England who scored the early try in the corner, converted by yours truly. No mud on the far touchline, oh I was pleased. The next time we ventured into the opposing twenty-two, a dropped goal – against the All Blacks . . . oh you false gods! New Zealand reacted unfavourably to the useless English having the temerity to take a 9–0 lead in their capital city. The inevitable fight broke out. Fourteen of them, thirteen of us. I never was much of a fighter. I could pin a man to the ground, was not averse to aiming a sly boot. In short, the average antics of a craven fly half in the days before corner to corner camera coverage. But what transpired, as the brawl escalated, has to register as the most idiotic few seconds of my rugby-playing career. Maybe my life and, like most men in their fifties, I have run up my fair share of stupid acts. There was one man it made sense to avoid: Mark 'Cowboy' Shaw. He was a legend then, still is, but not for the quality of his rugby. The best part of a foot taller than me, ranging, lean muscle, that glint in the eye, the 'get the hell away from' type of guy. But there I went, leaping salmon-like and unloading the best rabbit punch in my little locker. I caught him flush on the neck. From behind. While he was getting stuck into our unfriendly bobby, PC Wade Dooley. It was, at best, a gnat sting, an insult to his pride. Placing Big Wade on pause, he slowly creaked his barrel of a neck around to seek out the source of the irritation. He craned in my general direction, eyes not yet scanning downwards, as I, frozen in fear, went tumbling to the turf, knocked down by Steve Pokere, the All Black centre. A man of God, the fifteenth All Black to finally enter the fray, a player of delicate skill and feeling for his fellow man who had been shaking his head along with England's waspish pacifists until he saw my act of madness and the danger into which I had fallen. Or jumped. Trapped beneath Pokere, he punches the dirt. No hint of contact. American wrestling style. More fake! Still, I get one good punch off. He stares in sadness at me and my sheer stupidity. 'Whatcha doing, mate? Just stay there, I'm trying to hide you from the Cowboy. You're safe here until the fight is over.' I didn't move. Took a breather. Survived to tell the tale. In the post-match function, I tried to buy Steve a beer but Pokere, a man of the cloth, was averse to alcohol. As for the game and its outcome, we lost 42–15. Other than the scoreline it couldn't have ended any better. In my many years as a player, journalist and broadcaster it has come to my attention that it doesn't do to irritate an All Black.

Twenty years later, we are once more in Wellington at the new ground, the Westpac Trust Stadium. Athletic Park has been replaced by what locals know as the Cake Tin. You get the general shape of the stadium. Its stands are too far from the action. It lacks the atmosphere of Athletic Park, where the Millard Stand swayed with the breezes that blew off the Cook Strait. It's not one of the better places to watch or broadcast a game of rugby. Architecturally average, undeserving of the grandeur about to unfold. I'm miles from the touchline, tucked in the stands, Sky Sports microphone in hand, expecting the worst for the Lions. It's the middle of three Tests in the 2005 series.

Clive Woodward and Alastair Campbell came up with a ridiculous notion: that the best way to beat the All Blacks was to wind them up. Campbell didn't have a clue. Clive should have known better. Before the cold wind and rain of the first Test in Christchurch the Lions concocted a half-cocked plan to 'challenge' the haka by throwing a leaf or piece of grass in the general direction of the dancing Kiwis. As a piece of incoherent lunacy it wasn't quite up to the dodgy dossier standards at which Campbell excelled. But it too resulted in failure. Thank God this was only sport. The Lions were hammered in that first Test. Brian O'Driscoll, the superstar and tour captain, was spear-tackled out of the tour. Nobody has since thrown grass in the face of pre-haka All Blacks. But the media magicians weren't finished. The offending tackle was used to stir the righteous indignation of the British and Irish press. How many times did the massed media ranks see the guilty tackle? Slowed dramatically down, adding to the effect, to point out that this unpleasant epidemic of violent play had been spreading across the southern hemisphere for a few years was to go unheard. It still is. Grudges die hard. The All Blacks were bad. The Lions were the good guys. Black and white bullshit. But that was the line. What New Zealand actually were, was irritated. What the Lions management were, was misguided.

There was to be no punch-up, no posturing in the Cake Tin. Merely the most measured hit job in Lions history. Dan Carter used his boot, brain and body to beat them. Almost on his own. It was one of the soaring rugby performances of my lifetime. Poor old Jonny Wilkinson had been struggling with injury and he was left for dead that night. Carter shrugged him off en route to a splendid solo score. He would go on to seal his status as the twenty-first century's greatest. If Barry John had been christened the King by the New Zealand, British and Irish travelling press in 1971, Carter was elevated to an Imperial throne. The King was finally surpassed. Carter's international career culminated in a profoundly intelligent performance in the 2015 World Cup final. In the land of the Wilkinson drop goal, Twickenham, this running fly half stroked over a drop kick from forty metres out which ended any hint of Australian resistance. He went into the World Cup injured and out of form. On current form New Zealand's third-best fly half. But class is permanent. He finished the competition as the world's greatest player.

This was the All Blacks' third World Cup triumph. Their first outside their own country. Detractors were left without the semblance of a rational argument against All Black rugby hegemony. The traditional giants of the game had embraced professionalism and come through the experience with a new outlook and the old supremacy. The chorus who called them chokers had nothing left to shout. Not about their performances on the field. Off it, there is a smug sense of superiority outside the camp that can grate. But that's in the office of the administrators. Before we bid the Blacks adieu there's one more player who has to merit a mention.

The greatest? Definitely not. The most consistent? Not a chance. Yet his was the most famous rugby name and face on the planet. The late Jonah Lomu was a giant of a man, a mismatch for most of the world's wingers who had the dubious privilege of confronting him. Gentle off the field, he was the fifth horseman of the apocalypse on it. Amongst many great individual performances, one towers over all others: 1995, my first year retired, tapping away for the *Daily Telegraph* in the press box. In the historic stadium of Newlands, Cape Town. New Zealand face England in the 1995 World Cup semi-final. England had knocked the holders, Australia, out at the quarter-final stage. They thought they had a chance. So they did – a fat chance. Lomu scored four tries in the most rampant individual eighty minutes of them all. No one remembers that South Africa shackled him in the final. Nullified him. Outside South Africa that is. People only recollect a giant running through, over and around the England team. He stomped them into the dirt. I was pondering a piece on the runway of Cape Town airport the next day. Hyped up on hyperbole, I felt it was rugby's Michael Jordan moment, when one man turns a sport with limited appeal (outside America in the case of basketball; outside the old Commonwealth and France in the case of union) into a global giant. Did he change rugby? Not as much as the *Telegraph*'s hyped columnist anticipated. However, he was the face that signalled the end of amateurism and the beginning of professionalism. Jonah will always be one of rugby's foremost faces.

The All Blacks have become even more intimidating since Jonah jumped all over the entire England back line. Based upon results and trophies, they are one of the world's most dominant teams – in any sport – of the last decade. No comparisons with when a kid either saw or didn't see them beat Wales 19–16 on 2 December 1972. Awe has never been far from my blackest rugby thoughts but I'll end what has been something of an homage on a grudging note of disappointment. It is time to confess. The All Black magic is at an end. Maybe not for Kiwi kids who harbour the same sort of dreams I once had (the yearning to be an international, I just couldn't work out for which team) but for the rest of us. Dominance breeds resentment on one side, arrogance on the other. The bigger the blacks the more they command the world's rugby stage as a global brand. After the near-fatality of the last financial crash, the decision to allow themselves to be a marketing tool of an American insurance company that collapsed (and would have folded without the aid of the American government) is beneath an institution that yearns for respect as well as results on and off the field. When an All Black peers into a changing room mirror before a game and the player thinks of those who have come before, there's a company name to go with the black jersey. Before the 'profit over all else' era it was just the black and silver fern combination. The darkest yet purest rugby nation. Nothing else. I love watching the All Blacks play. Yet in a world where money swears, they feel a little less than All Black, no matter how black the magic. The squiggles of sponsorship change everything – at least they do for an old romantic. They are no longer that awe-inspiring black. Adidas, you can sort of understand the sports logo. But AIG? Those three letters spell the end of an obsession.

BASSALEG SCHOOL

BEEFY, RALPH, Plug, Mug and Tank. A Famous Five set of names for the latest Enid Blyton. Albeit the list is light on ethnicity and transgender. The quintet were to play a fundamental part in my fledgling footballing life, ensuring I had the rugby ball in my hands as much as possible. What else would any self-respecting back desire? My first front five. Where it all starts at every level of rugby, every week. From their sweat and graft we backs emerge, taking first tentative steps. The back row included Andy Young. There was Dave Weller – he went on to become a policeman – and a number eight by the name of Pearce. Pinky Pearce we called him. Nice guy, a bit too nice. No place for nice guys, not on the field. Nigel Callard was our scrum half. Part of a talented sporting family, Nigel played for the Welsh Schools and briefly for Newport. His younger brother, Jon, later joined me in the great escape from Newport. He too joined Bath, scoring all their points in the Heineken Cup final. Like me, Jon would also wear the red rose, kicking a late penalty to beat Scotland.

My first game of rugby was at inside centre. Eleven years of age, I didn't play there again until 1983. Then it would be against the All Blacks for the South and South West Counties in Bristol. By the second school game I was switched to the freedom of full back where a schoolboy career was to be relished, cavorting around in blissful broken fields. The anarchist in me loved it. Number ten and its bossy organisational requirements was in the far future. At school, the ten shirt was worn by Richard Jones. Slight, impish, he learned a sly side-step even before senior school. He had his family roots in west Wales. We had a reverence for all things from the West. Gareth, Barry, Benny, Gerald, the list went on. Julian Pole – 'Poley' – was my immediate replacement at inside centre. A stayer. Moved like he was running through mud but he had decent hands. Our version of a second five eighth. I don't remember who wore the thirteen shirt. Matthew Price was one of the wings – a big-shot footballer in the village of Marshfield on the outer edge of the school's catchment area, halfway between Newport and Cardiff. His dad was a pharmacist. A sophisticated family. On the other wing, Desmond Jones. Des was THE man. Famed for his extravagant stomping side-step à la Gerald Davies. He wore his collar up, hair long, Celtic cool. His dad was a rep in the beer industry with a garage full of Watney Red keyrings, little plastic red barrels. We couldn't get enough of them.

Apologies to the forgotten outside centre but this group constituted the core of the Bassaleg Under 11s, (we always pronounced the school as Baize-leg; friends from the West now seem to prefer the more Welsh-sounding Bass-are-leg) my first team. The Under 11s, the Invincibles. This should be one of those heart-warming sections when the writer explains it was here he discovered the importance of teamwork, of friendship and all those woolly ethics with which public schools love to tell us rugby, like the army, is associated. The eternal bloody brotherhood. But that wouldn't be true. I basked in the warm glow of this recently converted Grammar School. I entered the state system with an Essex boy's loathing for rugby. A whining kid who would not contemplate any sport other than football. All it took was a couple of coaching sessions, a bit of promise and – the clincher – my appointment as captain of our fledgling group. I was converted to the rugby cause. Over two decades ago, writing something that I naively called an autobiography, I doubtless reminisced over the first tackle, the first this, the first that. All lies. What I adored was infant POWER. Throughout the first, second, third and fourth form, I continued to captain the team as we tore into our teens. There were no fixed terms of leadership in Bassaleg. I was addled with authority. My voice broke early. A short-arse with bass tones and a Welsh seventies moustache, I always liked the sound of my own voice. (It took a career in commentary to sometimes get sick of it.) It was no coincidence that the most assured days of my adult career were the three years of captaincy at Bath. Jack Rowell knew an aspiring autocrat when he saw one. More than forty years later and all I crave is time, space, books and some Bob Dylan to keep me content. Power? Leave it to the politicians. My fundamental flaws were to be forged in those pampered, power-crazed early years. But that is getting ahead of the book. We are only on B, there's a way to go and plenty of possibilities for some self-flagellation as I expound my idea of the truth.

Back to 'Baize-leg'. There is a powerful memory from my second year, aged thirteen. A Catholic, confessional moment is long overdue . . . I recalled this lunacy in my first book, *Smelling of Roses*. Glorified it. An homage to the winning mentality. My fierce determination to win. Or not to lose. I'd hazard a layman's guess this psychological failing, this irrational inability to deal with defeat, damaged me – possibly as a person, certainly as a sportsman. The second year, a freezing bright blue winter's day. The middle-class boys of Baize-leg are playing away to Hartridge.

A rumour to us as much as a school. On the other side of town, most of us silently trembled at a trip to what we were told was the wrong side of the tracks. Scruffy and, in our eyes, crumbling council estates. Views down to Llanwern Steel when Newport's steel industry dominated the city. Steelworkers' sons, tough types, lying in wait for the 'posh' boys of Baize-leg.

Everything is relative.

The morning match dawdles around in the rear of my memory, waiting for odd recalls. Ten a.m. kick-off, no chance for the thaw to set in, the ground is frozen solid, rock hard, the pitch glittering, beautifully unplayable. Sporty teachers who refereed were tough and taught us to be like them. Times change. Sane people would have refused to tackle. On that day I made the startling discovery that our ranks were bursting with legions of the sane. Any injury was possible and what was possible, my mates contemplated. We waved the rough boys through our ranks. Thinking is a blessing for a good rugby player, a curse for a cowardly one. 'Torchie' was in the Hartridge ranks. The Torch. A blazing Newport legend at thirteen years of age. His dad was from Norway, a haggard, hard-looking man. Imagine the face of Auden as a steelworker. The son too, a man before his time. Decent people but intimidating, especially the Torch. A brute who stopped growing at fifteen. I hope he didn't end up another character in an Updike novel, trapped by a golden youth, giant promise unfulfilled.

Unbeaten for a year and a half, eventually we had to lose. But what did I know of these inevitabilities? Where better for the rude awakening than a frozen pitch? Against kids who would have scared us to death had we met them on a football terrace, I was burned by the Torch. Couldn't accept the defeat, couldn't take it like a little man. While most of the team hunched over in the cold changing rooms, comparing cuts and bruises, I cried, cried for the loss of my invincibility. I couldn't handle defeat.

Except for my time at Oxford, it would prove a hard habit to shake. In any walk of life. It stood me in bad stead. I shied from exams I might fail, deliberately stumbled in the blocks of 100 metre school sprints I was scared to legitimately lose. The risk of not winning was a scar, one that I buried deep. For much of my adult life I thought the greatest strength of the all-conquering Bath team was our fear of failure. Now, looking back on that distant past, I see this fear as the handicap it was. The loss of daring. Now, I see me not so much as a wounded thirteen-year-old warrior, shivering with anger and cold, but a blubbering baby, heartbroken by his ego. Something inside me had died. Invincibility. Idiot child, even Achilles knew he must die . . .

I hope you won't mind, but those memories lead us briefly away from Baize-leg and the babyish blubber to one of the more interesting sporting debates: whether it is the result or performance that matters more. It sounds like a loser's excuse, doesn't it, the latter, but if a team is scared of losing it will never look beyond the limits of its horizon. It will remain rooted in what it knows . . . and end up only squeezing out the next victory. Safe. Scared shitless within a cosy comfort zone. For all the brilliance of the coaching at Bath, we, as a group, were too often guilty – especially in Twickenham finals – of playing it safe. The word is anathema to creativity. Had we worried about ourselves and the potential expansion of our own game, more than the possibility of the odd defeat, we would not have won many more trophies, but maybe we'd have won them in style. We evolved year on year but the safety valve was locked in place for the Twickenham finals. Not every team can be like my now flawed former heroes from the Antipodes and play wondrous winning rugby. The pursuit of excellence takes dedication and imagination. It comes with the guarantee of the odd defeat. Teams will try too much, over-stretch, strain beyond the current limit of its capacity. That's how you learn. Not by some second-rate pedagogy. Rugby is too often taught by rote. I fitted in with men like Jack Rowell. He too had a psychotic urge to win. Defeat, more than anything scared me, scarred me. That changing room, high above the steelworks, the scene never left me. Petrified of losing, fear stifled my career. That frozen morning I dismissed Beefy, Tank, and Mug through my tears and branded them failures. Did it ever cross my mind that a few of them would sit and wonder about the silly, sulking sod in the corner?

Confessionals require pick-me-ups. An intoxicating gulp of the cosy innocence of the first form – and, of course, the joy of me as captain. Me, me, me. Only the Recreation Ground comes close to my first school playing field when it comes to happy memories. The first form pitch was separated from the rest of the rugby pitches, where the older boys and heroes of the first XV starred. A stream gurgled between the acres of well-manicured grass and the postage stamp pitch that was the stamping ground for our first comprehensive school year. The posts were not much more than a stubby letter H. There was no wasted material in the posts' construction. No need for Newport steel (they were, I think, wooden). We little goal kickers couldn't kick conversions out of the glue – the pitch was pretty much a mud bath from start to end of season. The mud stuck to the studs, the metallic taste lingers in the memory. Booted up, me in my ankle-high footwear that my English father thought differentiated rugby from football players. Forwards boots. Boots for Plug and Beefy! And Des Jones in a perfect pair of beautiful sleek Adidas boots. Three stripes, side-step and all. Ah, envy. We teetered, knobbly kneed, pale, hairless legs, out of the changing rooms, across a tarmacked area leading down to stream level. The field, the mud, the match. A road ran above it, linking the old 'Grammar' and newer 'Comprehensive' buildings which comprised Baize-leg school. Sometimes, during a midweek game, a teacher might pause between old and new, watch a game for a few minutes en route to another class. Older pupils ambled, giggling at the ant-like determination with which we ploughed up the field metre after painful metre, through the mud, through the opposing tacklers, everyone zeroed in on the ball.

The first game we played was against Queens. The school has long since disappeared from the face of the earth, an early casualty in the slow death of state school education. What is there to tell about my first game? We won 4–0 when it was four points for a try. Nothing else sticks. I did not score the try. My egomania would have insisted on that recollection. Doug Thomas, a ruby-cheeked English teacher who a few of us suspected had a touch of the Dylan Thomas in his belly as well as brain, took charge of the first-year matches. Did Doug bask in the reflected glory of his unbeaten, unbeatable boys? Doug supervised us, didn't coach us. He had to focus on Chaucer and his A level English class. Ron Lewis was the PE teacher with that privilege. A quietly spoken rugby player from the local Machen club, a hero to the older boys in the know. He developed our skills. Everything textbook. The angle of the body when receiving a pass. The position of the hands. There are many professional players and coaches who would be improved by a trip back in time to a Ron Lewis lesson. As for the tackle, the technique was pinned up on the gym walls. Tackling was taught in a way that brought the ball carrier to the ground without risking the health of tackler or tackled. Players have lost the art of how to position the head, to ensure it does not obtain the full force of the man being brought down. Professional coaches sacrifice their men while spouting 'player welfare' platitudes. Blokes are so big that every part of the body, including the head, is thrown in the pathway of these runaway trucks masquerading as rugby players. Sometimes progress has to make a U-turn to rediscover the right route. World Rugby's 2016 determination to act in the face of bemoaning coaches and lower the height of the tackle was a rare act of long-term thinking in our short-term world. As I write they are bringing the legitimate height of the tackle to the chest, against the wishes of many a narrow-minded coach.

But back to school. Before the 2017 Wales versus England international, Eddie Jones was wondering – in that fabulously inflammable way of his – how it is that a little country of three million beat big old England as often as Wales once did. I don't know the population of Eddie's Australia but it's an awful lot greater than another Antipodean country four or so hours south by plane. Both the Kiwis and the Welsh have rugby union in their blood in a way that the two larger nations do not. Both have produced high quality coaches at schools level. Historically both have punched well above their weight. New Zealand remain the sport's heavyweights. Professionalism and academy systems have been quick to forget the sport's subtler arts. The misguided global development of the 'gym monkey' has negated, to an extent, Welsh advantages. Wales, like much of the world, lost its sense and direction, suffering an obsession of muscle over mind. Let's hope the renaissance of the Scarlets will inspire Welsh rugby to return to their heritage. To be coached in Wales before professionalism, before Margaret Thatcher bit into the education system, was to be a fortunate rugby player indeed. The basics were our commandments. Julian Pole, as a child, ran and understood his rugby lines better than Will Carling as an international. Although Will was a little bit fitter, quicker and more determined.

Schooldays were a rushing stream of success. By the fourth year I was captain of Wales Under 15s. In the fifth form I was fast-tracked into the big league: the Welsh Under 19 schools team. I travelled to Ammanford, way out west, for the final trial. I was in the Possibles. Against me, Phil Lewis, who would one day play for Llanelli and Wales. Dave Jones, the Baize-leg wonder boy from the year above either made the team or bench,

I can't remember which. But he was a bright, well-balanced boy with a greater sense of perspective than I possessed. His promising career petered out at the level of English Students. Clive Rogers, a scrum half who represented Newport, made the Welsh schools starting team. I, along with Jeff Price, a centre, was the precocious pick. A sixteen-year-old in the Under 19 team. The schoolboy JPR. It might have been better had 'Snap', as the wafer-thin Lewis was widely known, made the team. Too much went my way too soon. Along with an inability to deal with defeat, entitlement entered the equation. Another unseen problem with which to deal. Too many people told me how good I was. Too many writers in the *Western Mail* and *South Wales Argus* linked in ink, a schoolboy, with an almost inevitable international future. Nothing could go wrong. When it did I wasn't ready. Perhaps I never was. I didn't like to fight in the dirt for it. It was 'the divine right of Barnes'. Now, after twenty or more years of professional rugby writing, I follow the wise words of Bob Dylan, 'The only thing I knew [make it "know"] how to do was keep on keeping on . . .' *Tangled Up in Blue*. One day it would be blue, black and white.

I was colour blind, never exactly sure of the school colours but deep blue with a wide yellow horizontal band is my guess. An art teacher once slapped my head for painting a purple sky, that too I remember. There's a black and white picture in *Smelling of Roses*, doubtless available somewhere for 99p. Beefy Lee in the team photo, top right, before our first game. The top does him no favours. I'm all simmering Jim Morrison with my long hair while glamorous Desmond Jones is Mark Bolan merging with Gerald Davies . . . as for Plug, in 2015 I met an aunt of his in Cardiff. She said he was still in Coedkernew, a little hamlet of council houses in the middle of nowhere. He had a beautiful way with words, most of them of the foulest nature. The sweetest of swearers. A clever bugger whose grasp of Latin was far superior to my stumbling efforts. We idolised a fat and corrupt cook who went by the name of Grumio in our basic Cambridge Latin beginners' book. A sly, slob of a man. A hero. Plug modelled himself on the cook; Plug, the leader of a punk band. Me, vocalist for one reason only. No instrumental skill. Plug was drummer, Danny Kilbride on guitar, band practice in Plug's garage. Our tight head's claim to fame was that Rat Scabies of The Damned was his uncle. He taught me how to gob, punk style, one evening in the garage. Am I imagining that? We played one gig at the nearby Rhiwderin Village Hall. A band destined for punk-like self-destruction, what with Plug adamant that our Dylanesque lyrical dreams be suppressed in favour of an ugly regurgitated imitation of his heroine, Poly Styrene of X-Ray Spex. Look her up on YouTube. As any of you who have heard my dulcet broadcast tones might guess, I didn't – and don't – have that sort of vocal range. That's punk for you.

Do I rightly remember Tank 'coming out' one night in The Three Salmons, a regular meeting place which sold cheap and weak beer? Its lack of any potency made us think ourselves heroic drinkers. I think he did. Over six foot tall at eleven years of age, a rhino on the rampage but Lord was it hard to make the man angry. He was a gentle giant, friend to all the girls when to us they were not so obscure objects of desire. After Saturday morning school matches he'd rather watch a film with them at the ABC cinema than rush to Rodney Parade for a Newport home match. Weird. Funny thing about Baize-leg back in the less tolerant seventies, none of us either knew or cared about things like homosexuality or Judaism. It wasn't until reaching the bastion of elite education in Oxford that I heard prejudice first hand. As long as Tank could run over an opposing player we loved him.

Baize-leg, winning memories, many victories, few defeats. School was a launch pad in the sense that men like Ron Lewis and Johnny Harris, the first XV coach, provided the basics needed to become a high-level rugby player. They equipped me with everything except a left hand for the purpose of passing. As a schoolboy sprinter my left arm flapped like the wing of a broken chicken. When I passed, the arm remained so close to my body that it was more a shuffle than anything else. Still the same when I deal a pack of cards. The right side's pretty good, the left useless. Why didn't Ron or Johnny get hold of me? Tell me to stop practising my right-footed kicking. Work on the motor neurone skills – or something – whatever the hell was wrong with the left side of my body?

Now for one of what will be a few brief digressions. I am in New Zealand with Sky, sometime in the 1990s. We are staying in a motel in Dunedin, some way south of civilisation, so I used to think of this city. A middle-aged cleaner walks into my room. I smile, say hello. She pauses, looks me over for a few seconds, 'Aren't you the five eighth who played for England here in 1985?' I was, and pleased to tell her so. I'd played one of my best games in an England shirt against Otago. She shakes her head, 'If you'd have had a left foot you wouldn't have been a bad player.'

Looking back on those schooldays it seems some of the best days of your life set you up for the nastiest future falls. There's a split level to success that's difficult to see close up. The immediacy of it immunises a man to those nagging whispers that warn most people. Entitlement is not just a class issue, it comes in many forms. I was massively entitled by the end of my schooldays. Head boy. Everyone loved me, wanted to be my friend, or so I thought. Life was never elsewhere, it began and ended with me. Baize-leg was the best and worst of times, it's just that I didn't comprehend the flip side at the time. That was for the future.

Holding court as we strolled leisurely out of school at the end of another day, some boy from one of the lower stream classes (there was educational apartheid even in a comprehensive school), not a rugby player, not an O level student, not anyone I needed to bother with, tripped me up for no reason. Next thing we were hammering away at one another in the concrete car park until a teacher intervened. I put it down as one of those mysteries. Mysteries make the world an interesting place. Who the fuck was this snarling kid? Some Nobody. As opposed to me, the Little Big Man. So full of myself. Impossible to imagine what it was like not to be me. I thought life was a matter of what you did and I believed I did a fair bit. As for it being a matter of who you were, let's just leave that inner monster imprisoned in the past – if that's all right with you. He's too heavy to lug around.

Success is counted sweetest by those who ne'er succeed . . . Emily Dickinson . . . To comprehend the nectar requires the sorest need . . . I didn't need it enough. Thought it was dolloped out on the plate right in front of me. As for the strains of triumph, they came too early, too resonant, and I lost the ability to hear clearly. Most of us have a bit of Jekyll and Hyde on the inside. It's best to locate your Hyde before Jekyll is destroyed while that good side of you gallivants elsewhere. Which brings us to the next stage of our alphabetic journey through rugby; enter, stage left, my dear friend, Gareth Chilcott.

CHILCOTT

EIGHTEEN YEARS of age, more likely nineteen . . . pretty certain I was a teenager. A much touted Welsh international schoolboy, a 'prodigy' in the overhyped world of the Welsh rugby media. I was good, just not quite as good as some said. I was either about to head for the luminous academic lights of Oxford or I was already there, gambolling around in that gown, anything but the intellectual Superman. Still, the world was mine for the taking. Youth and its follies, eh? School, parents, even the *Western Mail*, back then a Welsh bible. Admittedly there were a few disturbing hints of the hard times others measure the world by. Not picked instantaneously for Wales, meeting kids dressed as dons far cleverer than me. But overall the air I tasted seemed pretty fresh. An escapee from the grim reality of a darkening world . . . Thatcher, the Falklands War, the silent shadow of neo-liberalism set to swallow entire nations bite by voracious bite . . . ignorant, unaware of the gathering greed. That this was indeed the lifestyle for which Oxford was supposedly training me, such was the future I managed to miss, I am not what you would describe as impoverished but membership of the one per cent elite eluded me. Thank God.

Yes, there comes a time when reality hits and hits hard. It knocked me sideways, off my feet when, eighteen or nineteen, I was Newport's teenage full back. The Black and Ambers. A home match at Rodney Parade. The opposition a small West Country club. Some little city with a Roman history. We rested half our team. The visitors were English opposition, not to be taken seriously. Bath had the laugh . . . first and last. Black and amber lost to . . . lost in . . . the future ferocity of blue, black and white . . . the Bath show was set to begin. Jack Rowell and his ruthless regime had arrived. And here came reality, slow and sure . . . A kick across field, perhaps by John Horton. A good kick. It stopped a few metres short of the touchline, forcing me to carry it into touch. A Bath lineout. I did what any cocky Welsh-bred back would do and refused to hand the ball over to the opposition. Cool hand Stuart . . . next thing I knew I was flying through the air, heading, quite literally, for the advertising boards. I bounced into the boards, a Bath player stared down at me, snorting, twitching little nostrils, a fiery fat fucker. Hands on hips, breathing hard after jogging towards touch with that strange little trotting step of his. Me with my Welsh moustache; Gareth Chilcott, resplendent with his Bristol growth. Hardly love at first sight. I stared at this strange English abomination.

Here was the world with which I was yet to familiarise myself, coming at me shaped like a great big round cheese, maybe a Cheddar one. I petulantly flung away the ball. Kept the cheese comparison to myself. Only a rugby rumour at that stage – Gareth is now a West Country legend – a dark rumour to scare polite young men, the boy from Bedminster, Bristol, south of the Avon, a rough part of town back then, Bristol City territory. Most definitely the wrong side of the river, let alone tracks; Hartridge-like. The future British and Irish Lion, public speaker, pantomime star and entrepreneur is one of those players rugby's smug middle classes like to claim as someone saved by the game invented in an East Midlands public school. In this instance, rugby may have been right. His youth was dedicated to destruction. Football hooliganism. A place for young offenders, next stop prison. A frustrated but caring father, Dai, who was occasionally known to throw him out the family home, a mother, Doreen, who doted on him. The mummy's boy who headed home for a 'cwch' when dad was working.

Trips to Thailand, stints inside distant jails for alcohol-fuelled behaviour aboard jets. Scary stuff, even for The Cooch. Salvation came in the shape of a junior Bristol club by the name of Old Redcliffians (Old Reds as it is known throughout the city). An outlet for his violence. A home where his edge could be legitimately honed. Short, strong, hard to shift in the scrum, terrifying to the majority of rugby's participants. He worked his way from a Bristol junior powerhouse of a club to Bath. Born north of the Avon, maybe it would have been Bristol and another destiny, but south was Somerset and Bath was Somerset. And so the career crept forwards.

Early days and Bath tours – one to the East Coast of the USA, a tour I describe in some detail when I'm bribed into saying a few words at the odd rugby function. Here's a sample . . .

A three-team tournament in New England. Wasps, Bath and a Boston-based side. An unusual tournament, a fair play tournament, Bath won their two games . . . and came third in the tournament. Jack Rowell on the touchline screaming abuse at his rotund recent signing. There's a lineout in the early minutes of the match. Summer breezes are somewhere else, it's just saturating heat here and our new prop forward was without the stamina to travel far. A GPS on the Bath man wouldn't have measured a mile for his movement through the whole game, but then nobody was rushing through the scorch of the day. Gareth, at the lineout, puffing, hands as ever on hips, quietly contemplating some misdemeanour. A body-building American second row, six foot six, thirty inch waist, examines this old world torso, sees the lumpen Somerset proletarian curled up. 'I kick ass, fat boy.' He jumps, wins the lineout, sprints athletically in pursuit of the ball. Some would say stupidly, given the horrendous heat. Sly Cooch wastes no energy. Doesn't move more than fifty or so metres. Not until the ball finds its way into touch – not far from that earlier lineout. He's rested. Ready. The muscleman bends his powerful legs but before he propels his athletic frame into the air he is prematurely brought down to earth as the Bath prop wallops him with one of his specialist short arm punches. The legs weren't quick but the arms were boxer fast. The American collapses, the stretcher comes on, Bath's fair play tournament is in tatters. Cooch leans over the American braggart. 'No one calls I fat boy.'

The Bath boys head south. Florida and, few will ever know why, Disneyworld – or is it Disneyland? Who either knows or cares. Weirdly enough, many years later, Gareth and his late, lovely wife, Ann, joined the Barnes family on a Christmas holiday, our kids of an age to fall for Walt's many commercial wiles . . . anyway, the bottom line is that Bath are spending a day at the Disney Empire. The backs – so my after-dinner patter has it – are having a good time on the rides. That's part of the game's cliché: backs are the bright boys but utterly childish, not to be trusted to get 'the job done'. Meanwhile, the heatwave continues to ravage the entire East Coast. Cooch hasn't made much of the Magic Kingdom. He is sitting by the fountain near the entrance to Walt's world, the start of Main Street, USA. Head bowed, dripping sweat. The famed Disney parade pulses his way, Donald, Goofy, all the gang. Mickey in the lead . . . a Cornish winger by the name of Barry Trevaskis has peeled off from the rest of the backs having seen a chance for some mischief of which even that mythical Cornish man, Merlin, would have been proud. The winger slips into the chaos of Mickey's followers, just as the Mouse is inches from Cooch. He pinches Mickey's oversized, stuffed, Disney arse. The Mouse looks around and sees Gareth – head down – no one nearer the scene of the indignity. Well, he's a fair lump but this is Mickey's kingdom and no one takes liberties in the land of the Mouse, so he pushes Chilcott. Everyone laughs. How funny . . . everyone keeps laughing except grumpy overheated Cooch. The Bath man, humiliated, says, 'What's that up there, Mickey?' pointing to the blazing blue Florida sky. The Mouse makes a mistake and peers up, up and away as Cooch cocks his fist and catches him perfectly. Mickey goes down like the proverbial sack of shit . . . the American children screaming, 'Mommy, mommy, the fat man just killed Mickey Mouse!'

The story gets a great bellyaching laugh, whatever the audience. There's just the one problem: I wasn't on that tour. But like any good folk tale it was passed down through Bath legend and I appropriated it, made the tale mine, a little like Pete Seeger did with 'We Shall Overcome'. Did he actually floor Mickey Mouse? I have no idea, but there are a few thousand people who have heard the story and passed it on to friends. Maybe revised it. Told it as their own story as I have for twenty-odd years. Should I apologise to those people who paid good money for a few ribald tales? No. It elicited a laugh at the time. But what about my mate, Cooch? Has he and his reputation been betrayed? When does a folk tale become a distortion of truth and reality? I haven't asked whether he did in fact lay Mickey Mouse out cold on the hot, hot ground . . . and as for the body-building second row . . . call it collateral damage. What the heck. I'm sure the big man has taken my name in vain over the years. And it is not as if the story has any sort of negative effect upon his legend. The fans at the dinners cannot get enough of the rough stuff from the good old days.

Gareth, with his mastery of the malapropism and that mask of the 'muddled up old prop forward' he wears, controls the room. He has the comic touch: timing. One of the rugby dinner subjects that always crops up is violence. Why shouldn't it? Let's not pretend. My dear friend was never a man of peace. Intimidation was the starting point. Many a man has felt the full force of those powerful jabs, the cold-blooded footwork and other infamies too indescribably awful to recollect. He was a man of his time. Had he played now, with the vast array of cameras poking their noses into every scrum and breakdown, he wouldn't have lasted five minutes in a match. And he's not the only one. Jason Leonard, even more revered at a national and global level – to the extent he has been president of the RFU – was another shocker. He was a prop forward . . . what do you expect? He's another smiling assassin who has the crowd eating from his palm. The filthier the act of villainy, the greater the audience hilarity. Never mind the damage done to the poor bloke on the receiving end of the prop forwards' punchline.

The player who tells how he kept his cool under the greatest provocation isn't the one the paying audience want to hear. What a bore. Give them Willie John McBride eulogising how the forwards piled in on the call of '99' on the 1974 Lions tour of South Africa. The City sells out. Cheering and clapping the good old rugby speaker. A bit of hotel trashing too. No mention of words such as vandalism. On the recent Lions tour to New Zealand I declined over thirty invitations to attend various functions, any old Brit would do; rugby is awash with after-dinner speaking. In New Zealand many a tale is told of the late Colin Meads. The great second row held the distinction of being the last All Black sent off (in 1967) until Sonny Bill Williams came up with yet another way to grab a headline. McBride, Meads, these are men of warrior status. Much of what they did was beyond the pale of the permissible in those wilder, distant days. We should shake our heads, mutter our 'we are not amused' comments quietly, eyebrows raised. We should, but we don't. Not when the dinner jacket is dusted off. Anything goes. Hypocrisy reeks. Saturday afternoons, a shoulder charge here, a spear tackle there, condemnation everywhere. Rugby union is a physical game. Its laws were long ago designed to allow players certain leeway, to 'take the laws into their own hands' when required. Some of the world's best referees have told me, time and again, the game was cleaner and safer when someone on the wrong side of a ruck received 'a shoeing'. The crowds gasp when the replay of a boot on a back is shown. In black tie they roar. We are adjusted to the politically correct world of superficial order at the expense of a deeper prevailing understanding of what makes sport function. I'll go further into this subject when we get to the chapter entitled 'Injuries'.

Suffice to say, the 2017 Lions tour of New Zealand was on the edge, not of violence but anarchy – discipline the issue, not the odd haymaker. Better the day when The Cooch did something so savage I will not describe it, but suffered the consequences of a substantial ban and a good kicking from the opposing team. As my old university friend, 'Trotsky', a football fan, said to me many a year ago, 'The one thing everyone loves about rugby is the violence.' The public affection for the likes of Gareth, Jason and the rest of the hoary old front five legends is linked directly to what many of us of an older generation – me at least – believe to be a truth wrapped up in mankind's innate predilection for violence.

A man of violence with a gregarious, generous disposition off the field (rugby really did strip him of any anti-social behaviour beyond the rectangle where he ruled the Recreation Ground with his fists of fear), Gareth was once an inadvertent example of rugby union's middle- and upper-class stupidity. Like so much of Middle England that obsesses over examinations, it confuses intellect with education. Now, in no way, shape or form is my Big Buddy what even he could describe as an educated man. But he has an intellect capable of functioning with the smart set. Here's a little example. Dipping back into my box of unreliable memories from my playing days, Bath once stopped for steak and chips in Stow-on-the-Wold, en route to a Saturday afternoon match in Coventry. The dieticians who rule the roost of modern day rugby weren't even born. Simon Halliday of Downside and St Benet's College, Oxford, is searching for someone to play chess with, 'a quick game?' Cooch says, 'I'll give you a game, Hallers.' Simon expresses a certain surprise that the prop can even play. It doesn't last long. The Downside boy is routed. Just as well Simon preferred his steak rare.

Had The Cooch been educated at Downside and Simon at Cooch's state school/breeding ground for Bristol City hooligans, I reckon the prop forward would have ended up in Oxford and Simon somewhere slightly less esteemed. Rugby union's arrogant attitude towards football is driven by the same complacent narrow-mindedness. I would have been a very rich man if paid ten pounds for every time I heard a rugby supporter say rugby players are more intelligent than footballers. Not true. Rugby players were and remain much better educated. That's not the same as being brighter. Football is the national game. It is played the length and breadth of the country, in all areas, including the predominantly poorer parts of the land. Rugby is a popular middle-class minority sport. Its snobbery can be overbearing to those who would rather not be admitted to its 'clubby' spirit. Gareth was an outsider who found his home on the inside. When I watch Harlequins' Kyle Sinckler struggling with his anger and emotions I see a young Cooch. There are an insufficient number of such characters. When Eddie Jones talks about attitude he is talking about the vast majority of rough and rugged, below the middle-class line kids, who fail to find their way to unions.

Fortunately, my mate rumbled into the Recreation Ground and Bath Football Club (now known as Bath Rugby which makes a lot more sense); fortunate for both him and for Bath. He was not the quickest nor the fittest of players to grace the Ground. Whilst being far more adept with ball in hand than fading memories and legend allow, there were a few others with more skilled attributes. Short, which was a good thing for a technician of a loose head prop, fat, which I guess made him harder to move in a scrum but also made it harder for him to move (the mountains – or American second rows – had a habit of coming to him), he was an extraordinary influence. By all measurements Gareth should never have been a top class sportsman. Yet he made his debut for England the same day as I did in 1984 against the Grand Slam Wallabies. He toured Australia with the British and Irish Lions in 1989. In the 1993/94 season, he, Richard Hill and I retired. Between Richard and myself we had captained the club five straight years but it is hard not to see Cooch's influence as the greatest, for all the attributes Richard and I (well, I like to think) offered.

The players voted Gareth club captain ahead of the Entitled One. He declined the honour. All players who paid their subscriptions (which made them eligible for selection in the pre-contractual professional days) had a vote. Cooch was the heartbeat of the club, especially on the social level. Everyone who played for Bath loved him. Hill had nominated his friend as successor. The root and branch Bath majority didn't think twice. He won with a landslide while I, seen as the minority candidate nominated by an ex-Loughborough University coterie, looked set for the role of vice-captain. For whatever reason, Jack wanted me to captain the team. Cooch was within his rights to stand firm and captain the club he loved. Yet after a conversation with the Machiavellian mastermind Rowell, he quietly backed down. Like Mickey Mouse, it is not something we have ever spoken of. Jack wanted otherwise; Cooch obliged. As did I, most of the time. We both trusted Rowell. I was rewarded with a three-year stint as club captain. Gareth was my vice-captain. Together we went on to win the first English league and cup double. Ego fuelled, I was proud of MY captaincy achievement. My primary role was to guide our movements, shape the side on the pitch and speak, perhaps too often, off it. I laid out the cold tactical imperatives. Gareth managed the emotional needs of the club. We were a good balance. There's a photograph of the two of us together after we have claimed the Courage League. It's taken at the Recreation Ground. Holding the trophy, left and right hand combined, smiles broad, the night yet to come. Good times, great man. Perhaps we would have won the double with the captain and vice-captain roles switched. Probably would . . . almost certainly would. But Cooch did as his coach requested and in the process he missed out on an honour he most definitely deserved: captain of Bath. He spoke like a skipper, subtle and inspiring with his then mangled language. Whatever the circumstance. Here was an intrinsic part of his charm. There was nothing pre-prepared about him. He was always hot blooded, of the moment. You warmed to the man. The second and third team idolised him. The first XV had enormous respect. Yet not for every aspect of his larger-than-life being. None was closer than Richard Hill. None more dedicated to fitness than our scrum half. But in team warm-ups, we would only get halfway through a steady 800 metre looping run twice around the pitch before our prop forward would peel off with Falstaffian bluster to announce he would intensify his training while we jogged pointlessly on. He could be seen, sitting on the tackle bags, 'working on his "abdoms"'. He didn't care a fig for fitness. He was good in the gym, I'll give him that. There was always the suspicion the gym was somewhere he could hide from the running.

It cannot be said he set an example on the training field but that didn't diminish the enormity of his influence. Statisticians and dieticians take a pause. Rugby union is not merely a matter of measurements. Speed, stamina, overall fitness, lack of fat . . . of course rugby is now more dependent on these foundations than it was in our playing days but spirit remains rooted to the success of a side. Saracens taking time out mid-season to go on a binge in somewhere as hedonistic as San Sebastian – it's all part of the essence of the game. Statistics, with their deceptive, slippery truths cannot grasp the larger intangibles of the great men who hold teams together with personality and determination as much as any superhuman abilities. So it was with Gareth Chilcott, an underrated tactician whose rugby brain is as sharp now as it was in his playing days. If I want a word of wisdom on the dark arts of the front row he's the man I call. He'll let me know what is going on there. And much besides.

Much besides indeed. Rugby changed his life. For the better. Nothing better than his marriage to Ann, and their two children, Chloe and Ethan. Within a year of Ann's death, the children looked as if they could lose both their parents when a rare liver disease threatened to claim The Cooch. He was in Southmead Hospital, Bristol, while I was in Australia on the 2016 England tour. Richard Hill warned me – I would be shocked when I saw him. Horrified was the word. He had lost a frightening amount of weight. The light was going out in the eyes. But being who he is, his only concern was for the children. At times his friends thought 2016 would be the last the world would see of GJ Chilcott, yet in the nick of time a compatible liver came to the rescue. A miracle for Gareth, a tragedy for someone else's family. He thinks of that family often. He's not yet reached 'a liver for life' but it is impossible to believe the Big Man isn't set for a long run. Initially targeting one Lions Test in 2017, long range from his hospital bed in the summer of 2016, he was there for the entire three-Test duration. At lunch in Auckland he discussed work projects. In his hospital bed he had bemoaned the fact he would never work again. But he is back. Bossing one of Bristol's best music venues, The Tunnels. He told me he was getting out of the travel business. At the time of this rewrite he's checking out Air India as a possible carrier for the 2019 World Cup and there are numerous other work projects. The narrowed eyes – once a sign of serious impending violence – have been replaced in the autumn of his life with wide smiles, a cheeky grin and the warm handshake. It is easy to see a complete transformation of a man. Easy but wrong. He was never quite who he seemed. It was no surprise he played the Bath Theatre Royal, once in pantomime, another time with the Hull Truck Company in a rugby league play called *Up and Under*. Here is a friend who was always comfortable wearing a mask. One that fooled friends and enemies alike.

From childish thug to rugby hard man, he has made his way through a memorable life. He is a fantastic father and a fine friend. In true Bath fashion we don't see each other quite as often as we might like but when we do, the laughter is unleashed and the tears roll . . . a little gentle humour and a lot of savage wit. Beneath that smiling face there's still a big old bastard growling around. Looking to hurl the next cocky back into the advertising boards.

DROP GOALS

THE BEST drop goal I have ever seen? Not the most famous . . . we'll let England supporters fight with Irish and South African fans over that one . . . but the best? Travel back in time to 13 December 2008. The teams involved, Harlequins, at home to those fancy Dans from Gay Paree, Stade Français, in the fourth round of pool matches in the Heineken Cup. The star of the show, Nick Evans. A class Kiwi act. A drop goal struck through the mud and mire of a miserable winter's afternoon at the Stoop, tucked away in the shadow of Twickenham. The first act of this memorably underscored rugby drama began when Sergio Parisse – nominated as one of the world's five best players that season – sliced a clearance kick to touch. The curtain came down five minutes and nine seconds later as an inebriated-looking rugby ball wobbled its way over the crossbar. It transformed a two-point deficit into a one-point win. Rugby's ultimate 'drive'. Each and every one of the forty-odd metres Harlequins made to put Evans in position to win it was ferociously fought for, forwards going at it, hand to hand. No sporting armistice. Rugby doesn't have the luxury of American football's head-clearing time-outs. No chance for Dean Richards, the Harlequins director of rugby, to signal Evans to wave his arms around, fly half and quarterback rolled into one, to take a calming pause. No getting in a huddle, gesticulating, specifying each man's role. Clock on, start again. None of that. Time was ticking away from the Londoners. With the final play of the match commencing at 78.48 there was no time for indecision. Yet Harlequins and Evans took their time. Time for visions and revisions. The perfection was in the poise of it all. The forwards drove, dependable, determined, protecting the ball like a new-born babe but Stade Français were not for a spineless retreat. Something remarkable was required to enable the Harlequins push to force a position for Evans to drop that goal out of the mud and into Harlequins legend. They had that remarkable something, their New Zealand fly half, Dan Carter's one-time attendant ascended to fleeting centre stage with the most sensational mix of decision-making and sudden leaps of pace to march his men within striking range. Then it was the mere matter of bisecting the posts. Nothing mere in this mire.

From the commentary box I giggle nervously as the clock ticks past seventy-nine minutes. One eye on the pitch, the other on the screen. The broad panacea and the individual detail. In the top left-hand segment of the screen is the match clock. Every second important. The inexorable passage of time. The Harlequins lineout throw from the sliced kick finds an unconvincing, inaccurate way above and beyond its intended target to the back of the set piece where, fortuitously, it bobbles into home side hands. Harlequins have it, 'Somehow,' I chortle, 'somehow.' As the attack progresses I lose control of my commentary faculties, something close to full shout mode, 'Evans is way too far for a drop goal. He's gotta get a lot closer than this . . .' My partner for the day, the loquacious Ulsterman Mark Robson, notices the ball knocked backwards by a Harlequins hand. He interjects,

'But Harlequins are going backwards with ten seconds on the clock.' Stating the obvious I say, 'They've got to generate some momentum.' Robson: 'Here comes the surge.' Does their pack have the strength to force this moment to its crisis? Wish I'd said that. But I don't, I holler. The England scrum half, Danny Care, has the ball. Protected from the French by a wall of eight muddied men, it's only the seventh phase. 'Look at Nick Evans,' me shouting with either a sudden gift for insight or lip reading, 'He's saying, "I don't want it, it's too far out" and Care wanted to give him the ball.' But four phases later Care can't resist the pass, Evans is on the wrong side of the ten-metre line, 'It's too far,' I reiterate, now immersed, personally furious with the scrum half. But Evans stays cool. He feints, breaks a full fifteen metres between the French defenders, a scramble which shoots off to the right side of the field. The forwards churning through the mud to keep their hands on the ball. Keep control. Keep the chance alive. They keep on. 81.47 on the clock and Robson is bubbling up, 'He's in the pocket.' The American football phrase is now a universal rugby cliché but in this instant it is well chosen as Evans conjures another moment of his own All Black magic. Instead of shaping to pass like some quarterback, he dummies for the drop kick and 'slices through'. He leaves four Frenchmen flailing. Takes the drive another – a more direct – fifteen metres downfield, the attack in full flow. The visitors in retreat. Phase seventeen, inches from the try-line. Robson conjures a beautiful line of commentary. Jordan Turner Hall is 'Right on top of the line, blades of grass for Harlequins . . . one pick, one drive, one flop.' Almost Walt Whitman. By now I am demented, 'Give it to Nick Evans . . .' It is the twenty-first phase and there's a five-on-two overlap. The pack cannot part with their precious possession. Twenty-third phase, they've only advanced millimetres but they are millimetres only from the line. 'Impossibly unbearable,' says Robson. Twenty-seventh phase and the Harlequins are going backwards, the crowd breathless as they retreat. Then Tom Williams, later to become part of rugby history with his role in 'Blood Gate', 'weaves in a huge parabolic loop'. Mark is having a mighty match behind the microphone.

'It's time for Evans to wonder, does he dare, the moment of his greatness is flickering.' If only! Oh, for TS Eliot in the commentary box. Instead there's an excitable ex-fly half, 'Drop a goal, now, Nick Evans,' as if he can hear me. The ball spins its way from Care to Evans, the universe squeezed into the ball, the boot makes an unclean contact from about twenty-five metres out, Robson again, 'Look at the All Black, here it comes, this is it . . . oh . . . oh, he's going to the TMO.' We're both sure it's over. I bellow, 'Nick Evans has been a genius for the last minute and a half . . .' I stare at the television replay and the super slow-motion flight of the ball, 'A drunken kick, it's going, it's going, it's OVER, he's done it, Nick Evans has done it.' Harlequins – players and fans – hugged one another. Stade players fell to the ground, muddied in despair. The commentary team combusted, the mermaids sang.

It wasn't a World Cup final, a Six Nations game, wasn't even any old domestic final. It was the balance of rugby at its best. One man's class and the slog of the foot soldiers. The ability to hold the ball for over five minutes. Under immense pressure without league's liberty to take a tackle, pause and push the ball through the leg. This homage was written in the autumn of 2017, before the Sexton strike in Paris, the beginning of the Ireland Grand Slam march when it was seconds from a premature end.

In union, the isolation of the individual who goes for solo glory can spell the end. Every pass, every metre made has consequences. Ireland went through forty-one phases in the lead-up to the Sexton kick, one millimetre away from support and the 2018 Grand Slam doesn't occur. Especially when the contest is as tight as the Ireland and the Harlequins games were.

Rugby union at its purest. As for the subject of 'any old domestic final', a quick word, if I may, on my most famous moment in Bath colours. Harlequins this time cast as victims. If you have been paying attention you will remember the early reference to a drop goal against the All Blacks. We are only up to D and here's another authorial drop kick. Rewriting history with me as the drop goal king . . . this is not so much an alternative fact as insanity. I was probably dropped by England more often than I dropped goals. So I beg your indulgence. We head back into the twentieth century. Not in the commentary box but on the pitch. Exhausted. The heat of the battle. We are in extra time, Bath lucky to be there. Harlequins have outplayed us for the regular eighty-minute duration. But under the fierce mental pressure of a final and full house at Twickenham their kickers cracked. A bad case of the moving posts. When the pressure gets too great, posts sometimes move. Or they narrow as you eye them up . . . I swear they have some shape-changing quality . . . anyway, I have been harassed to hell and back by that silent assassin of an open side, Peter Winterbottom. I was unbearably useless – but there's a couple of minutes of extra time left. Bob Marley . . . *Redemption Kick*. It's 12–12. All my moment has in common with the Nick Evans masterpiece is its genesis from a sliced kick. On this occasion from Harlequins winger, Mike Wedderburn. The calamitous kick presents what will soon be the winning team with unearned field position. A lineout throw between the twenty-two and ten-metre line. I am standing on the ten-metre line. What are we going to do? This is what I am paid 12p a mile petrol for. To make the big calls. Keep the nerve when those around me are losing theirs. But the spirit isn't willing and I don't believe in miracles. I am flustered, all right . . . fucked. Bent double. Blowing. Too buggered to accept responsibility for one longish-range drop kick. That is if we should win the lineout, a rarity that afternoon. Gulping for air, informing Jerry Guscott of the plan. An 'up and under'. Get ready to chase. Win the kick and chase and it's a closer-range kick or maybe a disorganised Harlequins defence to attack. High balls down the middle make a mess of organised rearguards; they are under-utilised in these over-plotted times. Jerry stands tall while I slump. Stares at me with complete contempt. Wounding me with his withering, 'If you haven't the balls to do it, let me have a go.' The faint sneer of which he is master. Well, fuck you, Jerry. This is Bath, not England – my domain as much as yours. Yes, fuck you twice. Hill's pass is perfect. Time to set. Too tired to rush the swing of the boot in hasty panic, the contact clean. A fairly flat trajectory but never in doubt. As soon as I struck it, all right it wasn't the old Tiger Woods, but it would do. Stood there staring. The hopeless hero of the moment. Our fans delayed their celebrations a split second. Oh ye of little faith. The players did not. Redemption. We always believed we would get up on the line. It is what made us serial winners. The ball had no options, it was under instruction. It had to make it through. A draw isn't a win, it's our version of defeat. And we don't lose finals. Bath logic. Tired (it had a shade more elegance than the Nick Evans strike), but it made its own sweet way to its desired destination. I stand rooted in whacked-out wonder. Guscott, the first to congratulate me. I should have thanked him for his glorious goading.

Please don't think this last paragraph, the bit about my ineptitude, was a paragon of self-deprecation. This truly was one of my poorest performances in a Bath shirt. I was rank but the next day's newspaper headlines were all focused on the hero of the hour. 'Barnes Stormer', the headliner, scrawled over both broadsheet and tabloid. I had a beer by the name of Barnes Stormer named after me. It must have been some kick. For the vast majority of us, these highs dwindle with time until only fans and friends remember. Quite right too. Shall we focus on a few other drop kicks that send my little effort swerving and swaying its way towards anonymity?

The forever drop kicks. Let's consider them. Jonny Wilkinson's effort on my birthday for one. 22 November 2003. The World Cup final in Sydney. There's not a dreg of patriotism in the bottom of 'The Barrel' (a nickname that has stuck, earned for a slide in and out of a pool of water on a Bucharest pitch – not for my shape, nor penchant for a pint, although both are perfect justifications for the name 'Barrel' in their own ways). Ah, but when the opposition is Australia and the venue is Sydney, any of us can be forgiven for seeking the scoundrel's refuge. Like my 'epic', this one was towards the end of extra time. Unlike mine, it was meticulously created. Matt Dawson made the break, deep enough into Australian territory. Deep enough into the twenty-two for Wilkinson to take his chances. But with the scrum half trapped at the bottom of the breakdown the risk of a slow pass being charged down was magnified. Martin Johnson made a typically good common-sense decision. He drove the ball all of two metres forward. Two metres and a few seconds can make all the difference. In that time Dawson was back on his feet, Wilkinson primed to drop the goal with his 'wrong' right foot for good measure. Another similarity between this kick and my 1992 vintage was the fact that Wilkinson was turned into the hero (admittedly on a slightly more stratospheric level) despite not playing well. Who remembers his failed attempts to win the game at an earlier stage? Well, who cares, history is mostly written by winners. The most famous drop kick in the history of rugby union? Try arguing with the English rugby version of the Barmy Army. But what about JPR Williams' one and only drop kick which enabled the Lions to tie the fourth Test and seal their one and only series win in New Zealand? A one and only drop kick if ever there was one.

Staying on famous Lions kicks, a word on Jerry Guscott's series clincher in Durban in 1997. Memorable but magical only for what it told us about Jerry (a chapter of which is dedicated to him). More interesting is his evaluation of the Sexton drop kick to beat France in 2018. 'One of the best strikes I have ever seen . . . if they win the Grand Slam it will go down as one of the great sporting moments in Six Nations rugby . . . if they don't, it becomes another statistic.' His relatively straightforward drop goal needed the moment in South Africa to give it the faintest glimmer of grandeur.

Sexton's kick was closer to the Evans score in terms of patience and difficulty. More pressure but better conditions – dreadful as opposed to diabolical. The Irish creation lacked those shimmering Evans darts. Sexton would not have saved Ireland's day from forty-five metres had the game been under Stoop-like conditions. His kick was a case of control all the way. Ireland were so professional you never thought they would lose the ball but getting it within range to win? It was a truly spectacular strike, soaring beyond even Ronan O'Gara's seventy-sixth minute drop goal to win Ireland's second Grand Slam in the first decade of the twenty-first century. Eight-two minutes and forty-two seconds were on the TV clock as the kick found its way over the posts. According to my former Bath team-mate, it took another four wins to become one of the great Six Nations moments and not just another 'statistic'. And there's always the other perspective. 'C'est terrible, c'est terrible,' were the devastated words of the French commentator.

South Africans will be getting impatient with all this northern hemisphere nostalgia. How can I forget 1995? The Rainbow Nation are tied 12–12. Again, extra time. An earlier World Cup final. Against what was regarded as an unbeatable All Blacks side. Joel Stransky the hero. The ball is won clean. Off the top of the lineout. To the scrum half. Then straight into the fly half's pleading hands. No messing about. No driving pack of green giants to commit Josh Kronfeld, that exceptional All Black open side. Just a swift, accurate service and a steady swing of the fly half's boot. The ball rose steeply, quickly. Undeviating.

Twelve months earlier I played my last game of rugby against

Joel, South Africa B versus England's midweek team in Kimberley. A groin injury and retirement for the one, Homeric glory for the other. Twenty-three years on I can see that kick making its unstoppable, end over end way towards its target with even more clarity than the Wilkinson one. Perhaps it was the glaring Johannesburg light. Or maybe it was the significance of the result. Not just for the global rugby tribe but an entire nation. It's a kick all wrapped up in Nelson Mandela and new beginnings for South Africa. So we hoped at the time. The ANC compromises with the ruling whites and forces of global order have made a mess of the post-apartheid years but you can't say Joel didn't play his part.

Four years later, another Springbok fly half should have been forcing the International Rugby Board – as World Rugby used to be known – to revise their thoughts on the merits of the drop goal. Jannie De Beer was the South African second-choice fly half but injury to Henry Honiball offered him his fifteen minutes of fame. South Africa beat England in a World Cup quarter-final. De Beer dropped five goals in eighty minutes, three in a ten-minute spell and a pair in the last ten minutes for good measure. Jonny Wilkinson looking on from the bench, dropped by Clive Woodward. His time was to come. In Paris, the City of Light, it was lights out for Woodward who had promised to deliver an English World Cup triumph. But clever Clive, he never said when. A lot of the 1991/92 legends wanted him gone. So much for legends. Ironically, one week later, Stephen Larkham's late drop goal sank the defending champions. Jannie only dropped the one goal that day. Shouldn't have used up his quota in Paris.

After the Jannie Parisian drop orgy, why wasn't the question posed: 'Is a drop goal really worth three points?' As recently as 1948 it was actually valued at four. Rugby rarely rushes its big decisions. In former days when someone set up the scoring system most rugby pitches were in a state of constant churn, all over the world. There is a valid debate about the value attached to something like the Nick Evans muddy masterpiece. Generally, even though the points for a try has risen, from three, to four, to five points, there is little justification for a drop goal's valuation at sixty per cent of a try (if not converted). Not on surfaces that don't suck the ball into the mire with the drop where defences are more daunting than ever. The easier accumulation of Jannie De Beer-style drop goals has somewhat faded for the time being. But sport is cyclical. Soon enough some smart coach will look back into recent history and think, 'Why waste the effort trying to score tries when we can pick an expert, à la Jonny Wilkinson, to accumulate the softer three-point option?'

The All Blacks used the drop goal to great effect in the 2015 World Cup after anxious memories of being camped on the French line in Cardiff in the 2007 quarter-final, not having the collective wit to drop a goal. The tactical aberration lingered in the land of the long white cloud, where the smartest rugby nation played with their heads in those clouds and lost their way en route to what should have been another World Cup win. Never again. New Zealand are the arch advocates of the attacking game yet the pragmatism of Carter in the Twickenham semi and final suggests that the drop goal era is far from done, despite the voguish desire to 'entertain' and score tries (which are not one and the same). In the 2018 Rugby Championship, New Zealand lost at home to South Africa by two points despite being camped just inches from the Springbok line in the dying minutes; Beauden Barrett, for all his genius, ignored the option of the easy drop goal and persisted with trying to create a match-winning wonder-try. It is likely that this moment will prove to be a turning point in New Zealand's drive for a third consecutive World Cup as they sacrifice all-out attack for more pragmatic decision-making. Barrett proved he had perhaps learned the lesson when he struck a drop goal (his frist in seventy-one Test caps) in the 16–15 win against England in November 2018.

Whether he continues in the vein . . . time will tell.

A drop goal is quite some skill but three points exaggerate its degree of difficulty. It is not as if the drama of the drop would be lost with diminished value. The Wilkinson, the Stransky, the Larkham, even the Barnes kick, all broke the deadlock of a tied game. In those matches, one point would have been enough. One point should be enough.

That is how it is with our near relative, rugby league. League noisily regards itself as a superior running and passing game. I believe those five minutes and nine seconds of action at Harlequins provides an eloquent counter argument. Yet league has relegated the drop goal to a scoring mode of last resort (as was the case in many of the aforementioned examples), not as a means to score without all that bother of running and passing. World Rugby wants to ensure the game is entertaining. The needs of appeasing the millions of couch potatoes was one of their *raisons d'etre* for the introduction of the bonus point system in the 2017 Six Nations. There were fewer tries than in 2016. If the sport's grandees want to make a principled stand in favour of hand over boot, downgrade the value of the drop goal.

League got their numbers – and with it their priorities – right, long before union. Union is a conservative sport. Almost Whiggish. Changes are slow to come. Why risk a revolution? League, of course, was that revolution with its demands for an equal playing field for both rich and poor. Working men were once ruled out of Test rugby because of the time required away from work. The men that ran the game probably thought 'just as well'. Let's swallow our pride. Since the game went professional and the pitches became pristine, the drop goal has become rugby's easy anachronism. On the pitch, in the mind. Don't all rugby supporters hope the next generation of fly halves will be tactical giants, poetic passers, and, down at the bottom of the list of attributes, decent drop kickers in a crisis? League fans sneer, say union is slow and stodgy. Until we drop the drop to a solitary point, on principle, at least, they have a point.

The drop goal has a greater degree of difficulty than the more prosaic penalty kick from the tee. The ball has to be dropped with precision to the turf. Pressure is magnified by the onrush of opposing players but – as with American football – teams have blockers and guards in position in a manner not envisaged when the drop was weighted the worth of three points and amateurs didn't train, let alone work on defensive blocks. This mode of scoring symbolises rugby's stuffy, often unadventurous past. Sanity will soon enough be restored. The drop goal will return to fashion as the natty three-point option it is. This will be to rugby's detriment. It might take another Jannie De Beer for rugby's administrators to admit league has it right, that a drop goal needs downgrading to one point.

One final reminder. I'll reiterate. Jonny's kick against Australia would have produced the same outcome, one point or three, so too Joel's. But the greatest drives of televised times both required three points to alter the outcome. Evans and Sexton's were exceptions to the rule, not reasons to remain so conservative with points-scoring systems. Wilkinson was the deadliest of the drop goal exponents. The clean-cut Home Counties hero. But come on, hand on heart? The killer boot didn't do a great deal for the game. Not on the global scale. When I'm old and grey and full of sleep and nodding by the fire I might giggle one more time at the memory of an inebriated kick against Harlequins. Yet the sport must one day consider the wider consequences for the game. Three points encourages kicking, one point encourages running. If these convictions represent a conversion on the road to Wigan, then I'll doff my flat cap to our friends from the north. Best drop goal I have ever seen? That Nick Evans one, Sexton's second. The best of them all will be the last one to cross the bar with a three-point value attached to it.

ENGLAND

THE YEAR of George Orwell, 1984. Big Brother was on the alert for any English rugby player doing anything out of the ordinary. It was a time to keep your head down. A training session in Stourbridge, Industrial Revolution territory – England's only session before we gathered the day before our autumn international. Just the one, back then. The opposition was Australia, Mark Ella, magic, mystery in the green and gold. It would be my debut for England. I was the only contender for the fly half position. The form with Bristol was not far short of as good as it got for much of my career. Conference organising – my day job – was put on hold. Out of the office and straight up the M5 to the Midlands, a serene journey in Austin Sheppard's hearse. I was still a Bristol player, a gullible twenty-one-year-old. I drove to Austin's home, Bristol's most capped undertaker. He asked me to reach inside a door to grab his kit bag. Instead there's a body . . . and with it the amused chuckle of an old prop's laugh. Why not, it was a good gag. The old ones are the best . . . rugby humour, nobody hurt . . .

somebody's dead. We were dead beat by the end of the evening. An evening devoid of invention.

Nigel Melville and I had been selected together, England's half back partnership for the first time. Two debutants. Nigel handed the captaincy for good measure. Both of us begging for a few minutes to acclimatise ourselves. The one passing to the other. I had twice played against him in Anglo-Welsh schoolboy fixtures. We had played together once, a pair of Barbarians at the Hong Kong Sevens. But sevens has more in common with league than union – one-dimensional, one line of defence, athleticism over intellect, let's call it rugby intellect. We were strangers in the floodlit Stourbridge night. Exhausted, occasionally exchanging glances. The training was torturous, a sequence of stamina tests. Way too late to make us into international athletes. International rugby players were not the same as international athletes. Certainly not then. Our coach was Dick Greenwood, former England international and father of future England World Cup winner, Will. Was the illogic of the dimly lit evening some sort of psychological trick? Training so hard it wouldn't hurt when the lungs started to burn in six days' time? If so, it went over my head. Then again, most things do. I didn't find out how far Melville could pass, he didn't fathom how flat I would or wouldn't take the ball. In those days I regarded myself as a darting, daring fly half. Ella was to expose my ignorance as to the full potential of the position. A bold attacking fly half in England was a conservative cretin in Australia. The Wallabies were finally on the move after being league's bag ladies for too long. They thought about the game. We huffed and puffed in preparation. Our worth measured by the cold air we exhaled, powering up and down the pitch, no rugby ball in sight. For all the press-ups and sit-ups, the squat thrusts and the 'two-minute run' (to each line on a rugby pitch and back to the try line within two minutes) we were well beaten by the Wallabies. 19–3. I was dropped. Dropped. Dumped. Devastated. The latter not for any patriotic reasons.

To think, I had dreamed of playing international rugby through my entire schooldays. No, expected. And this was it. Into and out of a useless side after one cap. I cursed my Essex blood. Like too many members of the England set up, Test rugby was personal. Personal in a way that representing any other team was not. Or never had been for me. England was where, so to speak, I had thrown my cap into the rugby ring. I cared less about our sceptred isle than my ego. It was bruised and battered. Add boredom into the equation and it's no great surprise things turned out as they did. Which was extremely badly. A wasted talent, if you wish to be generous, maybe. A wastrel, without doubt. Even in 1983, my first year on the bench when I hoped – rather than expected – to start (although I had no doubts I should have been picked), that edge of excitement, the urge to win, was elsewhere. We were all amateurs, those days of wilting roses. 'Amo, amas, amat' and all that. But there appeared little devotion to the red rose. Just an artisan's approach to the cause. To make a mark in the early 1980s you had to be exceptional or an insider. I was neither.

Players played the game, accumulated caps. Win, lose or draw, the result wasn't the point. It was all very clubbable. Especially amongst the forwards. The heartbeat of the team. A very slow heartbeat. In 1980 England had won a Grand Slam, their first since 1957. I remember the shock of watching an Englishman scythe through opponents, footwork like a Welshman (indeed he was educated in North Wales, a military school from which he persistently continued to run away). That man was Clive Woodward. He was to become one of the most significant names in English rugby history. It seems more than a coincidence that Woodward had so many problems with discipline in his early days. English rugby was based upon rigid hierarchies and an unquestioning ability to follow orders. The man who changed the face of England as a Test team was an outsider. Such an outsider that he ran away to Sydney where he formulated his rugby philosophy. An English/Welsh manager, an Australian cultural influence. No wonder his former colleagues and contemporaries were quicker to scathe than praise 'weird' Woody. He didn't play their game. Woodward was not a structured thinker, he was a man of maverick tendencies with an open-mindedness that didn't belong in the barracks of the English rugby brain. Rugby thinking and England, it was a cruel contradiction in terms for a boy who perceived the game as a cross between poetry and chess. Not that I could play the latter or write anything but execrable poetry in my younger days . . .

Drinking, not thinking. Here was the great pleasure to be had in the Anglo-Saxon rugby life. I readily acclimatised myself to Albion's ales. Staying at the Petersham Hotel, high above an oft painted ox bow of the Thames in Richmond. The lads were thirsty for a pint or five after team meetings, trying to remember what they were told, rote learning rugby. The forwards especially. And the embittered bench. In those days only injury enabled the replacement to accumulate caps. Drinking half a dozen pints or so the night before the game? Rugby didn't take such a physical toll when the backs were small and the forwards slow and frequently flabby. It was odds against getting into the action. Probably 10–1 against, maybe greater. Worth a pint or six at such odds. The Roebuck was our den. Dark and dingy with a publican loyal to the boozy big men and the attendant substitutes, sinking and slumping into our half-empty pints of bitter resentment often as not. England's management drank in the pub attached to the Petersham, as long as we were out of sight . . .

As for the games . . . the real action kicked off after the final whistle on the bus transporting the team, the committee and their wives to the Park Lane Hilton. Windows On The World.

Scanning the grandeur of Hyde Park. Committee wives were there, like the dinosaurs, long before players' wives. We sipped pre-dinner cocktails at the expense of the RFU. Downstairs, off the foyer, Arabs were drifting into Trader Vic's. Hypocrisy and hookers, not in the tradition of such front row technicians as Peter Wheeler and Brian Moore. The dinner in a vast and soulless ballroom was the point of the weekend. For the men who served their times on tedious committees to make it big, they had to make a Five Nations dinner. Take the wife to London. Sip sherry beneath a massive mirror ball. Black ties, ball gowns, free gin and tonic. Everyone – or nearly everyone – inebriated in defeat as much as victory. Few seemed to care. Players' wives slipped out of their stilettos and we poured champagne into them. Decadence signed off incognito in the guise of RFU dignitaries. Had we displayed the same style and invention with which we ripped off the union, England would have come across as a dashing team, full of flair.

One of us even saved a certain semblance of style for the Sunday morning run-around at Hyde Park. It wasn't so much the lactic acid from the game we were getting out of the system (I thought this an entrancing cocktail of milk and LSD when first I heard the phrase 'lactic acid' – so much for an Oxbridge education) as the session-binge quantity of grog from the Saturday night. On a magnificent Sunday morning the late Maurice Colclough, one of the more intellectual yet antediluvian of England's forwards, stepped into the plush Hilton lift, one floor below mine, ready for the run, resplendent in Dunlop Green Flash tennis shoes and dinner suit from the night before. For that alone, Maurice, you will never be forgotten, not by me. I believe I may have vomited into the Serpentine that morning, scaring off the swans and a startled Sunday School party as I hiccupped along. This could have been any England home game between 1983 and 1987. The year is irrelevant. The coaches changed. The mentality, the behaviour stayed the same. The 1980 Grand Slam was merely one of those blue moons you see lighting up the darkness now and then.

The first World Cup in New Zealand, when, to the surprise of few, England flopped – losing to Wales, a weak Welsh team, the utter predictability of it. Then the decision to appoint Bradford's Geoff Cooke as the next England manager. Obscure to the point of anonymous as far as the Bath boys were concerned, it was the beginning of a more meaningful, professional approach to international rugby. Geoff and I didn't see eye to eye on many rugby issues. His appointment wasn't good news for me. It was bad, very bad. And it was good for England in general. Where there had been chaos there was soon organisation. Where there had been parties and piss-ups, suddenly there was pride and practice. The advent of the leagues assisted in changing the mindset of England's best players. That new-found English determination dripped through from club to country. It was definitely a case of trickle up when it came to rugby union. The good times creaked, the wheels began to roll. In 1991 and 1992 England achieved successive Grand Slams. Cooke was the catalyst. Will Carling was the captain. His appointment made no rugby sense at the time. England's foundations were up front. And the forwards knew it. There was to be no power shift from forwards to backs but here was a twenty-two-year-old centre, still one of rugby's genuine famous names. Public school. Durham. The army. Handed the reins of power. Carling didn't change England's way of playing, but he altered the public's perception. What with winning, suddenly the red rose was sexy, bounding off the back pages – Dean Richards and his ursine presence or not – and Cooke was creating an organisation which was meticulous in its planning.

Carling was the cavalier captain of the tabloids, Cooke the controlling influence behind the scenes. The team was capable of some scintillating rugby but there was always too much of the cosmetic about their commitment to back play. In 1991, this weakness cost them the World Cup final against Australia. Shrewd leadership would have seen England stay true to the power of their pack. Instead of focusing all their forces down the narrow channel of a forward-based game, the underused backs suddenly ran free. The energy of the side dissipated. England were outfoxed by the Australian team in the build-up to the final. England were baited, they ran the ball in a way the Wallabies' David Campese claimed they couldn't. And they lost a game that was the England forwards' to win. Australia won with a losing hand. Had the wily card sharp, Richards, been captain instead of sitting on the replacements bench, England would have produced a second gear performance and inexorably ground the Australian pack into the Twickenham dirt. In so many ways Cooke had chosen the ideal captain but in a crisis Carling, with a limited vision of the game, was the wrong one. A 'follow me' type. Not the thinker England needed. Another Grand Slam followed for Carling in 1992. England were mean, muscular, sharp and strong. A superbly drilled, individually excellent side but grand as they were, as much as Cooke reinvented them, the seeds of English supremacy were not sown by this group. Cooke pulled England from the mire of European mediocrity. For this he deserves plenty of praise. But he lacked the devil and anarchic forces needed to take them to the top.

Clive Woodward would be plucked from his back-up position as Bath's backs coach, Andy Robinson's number two, into the role of England coach. The former London Irish coach replaced Jack Rowell. The Bath Machiavelli won a Grand Slam in his first year in charge of England. He made the semi-final of the 1995 World Cup. Woodward took six years to win a Grand Slam and was eliminated at the quarter-final stage in his first World Cup. After that searing disappointment against South

Africa in 1999, the chorus was legion. Woodward should go. 'Judge me on the World Cup.' Some did and he came up short. But in Fran Cotton he had rare support at the highest level of the RFU. Cotton, a major force within the union, was one of the few England forwards who stood by Woodward. One of the few who yearned for so much more than a few post-match pints. In professionalism's first few years, Cotton took country's side over club. The row is yet to be resolved. He stood behind Woodward and repelled any potential rebellion. An important, imposing background force. Had Woodward been run out of office in 1999, the northern hemisphere would still be awaiting its first World Cup triumph, for all the calibre of the squad at his disposal. Vickery, Johnson, Back, Hill, Dallaglio, Wilkinson and Robinson were all world class players when 'world class' was more than an unthinking cliché. The brawn and brain of Tindall and Greenwood was a fine foil in the centre. Given such riches wasn't 22 November 2003 inevitable?

Some of the players claim as much. But some of the players would. Some of the players didn't and don't comprehend exactly what Woodward did for them. There's a lovely tale told by assorted World Cup winners. It relates to one of their final training sessions before the final, Wednesday, Thursday, it doesn't matter. The coaches had a few details they wanted to iron out. Johnson sent them packing. From here on in the players knew what was in their tank, what was needed. Ergo, proof the coaching was overrated . . . wrong. Woodward systematically worked on them, game by game, year by year. Martin Johnson was converted from a thuggish second row to a thinking forward, one of England's greatest. It required someone to chisel out the big basic rugby brain from the mass of granite that was the Leicester lock. The Thinker was once one hell of a chunk of marble. Until Auguste Rodin got the hammers and chisels out it wasn't amounting to anything more than a bloody big lump. It took time. Sculpting does. Grand Slam games were blown at Wembley when England kicked for the corner (to stick the knife further into the Welsh opposition) instead of the posts. There was Murrayfield. When England threw to the tail and lost their bearings on a wild, wet day. Logic screamed drive from the front. Dallaglio and Dawson were the offending characters in those matches but in the end these mistakes pale. They won the World Cup. Unlike the Cooke regime that had so much under-utilised firepower, Woodward encouraged his team to explore their limits, to expand them. To full potential. In the course of this journey they made the sort of errors explorers make. Uncharted territory. Ones that cannot be avoided in new terrain. Ones Cooke's England could have done with making. Grand Slams sufficed for the one regime, but not the other. 'Judge me on the World Cup.' You can judge England on their victory in Australia and their 42–6 demolition of Ireland in Dublin a few months earlier. The Grand Slam, at last. The World Cup and a rare win in New Zealand. All in 2003, the greatest year in English rugby history. A rare statement.

Brian Ashton, Woodward's inventive maestro, was discarded before 2003 but this clear-minded thinker (not as marble hard as Johnson) was back after the embarrassment of the Andy Robinson years when England rediscovered the art of losing on an industrial scale. His wife, Samantha, believed his old Bath team-mate had a role in his dismissal but commentators and columnists meant nothing next to the negative results ledger amassed by Andy. Touching, I suppose, that Mrs R thought me so influential. But I know my position. Don't shoot the messenger . . . Ashton, yet another Bath man, made the final of the 2007 World Cup. He produced a miniature masterpiece of managerial genius halfway through the tournament. A man who encourages players to think for themselves, such a task was beyond this non-vintage crop. Admittedly it had been foolish of Ashton to have believed otherwise. Eventually there was only one thing for it. He let them lose their way sufficiently in order to unite as a group under Phil Vickery. Between them the players formulated the style that most suited them. The squad berated Ashton, as did a few of the coaches. The north Cornish captain, Vickery, in contrast to coaches and veterans like Lawrence Dallaglio and Mike Catt, was loyal to the manager. He returned from France 2007 an outstanding man, like Cotton a crusher of rebellions, a fine captain. His was an average team but they thought, fought and kicked their way to a final. Ashton, the catalyst, was immediately and indecently kicked out. It's true this most original of rugby thinkers wasn't managerial material. Ashton lacked the tenacity of a Woodward. Lacked the will for the fight. Unlike Woodward, he would not have ensured the considerable financial power of the RFU found its way to the playing side. Money was part of the 2003 side's advantage. It had to be fought for. Brian was never that politician. Too reasonable a man. Clive went out on and, when he had to, over the edge.

When Woodward fell from that edge where did it all go wrong? How did England take another twelve years to win a Grand Slam? Rudderless, a lack of ruthlessness. I remember his final press conference. He spat out the word 'compromise' like it was bile. 'Woody' was not a man for compromise, not one for sitting round a pub with a pint and ploughman's in hand, giving here, taking there. There was something of the Margaret Thatcher within. Confrontation was his modus operandi. The RFU, in contrast, a body from the shires, has more Edmund Burke in them. They worried about the potential sporting conflict between club and country. Woodward was all for bringing it on. He won a World Cup. He could just as easily have started an English rugby civil war. Woodward was not to be succeeded by a kindred spirit for well over a decade. What an irony that Eddie Jones, his greatest of verbal sparring pals, was to be that man.

Why did Woodward recommend Robinson? It was the beginning of the slump. The number two had studied many years at the feet of the master. Continuity was the key word. And an arrogance on the part of Woodward. To retain Robinson was in some ways to stay as close as possible to the Woodward years. Lurking inside the rugby knight there's even more Blair than Thatcher. He walked away but that was not the same as letting it go. This was to be his worst decision. Woodward – as he illustrated with the Lions in 2005 – had one way to rule the world. Only the one. As Lions manager he headed for New Zealand intent on teaching New Zealand the same lesson he had taught them with England. The All Blacks had moved forwards and Woodward's thinking had been overtaken. Robinson, alas, lacked the electricity Woodward brought to a room, lacks originality as a thinker. A stuttering selector too, which was terrible news as it is the first priority of a manager. My former Bath team-mate was a good number two, an excellent coach. Good number twos do not necessarily make good managers.

Then Ashton. Then Martin Johnson. The RFU's moment of capitulation to the Twickenham version of Barbour-jacketed populism. To the west stand he was only ever 'Johnno', always the inspiring World Cup-winning captain. Rugby union's Bobby Moore with half a ton more beef. England's greatest captain. Where he led, his lads marched behind, trusting, obedient. In the trenches he would have been quite some man. But the manager isn't in the trenches. He's not leading from the front or by example. He's cool and calculating. He's back behind the front line. Maps, messengers coming in. Readjustments here and there. Shifts in strategy. It is possible that had he stayed within management Johnson might have acquired all these ingredients nobody knew if he possessed or not when appointing him England's saviour. But his failure in the 2011 World Cup ended the debate. Johnson's era ended sadly. Grumpily. Inevitably. Good captains do not necessarily make good managers.

He gave way to caretaker manager, Stuart Lancaster. Inexperienced at international level. A career coach. An RFU coach. Versed in coach-speak. From opting for someone with immense experience as a player and none as a coach, they switched to a man with no real playing background but all the coaching badges the RFU could invent. There can't have been many RFU courses Stuart hasn't been on. On the day of his official appointment Lancaster sounded like an engaging polytechnic lecturer. It was the language of progress, process, decency and pride. Clipped phrases, comfortable with the latest cliché and communication tools. Johnson despised the press. Lancaster embraced us. No mumbling and dark-eyed stares to melt a media pack. Lancaster was the light. Stuart was going to make English fans proud of their team. He played a clever card, intimating England's greatest failure in New Zealand was off the field with dwarf throwing, jumping off ferries, whatever the tabloids could get their hands on. But the real problem wasn't discipline. Johnson wasn't a manager, wasn't a selector, and he didn't get the balance of his team right. The team was terrible in New Zealand, on the field. It is always primarily about what happens on the field. Had England won the World Cup, nobody – or very few people – would have tut-tutted about the off-field behaviour. We'd all have been pitching ourselves off ferries. No criticism until the sheen wears off. Then anyone becomes fair game. That's the game we play. As for on-field manners? Lancaster's pride in his players preceded the fall. Year after year after year. How delightful to find decency the key to winning. That dream died. England were nice. But dim. They needed a few bastards. So Lancaster bombed out, like Robinson and Ashton and Johnson. Like Robinson, he was not a good selector, like Robinson he is – as he has proved in his work with Leinster – an extremely capable coach. In the end he was probably too decent. Certainly too thin-skinned. Good men don't necessarily make good managers.

Enter Eddie Jones, a man proclaimed too nice by few, for all the cheeky Antipodean grin. Jones picked Dylan Hartley, the media and public's Playing Enemy Number One as his skipper. Selected the same men who had made such a monstrosity of the 2015 home World Cup, as if to say, 'the problems were not the players', the Grand Slam a two-fingered salute to the flaws of the previous management, even as he politely praised them. Hard-nosed straight-talking thinkers have it in them to be good coaches. For a while . . .

THE FRENCH

PUT YOURSELF in my boots, Nike at the time. The Greek goddess of victory. Not this afternoon. Not as far as England are concerned. France were the opposition. France on form. This Saturday afternoon they have shrugged their collective shoulders and thought, 'Why not?' The backs are running full tilt from the first minute onwards. It's a good day to be a replacement. Make that a great day to be a replacement. There are no tactical substitutes in March 1986. I wouldn't have minded a chance to get a run at fly half. What I did not want, what I dreaded, was an early injury to our full back. Myself and John Palmer, Bath's gifted, gambling, smoking centre, were enjoying the jelly babies an awful lot more than the opening exchanges of this game. Not that we weren't bursting with admiration for some of the French back play. English or not, had we been sitting anywhere but on the replacements' bench we would have relished the treat of seeing the fabulous French backs at their elegant best.

I was just about to get stuck into my favourite black jelly baby when Brian Ashton, the backs coach, snatched the sweet from my hand. 'Get on, Stuart.' An injury to our full back. Shit. There was no rush. Slowly, slowly, I peeled off the tracksuit top, hoping the zip would jam. I yanked down the bottoms, ensured the socks were neatly tied at the top of the calves. Knot and unknot the short cords several times. Fuck it, there was still an hour to go, there was no getting out of this.

Full back is a peach of a position. I had some great days there in my youth. Especially when the pack was on the front foot, when the midfield was full of threat, the opposition struggling. I side-stepped onto the field and pranced into the drama. Surrounded by the architecturally brutal concrete bowl that is the Parc des Princes, *La Marseillaise* echoing around this stadium of pure sound. So much colour. The senses took it all in. Thrilled. Scared? Mistype scared and you come up with sacred. Maybe. England were awarded a penalty. Rob must have been having a bad day, I don't remember, but I was asked to kick for goal. Thirty-five metres or so out, late into the fray, hamstrings a touch taut. The Adidas ball. Black at each end, and something between an orange or brown in the middle (I told you I'm colour blind). Part of the romance of the French game . . . a plump ball, giant sweet spot, pigskin? It travels a mile. 'Try for goal, Barnesy?' Damned right I will . . .

. . . The Alcan rugby field, Newport. Halfway between home and school. Alcan is a company that had (I assume the company and its jobs are long gone now) something to do with the steel industry. I'm not sure what. Take a narrow dirt track off the main road and it is a few hundred yards to the car park. Through an avenue of trees. There's heaven on earth. My own private pitch. Surrounded on three sides by trees, on one by a stream. Cross the watery border and you were on your way to Rogerstone. I never saw another soul, bar me and my father. I think a supermarket has swallowed this particular field of dreams. John, my father, drives the mile or so from home. He stands behind the posts in his sheepskin coat and boots the ball back to me. Ever encouraging, dreaming as much, if not more, than me. Our rugby ball is cheap. Not the narrower Mitre brand which does not allow much margin for error if mishit. No, we have a big fat unbranded pigskin ball. Shaped like an Adidas ball. Flies a mile if you make a true connection. I kick penalties from my own ten-metre line. Sixty soaring metres. Further than the then current internationals kick. Playing at a Celtic version of Icarus and Daedalus. But I don't know that myth yet. Crash and burn. Not yet, not in those teenage years of wild delusion and borderless imagination. The dream lived. For father and son. I carried his dreams with me. Aeneas in a pair of rugby shorts? I took those dreams to Paris. From playing at the Alcan rugby ground, it was less than a decade. Now the pretend pigskin is the real thing. No longer the secluded woods. Pretending to kick the winning penalty for England against Wales. The perfect strike, the real thing, sweet on the sweet spot, three points . . . a fine feeling. Unfettered fucking youth. Full back or not, it was now officially spring time in south-west Paris . . .

. . . But not for long. Clouds emerged from nowhere. Well, the other end of the field; dark blue clouds, lots of them, in the shape of the French back line, pouring through our midfield. Yeats was right, the centre cannot hold. Not that day, Willy boy. There I was, Wales' most capped schoolboy full back – but that was then and this was now, and besides the wench is dead and I'm thinking of Marlowe, anything but my forlorn predicament as the forces of fair France swarmed through the English breaches. Shit, but where were you Shakespeare when I needed your fifth Henry to help me? The try line, seventy metres wide, and Serge Blanco running straight at me. Philippe Bloody Sella on his shoulder for good measure . . . and a few others. No sign of a red rose. Just me to protect our line. Blanco was so beautifully balanced. He held the ball in the palm of his hand. All the swagger of a French waiter in a high-class Parisian restaurant, swerving past Englishmen as if we were no more than slightly sweaty tables of foreign tourists. Devouring strides. Glorious. Twenty metres from the try line, his support cast either side. I faded to step inside. Make him think I am going to (attempt to) tackle him. I shifted late, hoping he will throw the pass, aiming to intercept what was otherwise destined to be a try-scoring pass. Yes! He passed a split second too soon. The ball bounced into my left palm and up. Nearly 50,000 people should have seen what a sharp-witted piece of play I pulled off. What a hero! The ball dropped back into my hands, I stepped into the safety of touch. Such are the incidents to earn a replacement a recall. But no, the referee was signalling towards the posts for a penalty try. Against me. Deliberately knocking on. No! Oh, for video technology. I could have been a temporary hero. Instead I conceded the only penalty try of my career. Good a place as anywhere to be criminally misjudged. France went on to win 29–10. Blanco and Sella were acquainted with me far too often that afternoon. Lights out in Paris.

Outplayed, punched out, it all came the same way to France. As a child, one of the most beguiling aspects of the French team was the violence that simmered below the surface. Inches below. I loved the way television unerringly shot a close-up of the sweating lock forward, Jean-François Imbernon, crossing himself and mouthing prayers to the Virgin Mary moments before stomping onto the field – sanctioned/sanctified by the mother of Jesus to do as much damage as possible to the obviously disbelieving opposition. Violence, intrinsic to the game. Who doesn't like a scuffle in these watered-down days? Who didn't thrill to the closed fist ferocity of rugby in the good old bad old days? And there was nowhere more bloodthirsty than France. Monsieur Gouge from Gigondas, Monsieur Testicle Twister from Toulouse; the contrast was magnificent. Forwards fought, backs ran. French backs ran like no other three quarters. Deeper and more lateral. Drifting with the floated pass of that bloated Adidas ball, as if caught helpless in an Atlantic rip tide, until someone cut the line, changed the angle, broke through the defensive wave and all of France was suddenly flooding towards the full back on the breakers of wave after attacking wave. I do believe the angels will stand by the French backs of old and the demons by the thuggish beetle brow forwards. Angels and demons thrive where political correctness finds few footholds. You'll find them still in the south-west of France where rugby defines its districts and denizens.

Political correctness struggles in the south of France. French rugby has soul, albeit a dark one, an intriguing one. Milton's Satan had all the best lines. The greatest crime committed on the field in France though wasn't any of the notable nefarious acts over the years. No, it was the day Bernard Laporte – then coach of France, once secretary of state for sport and now president of the French Federation – came up with the calamitous plan to strip France of its unique rugby soul. A soul originating in the small towns of the south-west. A declaration of old France. Laporte demanded that French elite players should imitate the discipline of their English opposites. It didn't work; it won't work. In the quest for discipline France froze. The forwards stopped intimidating and the backs ceased scything.

Oh, for the days of the 1930s when France were ejected from the Championship (the Five Nations) for the twin vices of violence and professionalism. Pompously amateur in Great Britain and Ireland, French semi-professionalism sent them into disgrace and exile. It was to be quite some exile with the Second World War ending all competition from 1939 until the termination of the war. During occupation, the French Federation saw an opportunity to rid themselves of the growing threat from rugby league. The rival code was known simply by the number thirteen, a reference to the number of players in a league team. This shameful period of French history proved to be more than merely unlucky for league. In collaboration with the Vichy regime, union confiscated league's assets. They were not readily returned. Not to even be acknowledged until 2002 when an apology was belatedly issued. This is a rugby land where poets and the Prince of Darkness kiss and make up, over and over.

Where were we before the Vichy regime so rudely interrupted our musings? Ah yes, the quest for discipline. Laporte looked on in horror as the nation of shopkeepers (Adam Smith coined the phrase, not Napoleon) showed the world how to win. He didn't register the fine balance between backs and forwards. Or the development of English attacking play under the gaze of Brian Ashton. Only the Anglo-Saxon capacity to play to – not by (major difference between these little words) – the rules. France's coach tried to convert the French rugby team into an ill-fitting English one. A decade after Laporte had departed from the Test arena, Philippe Saint-André took charge, Round Table like, pursuing the same Holy Grail. The same sixty-nine-times capped French winger who once said to me, 'Stuart, the difference between the English and the French is this: if a policeman blows his whistle and gesticulates in England, everyone stops and stands still. Awaiting instructions. In France we will run away in every possible direction.' It was a shrewd observation. English rugby teams were not averse to being told exactly what to do. Laporte set about making France the continental equivalent of England. I wonder how deeply the quest damaged the psyche of the French game? Even now, in 2019 my great friend and former half back partner at Bath, Richard Hill tells me, 'The coach is "Le Patron". He decides what goes and what doesn't. Players keep their heads down and say nothing even if they don't agree. In a team meeting no French player will say a word.' Richard is coach of up and coming Rouen. The malaise has permeated deep. An epidemic spreading from the Test team through the rest of the country. The negative impact of the vast number of overseas players in the club game is the 'official' explanation when one discusses the failures of the French national team but the implantation of an alien virus into the very DNA of French rugby has done untold damage to the French game. Overseas players are a fact of French rugby life. An easy answer for the years of failure. In France it is regarded as a self-evident fact. Fuck the facts. More truth may be discovered by sticking to feelings.

Long before Laporte, there was Toulouse. The nearest thing in rugby-mad south-west France to aristocracy. The dominant force in both French domestic and European rugby. No club in Europe has a finer pedigree. The first European champions, four titles to their name. Guy Novès played for Toulouse, he coached Toulouse. He *was* Toulouse. Until recently he was charged with restoring pride and eventually results to the French national team. It was a strange appointment. One either rewriting or ignoring the last decade or more of his time in charge at Toulouse, when the French giants lost their style and, eventually their way. Novès forgot about the tantalising touches of the Toulouse back three on the counter attack. The majesty of a midfield with the bejewelled brilliance of Yannick Jauzion at the centre of everything. Suddenly only size counted. Slow. Ponderous. Toulouse went from being feared to being fat. And France appointed the man who presided over this dumbing down as their coach. My feeling is that the national team's experiment with discipline, which discarded words like 'flair' and 'risk', was a contagion in the very body of the French game.

True, Toulouse continued to win titles even as the magic faded. But their two most recent European triumphs against French teams, Stade Français (2005) and Biarritz (2010) were down to aura as much as ability. Toulouse were Toulouse. Other French teams didn't beat them in European finals. The same occurred in the 2002 final in Dublin against Perpignan. All three all-French finals were dreary affairs. At Bath, we too benefited from the great intangible of being the side that always won finals. For all the talk of tactics and technique, sometimes the belief that one side possesses and the other does not overwhelms all other factors. These are the days when you believe and talk of the rugby gods. So it had been in 1992 when Harlequins did everything but drop a goal to end our unbeaten Twickenham run. But belief alone cannot sustain a team forever.

In the distant days before Novès and his replacement, Jacques Brunel, there was Pierre Villepreux. The Cardinal Richelieu of French back play since his buccaneering days as a long-striding French international full back. The professorial mastermind at Toulouse. We played (and beat) Toulouse in a four-team tournament pre-season in Brive. Down in Le Corrèze. Proud of the result. Toulouse were, after all, Toulouse. We were also delighted with the fact that the day after the match the Cardinal worked with our backs and Jack Rowell with the Toulouse forwards. These were days of open-mindedness. Good days for the game. Open borders and minds. Now there is globalisation. Coaches and players travelling from all over the world (predominantly New Zealand) to earn their income. But instead of expanding the game, too much globalisation shrinks the sport. If New Zealand can induce the rest of the world to play like Kiwis, there is no hope for the planet. To beat New Zealand, not mimicry but originality and variety is required.

French rugby has an obsession with thr All Blacks. Not unlike my old one. That France became their bogey team is no great surprise. France is a little more extravagant in everything it does; daring to do the unexpected (except on the field these days). Wearing bow ties in a final in front of over 70,000 people. Such was once the way of Racing when they were Metro and not 92.

The patrician Parisians took the Bath ploy of wearing pre-match bow ties at Gloucester to another dimension. Took it to the field in a Top 14 final. Exotic. Extreme. Put Bath's idea of the louche and libertine in its little Beau Nash place. Too Molière for the English language. Yet Racing and Stade Français stand in the starkest contrast to the rest of France in their penchant for pink and their homoerotic nude calendars. Cosmopolitan with a capital C.

At the other end of France, at the other end of the spectrum, stands Toulon. A Napoleonic naval port on the Mediterranean. Three consecutive Heineken Cup trophies from 2013–15. One of the most amazing institutions in the world of professional rugby. Their president, Mourad Boudjellal, does nothing by the text book. Everything comes out of his crazy comic book logic. Coaches are appointed after players. Coaches come and go. As I first wrote this chapter in March 2017, Mike Ford was leaving to be replaced by Fabien Galthié, the former French scrum half and Montpellier manager. What odds he isn't there now? That is what I wrote in 2017. He's gone now. Toulon are in free-fall. The 2013 team stand alone. Boudjellal assembled rugby's version of the Avengers with Jonny Wilkinson as the clean-cut Captain America figure, holding the collection of egos together. Theoretically the most English of fly halves, with his conservative kicking game and his chiselled looks, he should not fit into the Toulon template. Rather the non-template, the anarchy of the individual. The comparisons with Real Madrid and their 'Galacticos' had been right up there near the top of the cliché table throughout the Toulon era. But whereas Real sign many of the world's leading footballers, Toulon cherry-picked men who were broadly perceived as past their international prime. Until we had to write those clichés. Wilkinson, Bakkies Botha, Ma'a Nonu, Ali Williams, Juan Smith, all these men were former World Cup winners. Their best days should have been on DVD. Yet Toulon, with a laissez-faire approach to the gym and a deep-rooted trust in the decision-making prowess of these supposedly dated superheroes – who knows – maybe inadvertently questioned the very foundations of rugby's new age professional logic. The importance of a player's mental strength (as opposed to the physical obsession of the era) is so far out of kilter with the world of the professional European game that Toulon has to be sidelined by the establishment as a freak show with a freak comic book owner. One day their achievements might cause a rethink in the way rugby is coached. They were so much more than a Stan Lee Saturday morning Marvel magazine through those glory years.

I'll admit to a soft spot for Toulon. In my first year as Bath captain, 1988, we returned from a Far East tour; anything but fresh, but fit – despite the terrifying amount of alcohol that had to be consumed on a tour. We had been in Malaysia, Thailand and Australia. Now we were back in Europe – Amsterdam to be precise. Where else? The Dutch champions and runners-up and the top two sides in France and England, Toulon and Bath. Éric Champ, tough guy. Toulon, tough team. Toulon tore into us in the final. They had an open side flanker, could have been a young Apache out to make his mark in a Hollywood Western. Torture on his mind. That is if he didn't kill me straight out. I caught my first pass, kicked downfield, stopping to admire my work as a set of studs grazed my jaw. Only a glancing blow but an unusual one. The solitary occasion on which I was karate kicked. It was ample excuse for an all-in fight. I could write 'frightening' but there is something quite undeniably exhilarating when a man tries to break your jaw with his boot. Frightening? No, it was freedom. JG Ballard madness. Great fun while the adrenaline lasted. In this instance that was maybe twenty minutes. I called the team over. All chasing a chance to kick someone in the head. Enough, neither Toulon nor us were doing anything except beating the crap out of each other . . . let's do something radical . . . like concentrate on the rugby. What do you reckon, men? By the time Toulon worked out our clever little ruse we were twenty points clear. Late that night I was drinking with their coach, a legend in Toulon, Daniel Herrero. The Toulon family. Bushy grey hair, red bandanna, big beard, a Mexican bandit landed in Toulon. We drank late that night as he toasted Bath for 'understanding the purity of violence'. Outside rugby, Herrero is on the side of the angels. He does notable charitable works. On the field, he was the quintessential French rugby man. He still does some radio work. Occasionally we bump into one another, huge smiles and open arms in the press box, bonded together by a love of a violence that can no longer speak its name.

Boudjellal was preaching to the converted in 2016 when he said, 'It's a difficult time [he was referring to the spate of terror attacks in Paris and nearby Nice] but in the stadium, people of every religion come together under the name Toulon.' This is as neat a summary of the virtues of community as you could wish for. To have seen Captain America and his superheroes achieve the astonishing feat of three European titles was right up there with the antics of Spider Man, to whom Boudjellal compared Wilkinson. Hmm, the troubled youth with super powers that was Peter Parker or Captain America, the all-American action hero without half the power of some of his mates but an innate ability to pull it together and prevail . . . you decide the more appropriate comparison. The ragged orange glow on the peaks behind the stadium, the harbour and the Mediterranean waiting for you, Africa out there, beyond the other set of posts. This is as dramatic a backdrop in rugby country as you could ever wish for. The sun goes down red here, blood red. Hemingway would have got it.

Perhaps another of the snapshots that summed up the best of French rugby took place on the first day of the 2007 World

Cup. The theory went something like this. France kick off the tournament on a Friday night against Argentina. The Pumas are good. Will make a game of it but not much more than that. France march on. Scotland in the quarter-final. The Springboks in the semi and then the game of French history, the All Blacks in the final. In Paris. The plan was a good one, until the host team froze in the spotlight and lost to Argentina. I was commentating for ITV. Quite a way to kick-start the competition. Stunned, silenced in the architecturally impressive but deflationary atmosphere of the Stade de France spacecraft. Dreams dead before they were born (they were, typically French, to famously beat the All Blacks in a quarter-final in Cardiff, of all places), yet when a band of Argentina fans danced and sang their way around the stadium after the game, the French fans clapped. Cheered. Shared their finest Calvados. Nothing reflected better on France than the reaction of their fans that night. On the field, 2007 was not a memorable tournament, off it France revelled in the same flair and exuberance for life their players once displayed on the playing fields. If the French team could perform with the verve of their supporters, it wouldn't matter how many Georgians, Kiwis, South Africans and Fijians filled the professional ranks. France would be back. All rugby fans should eagerly await that day.

GUSCOTT

THE SARACENS press room on a Sunday. No one seemed too interested in the afternoon's European Champions Cup quarter-final. Saracens versus Glasgow. The English press assumed an English club win. Come to think of it, so did the Scots. An hour and a half until kick-off. As far as Sky went, the commentary checks were clean. We could all hear one another, producer, director, commentators, graphics, replays; all hunky dory. What better way to kill time until kick-off than filling my face with one of the many meaty pies warming and waiting for me at the far end of the press box, burn the roof of your mouth-type warm. An anti-epicurean experience. Everyone else is talking about the impending World Cup draw and the cost of flights to Tokyo.

Then I saw him. My old companion from the days when Bath, not Saracens, were the team the press were sent to cover. Jeremy Guscott. Do I see or hear him first? 'Stuart,' he was smiling, waving, like he couldn't be happier to see anyone else on the entire planet. Something was up. Smiling, waving, using my first name . . . Barrel, Barna, you old bastard, anything but Stuart.

I don't recall Jerry ever calling me anything as friendly as my first name. 'Hi Jerry, good to see you, how's it going?' It turned out everything was great, other than the fact Jerry had driven to Barnet from Bath without his wallet. He was short on funds to fill the tank after the game, to transport him back to the civilisation of the West Country. Away from BBC radio duty. Big grin, perfect teeth, that old evil laugh, grey hair these days . . . he knew I knew he was after something from me. 'Sixty quid will do.' I had a wad of notes left over from a successful four days at Cheltenham races. For once. In true Bath fashion I handed over five ten pound notes. 'Drive slowly, save the fucking planet, Jerry. And don't call me Stuart again, it gave you away.'

We live less than half an hour apart. We don't meet up. Away from rugby we don't share the same passions. On a team bus Jerry used to say, 'he's deep' if I dared open a paperback before the three-card brag session warmed up. Even if we did have more in common, we probably wouldn't bother. It's the Bath way. We are not soul buddies, we are mates. He's one of those men you can see once a year and pick up the thread. We had a helluva night out in Cape Town on the 2018 England tour. Probably won't drink together for another year. But it's always a delight to see the Prince of Centres as someone once pronounced Jerry. It may have been Jerry himself.

Our relationship wasn't always this warm. The former bricklayer and briefly Bath Badgerline bus driver (the players liked the nickname 'Buscott' considerably more than Jerry did) would have preferred the Oxford University 'ponce' to have stayed in Bristol. Having one Oxford type in Simon Halliday at the club was bad enough. A pair of Varsity snobs? Too much. A local lad, mucked in with the Bath boys. Didn't initially care for outsiders. Especially when they played in his favoured position. A rumour doing the rounds long after Jerry established himself as one of England's greatest of centres was that he thought he would take over as Bath's fly half when one of the heroes of Bath, John Horton, retired from the game. Suddenly some stuck-up bloke from bloody Bristol – of all places – is recruited. An England international, just twenty-two years of age. Never did ask Jerry if he pined to play ten. Maybe I'll ask the next time we meet. Though I doubt it. Our Bath generation aren't big on questions and answers. If true it might explain the coolness of our early relationship.

Coolness is kind. When I pitched up in the Georgian City, the autumn of 1986, he hadn't yet made the big breakthrough. Horton, Halliday and John Palmer was not a midfield a teenager waltzed into, even one as gloriously gifted as Guscott. Outside Bath now, Palmer has already been swallowed up in the mists of time. Let me shine a torch briefly back into the distant past. 'JP' was bandy legged, had never seen the insides of a gym and had something approaching a stoop in the way he walked, bending into the breeze, keeping the cigarette from being blown out, *Racing Post* in kit bag, worried lines on his brow . . . except I don't think John worried a great deal. If he had any ambition he kept it hidden in the pages of the *Post* somewhere between Fakenham and Fairyhouse. He had no great pace. Not much power. But he was pure genius with a ball in his hand.

Getting ready for Cardiff. A big game in those days. The midweek match under floodlights. You could buy postcards of the event. We prepared for it like a cup final. JP and I worked on a move. He would run straight into a Cardiff tackler and, at the moment of impact, flip the ball into the air, behind his back. At the last second I would loop around and scuttle between the posts, not a Welsh hand laid on me. Jack aimed abuse our way when he saw the backs 'playing around' instead of taking the training session seriously. Waved his forefinger, 'That'll never work.' These were days when rugby league professionals were not yet off-loading out of a tackle, let alone one-handedly behind their back. It came on like a circus trick and of course, it worked. The crowd cheered as I darted beneath the posts. What a great player I was. People patted my back. John Palmer, pint in hand, chuckled in the clubhouse afterwards, 'That worked all right then.' Understated, a star for those who knew their rugby astronomy, not of the stellar variety for which Jerry was destined.

I don't like words like 'destiny', not much is inevitable in this life. Not many see that awfully adopted word, a 'pathway' that will open up their blazing trail to the firmament. But Jerry did. His self-confidence masked by a youthful arrogance which didn't impress everyone. But he wasn't that impressed with the rest of the world. Jerry had an edge. His mother, Sue, sadly now gone, was the daughter of a military man. She took no shit. Great sense of humour, sharp tongue. Like mother like son. As for his father, Henry was Jamaican. Henry was – and still is in his 80s – elegant. Very suave. Word was he worked as a porter at the Bath Royal Infirmary. He carries himself with great distinction. A proud man. A sharp-eyed man. He identified an insult in the blink of an eye. Or a newspaper column . . . in my first few years with the *Daily Telegraph*, I picked Jerry out as a player past his prime. Henry was unhappy. He let me know over a pint in the clubhouse, in terms of great certainty. I didn't mind. That's what fathers are for. Chastised, I staggered, drunk with insults, from the public to the members' bar. Walked straight into Sue. 'Ah, there you are . . . I want a word with you . . . thank God, somebody can tell my son he's not perfect.' We shared a gin or two. Jerry had Henry's spike, a point to prove to the world on the field. Off it he had his late mother's straight-talking integrity. Mum and dad gave Jerry the perfect mindset to become a great player. All that was needed to go with the mental strength and determination was the natural talent.

In the mid-1980s there were far fewer black rugby players than there are today. *Swing Low* was first heard at Twickenham when the Nigerian winger, Chris Oti, scored four tries for England. White men singing Negro spirituals. I'd like to think a rugby club and public school song, replete with obscene gestures, was an honest attempt at reverence. Somehow I have my doubts. Rugby wasn't racist but nor was it colour blind. Even now the sport sees rugby in black and white. When Jonathan Joseph, the Bath and England inside centre, tore Scotland to shreds in 2017, the unthinking comparisons with his Bath predecessor filled the sports pages. Yes, both men played outside centre for Bath but their running styles and their defensive games were nothing like the other's. Had one of them been white and the other black, there would have been few if any comparisons. Lazy journalism. A generous term for the clichés.

Emotions ran deep with Guscott. When they erupted, it was smart to stay out of range. I recall his stag night. Beers in Bath. Late night nightclub, nothing out of the ordinary. Nothing except the fact that I was one of few first team members invited. Despite the obvious antagonisms. The night staggered towards the dawn. I was propping up the bar, wondering why I was still out, twenty miles from home in Bristol, in an otherwise empty room had it not been for the Guscott party. The stag eased his way towards me. Leery. Uninhibited with alcohol. His short fierce fuse. He let fly a volley of the purest vitriol. I slurred out clumsy words, eight-pint abuse. Push, shove, roll on the floor, pathetic punches. Nobody, nothing hurt, except pissed-up pride. Jerry's best mates looked on in momentary confusion and saw no damage had, or could, be done. The pair of us were picked up and dusted down from the dance floor as the feeble fight reached a painless finale. The music thudded monotonously on. If there were broken chairs it was where we fell off them, not smashed them over the other's head. As fights go it was feeble, no stunt men needed. But it broke the ice. Better to break the ice than a skull. Had he fought as he played the game, he'd have killed me. Strange evening. But I liked the fact the stag night party was predominantly made up of his drinking mates. Not the big names of the first team. You can judge a man by the friends he keeps. Jerry, through the glory years and beyond, never deserted Chalkie, Pete . . . all his Bath boys.

And oh, were there to be glory years. Rugby records will note a hat-trick on his debut for England against Romania. May 1989 if my memory is playing straight . . . the moment when the transition from bricklayer to Prince of Centres began. But see if you can find Bath's first match of the 1988/89 season somewhere in the maze that is the internet. Just back from a booze-ridden tour of the Far East. Toulon as a 'warm-up' game. The tour I started to appreciate what Jerry was about, on and off the field. He liked to laugh – with the world, at the world. All the same to the Prince. The Far East to east Wales and Pontypool, the top Welsh club. A huge pack, horrible, hairy, fairy-tale baddies. They ate up the entire rugby world at their scenic ground with their great, grassy bank. Expectant home fans saw teams dispatched . . . Fee Fi Fo Fum, I want to fuck up an Englishman . . . the boys of Bath strode onto the pitch. Warm autumn, dry summer, bone hard pitch. 'Pooler' didn't know what hit them. He slashed them until there was nothing left but staggering giants, deflated with defeat. I stood flat and threw passes as hard, fast and flat as I could. Stood there and delivered. There he was, gliding onto the ball, ghosting past defenders. Impossible to realise the speed and timing of his runs. As if Medusa was on our side, turning the opposition into statues. Bath scored more than forty points. You didn't win in Pontypool, let alone score forty points. On a dry surface he was a good man to have on your side. He wasn't bad in the soft.

This was my first official game as Bath captain. A bittersweet return to my old stamping grounds. I finally understood what natural talent truly was, seeing it at close range. The rest of us were going to have to work our asses off just to keep within breathing distance of the Prince, the little shrug of the shoulder and hip, the dip that eased him past hands snatching at thin air. His future was inevitable. We were celebrating the first league and cup double on a

Sunday in Bath when Jerry was informed that he had been selected for a debut in Romania. A hat-trick in Bucharest, an injured Will Carling and the Lions legend was ready to emerge from his chrysalis. This haughty and humble, all at the same time, local lad.

The second Test and the Lions led Australia narrowly. Five metres from the Wallaby try-line and Jerry dropped his foot on the ball, a delicate grubber. He eased behind the Australia midfield defence. Regathered. Touched down. The series would be won by the might of the forwards but the memory was of the Prince and his poised kick. A three-tour Lion and twice a winner, it was the Lions, more than even England that defined the Bath boy. In 1993 he played all three Tests in the losing tour to New Zealand. Four years later, in his thirties and past his peak, Ian McGeechan selected him for South Africa. McGeechan had been his manager in both 1989 and 1993. Jerry was his man. Call it some sort of sixth sense. The Scot stayed true to him when the easy option was the axe. Time was beginning to catch him up in a way few defenders had over the years. The star centre, in many ways the star man on the tour, was Scott Gibbs, whose ferocious tackling stopped the Springboks in their tracks. A psychological battering ram. Gibbs' defence was nearly matched in the midweek matches by the attacking guile of another Welsh centre, Allan Bateman. If there was any justice, if form was to play a part in the selection process, these were the right men to include in the Lions Test team. But McGeechan had a hunch. He stuck with Guscott. Trailing 7–6 late in the second Test, King's Park, Durban. One Test up. Guscott popped up in midfield, paused, a lazy swing of the right boot and the goal was dropped to clinch the series. He wasn't supposed to do that, to even be there, but this was Jerry; the ball sailed through the posts. He is standing still, arms at right angles, the crazed Guscott grin . . . Straight afterwards I saw his mother in the tunnel. We hugged . . . she shook her head in proud disbelief, 'Typical of that bloody son of mine, isn't it?'

Some people were born for sporting greatness, not many. Jerry was one of them.

The only mistake I recall him making in the red of the Lions was an occasion when he dropped the ball against Canterbury in the 1993 tour. His club fly half had made a smart break. Still trying to play his way back into Test contention, I needed Jerry to turn my touch of skill into a score. He was clear, away. Inexplicably he dropped it. You bastard! But what the heck, he goaded me into one of the most famous moments in the annals of Bath rugby against Harlequins and he didn't let me down against Scotland in 1993. If he'd dropped that pass you wouldn't be reading this book. It would not have been written . . . *The Memoirs of a Building Society Man Who Should Have Kept His Mouth Shut* . . . lacks a ring, don't you think?

Maybe I wouldn't have even played against Scotland was it not for the half-joking, half-serious sneer of the centre in the Bath training ground back in 1991. I did something cute as I had a habit of doing at a Bath training session. Safe by the hearth and all that. Maybe it was a left-footed drop goal . . . I don't know. I do remember Jerry standing close, whispering, 'Pity you haven't the balls to do that away from here . . .' Was he calling me a coward? In concert with that inner voice of mine. The one afraid of failure? Just as he hit the right spot against Harlequins one year later, so he infuriated me into a response without which the inner coward might have stayed safe in the west. I traipsed home from training, tamping mad. Told my wife, Lesley, about the temerity of 'that bastard Guscott'. In the same breath I was phoning Geoff Cooke to make myself available after a petulant second bout of international retirement. Jerry lacks the medical qualifications but I reckon he could have been quite some psychiatrist. It was kill or cure with Jerry.

Jerry had attitude. Easy to love. Easy to loathe. He didn't attempt to hide his arrogance. Why bother? Anyway, it wasn't as if the strangers who tried to ingratiate themselves into his circle on a Saturday night were doing it for his benefit. Everyone in Bath – or an awful lot of people so it seemed to the rest of his team-mates – wanted their slice of him, for their own egotistical reasons. Sad pub bores living on their lies in which he is transformed to great guy and friend. If no more than polite to them, he's 'that arrogant tosser'. Yes, why bother? He frequently didn't. Nobody breathed Bath Football Club in deeper than Jerry. He had risen through the junior ranks. Bath born, bred, proud. But it did not prevent him from becoming distracted during the great days of his international career. The first team squad resented the lack of effort he was putting into his performances. I told Jack it would be best if we dropped him for an important cup tie. Jack didn't like the thought of the bad PR. We went through with the decision anyway. Jerry didn't shout, rant, didn't do anything but walk away. I don't know whether he thought I had no right to tell him he had been dropped, no idea whether somewhere a penny dropped. He went away with England. Came back to Bath. A strange silence about the decision to omit him. I think he may have been hurt for one of the few times in his playing career. Then again, he might have thought, 'Who the fuck are you to drop me?' Who knows?

He was the most uncaged of rugby players. His stride, like Hughes' Jaguar, had 'the wildernesses of freedom', his eyes would drill a man with contempt. It was the otherness of the man people disliked, feared. Here was a normal human being with an abnormal ability to play sport, to take a game that was essentially born from the muscular Christianity of the public schools and transform it into lines of poetry. Jerry even cadged fags from my wife with style. His purring presence, a sleek panther in a traditional England shirt, freed England from its conservatism; for a while. To feel the throaty roar of his filthy laugh, a face that could freak out in horror like something by Bacon, was to remember that this bloke who played rugby like a god was very much human; flawed, imperfect, deliberately arrogant but warm, generous and impulsively fun at the same time.

The best player I ever played with but was he the best Lions centre of even his own lifetime? The series-winning drop goal was his Lions epitaph. Four years later and he has been replaced by Brian O'Driscoll, *Waltzing O'Driscoll* the red horde of Lion fans sang on the night of the first Test against Australia in Brisbane. 'In Ireland they call him God, he's a better player than that,' I screamed into my microphone as television reran the replay of his half-the-length-of-the-pitch try at the start of the second half.

But O'Driscoll or Guscott? Probably the Irishman on the balance of his all-round game. Jerry was easier on the eye with his sinuous outside break but O'Driscoll had a little shimmy and a swerve and a sneaky offload to match those surgical soft passing hands of the Bath and England man. In defence, O'Driscoll wins it hands down. Not just the tenacity of his defence but the way he worried opposition off the ball around the tackle. He and Gordon D'Arcy were a match for any back row at the breakdown, in a way that would have repelled Jerry. He would have been contemptuous of such hard sleeve-rolling work.

It's the difference between one player whose playing days were ending as professionalism was finding its wailing way into the world and another who started his career in tandem with the new professional era. Two different cultures. It is inane, perhaps insane, comparing era with era. One of them gave me much pleasure, merely watching from the commentary and press box. With the other I shared the same changing room most of my Saturdays. Jesus, you could hate him . . . but you loved him even more. It was one of the pleasures of my playing career to share the field, if not the headlines.

He paid that £50 back too. Is he finally getting soft?

HALF BACKS

'YOU CHUCK it, I'll catch it.' Apocryphal? We will never know. This is what Barry John supposedly told Gareth Edwards the first time these legends of the game met for a practice. As a child I devoured the sentence in Barry John's autobiography, *The King*. Thereafter the words were never far from the forefront of that bit of brain that ruminates all things rugby. John is idealised as one of the great rugby romantics. The outsider, the one-off, like Oscar Wilde unafraid of declaring his genius.

For most of us imagination is everything when the subject is Barry John. He retired in 1972, one year after he conquered New Zealand with the Lions. The one and only time. It is rumoured he had assistance. He was aged twenty-seven. Retrospectively, retirement appears almost obscene in its wastefulness. Just twenty-five caps for Wales, five for the Lions. I hadn't got around to even picking up a rugby ball by the time he walked away from the game, the payment from his autobiography condemning him to an exile he surely must have regretted. But those were the draconian laws the amateur administrators imposed on our sport's heroes. I have seen John gliding through a gap in the black wall, an unlikely hand-off, this ballad of a thin man scoring a try in Lions red. And that is it. Nothing else. The end. Yet when I am asked to list the greatest players of all time, John jumps ever into contention. When asked this question, I add the caveat – the greatest I have seen. Forever is a long time. Barry belongs to the ancient era of forever. He always will.

The John line to Edwards is so famous it might have become an undeniable truth within his private world. All these years on, does he rely on the book or the memory? Whatever the facts of their first meeting, one of the most perfect half back partnerships of them all must have based its foundations on more than the instinctive genius of the one. Gareth, in stark contrast, was a 'practice makes perfect' man. He may have burst onto the international scene with an innate gift, that missile projectile pass of his with its built-in tracking in the pre-computer age. It was, however, a genius, grown from hard graft. Edwards grafted at his genius with his coach, Bill Samuel. Behind the brilliance of any half back partnership is work (even if the scrum half, in this instance, did the lion's share of it).

As for Edwards, he has longevity over the comet-like career of John. History has to adjudge him the greater, if less compelling, human figure. Gareth was one of us, normal yet great; Barry walked on air. No one else inhabited his stratosphere. The fly half was a poet who cut himself down in his prime. Chatterton. Close to tragic. Edwards was there in 1971 and there in South Africa in 1974 when the Lions went unbeaten. Blacks cheered them every step of the way. He was there with Wales through the glory years, the length of the field try in the mud against Scotland. And, of course, he was there in black and white, vivid colour on the TV screen, at the National Stadium, 1973, arriving like a rocket, undeviating as one of his passes, propelled into the corner against the All Blacks. Grant Batty's desperate dive to no avail. He made the Barbarians in this moment. The most famous try in the history of British rugby. Instead of Barry it was Benny making the plays, side-stepping past numerous New Zealand tacklers. From his own twenty-two. The King had abdicated but fresh royalty had ascended to the throne on which Welsh fly halves sat. 'Go out and show them how good you are,' Carwyn James reputedly said to Phil Bennett on the day Llanelli beat the All Blacks. He did. And how good was James? The man who never coached Wales. Steered Llanelli and the Lions to victory against New Zealand. As for the players, Benny was brilliant but Gareth was the god of those rugby ages. He was fast, fit, with the perfect physique. Nature and nurture combined to guarantee greatness whereas Barry was impossibly thin, even for the late 60s and early 70s. An elfin spirit that glided mysteriously, magically, vulnerably through matches.

But sprite or no, I bet Barry's hands were blistered after Gareth's passing sessions. I am not, I promise you, putting myself anywhere near Barry John (I remain childishly thrilled when he asks for my opinion on some rugby matter when we meet on match day in Wales on media duties). Yet I too have had tips torn from the rest of my fingers as a fly half working with a scrum half. In this instance the scrum half was Richard Hill. He captained England. Not the most natural of talents, Richard was probably the most durable and dedicated player England produced in the mid-eighties to nineties period. Certainly as far as practice and preparation went. Feet planted wide apart. I still see him shuttling across the in-goal area of Bath's training ground. At the bottom of the A46. A hundred passes off the right hand, a hundred off the left. Then I would saunter out from the physiotherapists' room to play my part in the partnership of Bath half backs.

We would start our session on the twenty-two-metre line, Richard on the touchline. I would call 'deep' and he would spin the ball back into my regular defensive position. I would boot the ball away, every now and then feinting to kick, darting away from whoever we could enlist as a flanker, under order to pressurise me. The try I was credited with creating against Scotland, described later in this book, was no instinctive 'off the cuff' moment. Ten of these positional passes and we would shift into the midfield, 'kick right' or 'kick left' was a signal for an orthodox delivery into my hands and a clearance kick into touch, then I'd throw in a few 'late right' or 'late lefts' shifting from left to right, right to left, sprinting flat out towards the gain line . . . and so we advanced up the field. More attacking positions and he threw fizzing passes onto the very gain line itself from lineouts and scrums . . . from breakdown situations, a hollering sequence of delayed 'lefts' and late 'rights'. My panting voice cutting through the mists of the early evening air. On and on and on until I stopped to recover my breath before the team practice. Richard became so attuned to my shifts and my gear changes I didn't shout directions during a match. He was me; we were symbiotic. It was bloody hard work (like a schoolboy swot I pretended never to train while putting in plenty of hours) but when a late change of direction opened up an opposing defence and Jeremy Guscott or Tony Swift was passed into a hole of our creation, the satisfaction made the hours with Richard worth the sweat. Make your play as late as possible. The modern jargon is 'scanning'. The later a fly half waits until he reveals his hand, the less time there is for a defence to adjust. When you had the calibre of backs that Bath possessed, we looked the part when the fields were ripe for running rugby. From September to October and the end of March onwards, Bath's backs swaggered. For the rest of the season the mud tended to turn most matches into a slog. If there is one thing about the modern game of which our old generation should be envious, it has to be the quality of the playing surfaces. We would have had some fun on the bowling greens of today.

Scanners were not the norm in the English game. Mired in conservatism, there were few fly halves who sought to outwit an opposing defence. The preference was to bore them to death with kicking. An honourable mention to Les Cusworth, a true prober for the gap. He was one of the exceptions. Here is a typical example of how the metronomic by numbers rugby worked in practice. An England training weekend at the Petersham Hotel. We were sitting tracksuited in the team room. The whiteboard. Discussions with forwards as ever the pre-eminent voices. I was on the bench. Now and then slotted into the starting fifteen. Just in case. The game plodding towards professionalism. There's a line drawn on the whiteboard. Black line, representing a lineout. Dick Best, England coach, drew a parabola to signify the ball being thrown and caught at the back of the lineout. He pinpointed the next pass to the inside centre, there's an explosion of marker pen squiggles as our man runs into a few opposing defenders, midfield . . . 'What are we going to do next, Stuart?' Shit, wake up, Stuart . . . I looked at the whiteboard scenario, thought myself onto the field and said the only thing that made sense to me. But it was not the answer I was supposed to spout. 'I'll wait and see what the defenders do and pick off the weaker area.' Or words to that effect. Scanning, but I didn't have the phrases; anyway, what many knew as 'heads up rugby'. This was the wrong answer. The opposition were located where we expected them to be, at least on the board, and I was supposed to do exactly what the other fourteen England players expected. The forwards needed to know in advance in order to make their support runs. Everything was pre-programmed. Coaching was beginning to 'advance'. In other words, the coach was telling the players more and more. Those early days, confused days, confusing to those with an individual vision, being asked, not as a fly half, but rather the next cog in the machine, what happens next. Artificial intelligence before the term became so familiar. This wasn't rugby thinking but rugby memorising. A kind of primitive coding. It is now perceived as advanced. Back in the twentieth century forwards were 'fat boys' who were not supposed to think. I thought, 'Give me the ball and let me get on with it.' The England management thought, 'Let's create a system in which we can operate with some degree of structure.' It was a groping stage in English rugby's evolution, one that mitigated against instinct. It went against everything taught to me in my Welsh upbringing. Sure, familiar playing patterns did create a sort of backbone from which the odd individual riff could be performed but such free-form rugby, especially within England, was strictly within limits.

There should exist a tension between the team strategy with its in-built restraints and the freedom for the fly half to act as he sees fit. For this is the timeless essence of the outstanding tens. It conjures a balance between the collective structure and the chaos an exceptional player can cause the most organised defence. Impish originality. Beauden Barrett. The best teams appear to have the least structure. Too much will numb the mind. Too many coaches don't fathom this eternal imperative. Barry, Benny, Cliff Morgan, it was their show and so it should be. There's no better seat in the house than the fly half's. With the privilege of the best tactical view comes responsibility. The responsibility to make things happen. Even in this age of ultimate organisation and order, there's no doubt the fly half retains a pre-eminent position within the team. And therefore this chapter. New Zealand's stream of match-winning fly halves is not some sort of coincidence, some golden age that has been going on for over twenty years. Forwards do not win matches. They lay the foundations. The fly half, along with his mate at scrum half, has to build upon the foundations. Fly half is a position from where plays must be made. Judge a number ten on what he does right. In the process, an ambitious fly half will make mistakes. Barrett makes plenty. But without the freedom to operate as he sees fit, his team is tied to a template. It makes for mediocrity. Too often teams have not assessed their tens on what they have done well. Rather on what they haven't done badly. We should forget this double negative. It leads nowhere very exciting. When I was growing up, England opted for Alan Old and Martin Cooper, Neil Bennett, all accomplished kickers of the ball, all slaves to the obsession with forward-based rugby . . . meanwhile in Wales we were spoiled by rugby's radical firebrands who could create a kaleidoscopic chaos against the most organised of opposition. In my playing era, the foremost fly halves in Wales and England were Jonathan Davies and Rob Andrew. They both wore ten on their backs. They had little else in common.

The fly half must orchestrate his back line. In the amateur days the inside centre – in this hemisphere – was nothing more than the bloke standing next to him, a friendly shoulder. Days in which defence was a rather more gentlemanly, almost optional pursuit. The only defensive debate was whether a team rushed up to maximise pressure on a back line or drifted across the field, forcing the move to taper out in touch as tended to occur with most English back lines. A fly half used his centre to crash the ball over the gain line, or as an arrowing runner who picked late lines off the fly half. Mike Catt performed that latter role to perfection for Bath. Yet New Zealand reads rugby in another way to Europe. It always has. The clue has been there for all to see in the positional titling. We have the unit of scrum and fly half; Kiwis have half back and first five eighth. We have fly half and inside centre, they have first five eighth and second five eighth. The key link in New Zealand is between ten and twelve. When the game went pro and the fly half needed another pair of eyes to assist, New Zealand was ready with their second five eighth.

I digress. Yet again. We haven't finished with the fly half. Not quite yet. The most talented Bath (now Leicester) fly half of recent years is George Ford, a fabulous scanner although not necessarily an innate winner. Which is a worry for Eddie Jones who is a fan of the Ford/Owen Farrell first five/second five eighth combination. The most naturally gifted through my time was Catt. He could fling a ball half the length of the pitch with a one-handed flick. Punt it from Wiltshire to Somerset. But he wasn't a fly half to trust. While creativity is essential, they cannot lack a clean vision of strategy and the battle as it unfolds, from one end of the pitch to the other. First to last minute. If I had one significant ability, it was the capacity to come up with the right answer to the question being posed in front of me. Its why my moronic performance for England against Ireland in Dublin in 1993 so infuriated me. As if the Stuart Barnes of blue, black and white was possessed by a demon which drove all feel for the game out of his thick skull. Great fly halves make good decisions and execute the vast majority of them superbly. Good fly halves make good decisions. Even if not all of them are as well executed as the fly half would like, the team still has a winning chance because the decision-making is sound. The bad fly halves make bad decisions and no matter how skilful they may be, a team will not extricate itself from dire decision-making. Great talents do not always succeed as top tens. Game management trumps individual ability. Combine the two and you have Dan Carter. I was a good game-manager, most of the time. People think they are being kind when they recite my playing days back to me. Invariably cast – by those of a generous disposition – as a swashbuckler, a risk taker, a gambler. I was rarely any of these. Let's say I had the mind of an accountant, albeit a dodgy one with a penchant for the odd gamble on the horses. My bottom line at Bath was winning. Judged purely on that record I was quite good. Game-management does not mean risk-aversion. It requires a fly half to gamble when he knows the odds of the play coming off are good or better than good. Betting on 100–1 shots will cost you; work out how to turn the 2–1 shot into 1–2 odds and you are a

Test match rugby player. Too many people hear the word 'risk' and panic. In 1980s England it reached epidemic levels. It has also discoloured the glorious running red of Wales in recent years. Warren Gatland's management regime and players for too long failed to understand some of the native animosity to their crash bang wallop. They dismissed the Welsh feel for the game. Risk is a wonderful word. Without risk-taking the world is dull, we plod purposelessly on, going round and round in ever decreasing circles from cradle to grave. Or head down and straight in recent Welsh years. I am regarded by a few with creaking memories as a risk-taker of the reckless sort. Meant as a compliment but smilingly taken as a well-meaning insult. Game-management came first to me, the rest was a bonus. Manage a few fancy tricks with the ball in hand and you are boxed into the category of 'running fly half'. Kick like a mule and you are the very epitome of 'the English fly half'. So it was with Barnes and Andrew. I could kick and Rob could most certainly run (although he played it too safe for England). We are still pigeon-holed as such today. Ford has more than a few similarities with the way I played. Only his skill level is infinitely superior. I passed well off my right hand, diabolically off my left. He is a purist off either hand. Neither of us are giants, both of us were and are 'scanners'. Ford doesn't shirk a tackle, nor did I – especially in my younger days before some semblance of sanity found its way into my head – but I had and he has a far from flattering reputation in defence. Ford is all creativity. When he misses a tackle it must be highlighted. The same applies to Danny Cipriani in spades. Owen Farrell is a more direct, earthy fly half. When he misses tackles it is ignored by many commentators. We stick to our pre-ordained scripts.

So much for the fly half. He won't amount to much if his scrum half chucks the ball any old where. Barry should have treated Gareth with a little more deference. At Bath I did most of my thinking for myself but the runs and breaks and the shimmies and the delayed passes . . . without the searing speed of Hill's pass, little to none of this would have been possible. A fly half cannot compete on the gain line, not if he is waiting for a pass that is floating in his general direction. Strange then that the art of passing is so rarely mentioned within the media. Most of England's recent scrum halves have had a habit of throwing poor passes, of crabbing across the field. Occasionally to effect, usually not. The wide base of Hill is a thing of the past. The blistering thirty metre pass of Edwards all but forgotten. One of the reasons Conor Murray has made the leap to world class is because of his improved pass. Yet we only ever coo at his box kicking, breaking and cover tackling. Important as they all are, without a pass he would be less than half the player he is. Johnny Sexton performs the role of broad visionary and launch pad for the entire Ireland team. Murray is master of the pack with the silver service. A cracking balance. A Grand Slam combination if ever there was one.

The relationship between the nine and his pack determines the nature of a team. Frequently the nine is regarded as the servant of the forwards. In my England playing days, the doughty Dewi Morris was very much the poodle of the props. The pack petted him. Sat at the back of the bus with his big mates. He was a strong man, would break around the fringes, keeping the ball close to the pack. The backs – second class citizens sat squirming at the front of the bus – dropped deep and waited for a pass that was not as bad as legend has it but poor in comparison to Hill's. England played nine- and ten-man rugby. Few considered the talent being wasted in the wider channels. The same occurred in Wales throughout the Mike Phillips years. He was a powerful athlete in the mould of Terry Holmes. Himself a fiery if more limited successor to Edwards in the late 1970s. Phillips flourished, was a Test match Lion, as Welsh back play went into a decline from which it has struggled to recover. No coincidence. Only if a team has a powerful pack and poor backs is there nothing wrong with the 'ninth forward', inevitably a slave to the big men.

The better scrum half is the one that masters them. He demands, drives, slaps and screams at them. Treats them like mules. The world's leading scrum half of recent times, Aaron Smith, is such a player. Smith is not a massive man. Strong but pocket sized. A reminder that despite the cliché you don't have to be a mammoth to pull on a pair of elasticated shorts. This chapter started with the elfin charms of Barry John. It will finish with an even smaller half back. The late Jacques Fouroux played for France intermittently from 1972–77. It was not until he was elevated to captaincy in 1976 that the famous Fouroux finally stood, revealed to us all. Five foot three inches tall. Socks rolled down. Hair thinning. Muscles invisible to the eye. He was an impossible figure for a captain of a French team with as imposing a pack as existed in those days. He was mistakenly known as the ninth forward but his nickname gave the game away. 'The little corporal'. Named after Napoleon Bonaparte. Here was a formidable figure hidden away in a mere sixty-three inches.

He barked. Shouted the commands. The ultimate master of the pack. France won all bar one of their games in the 1976 Five Nations Championship. In 1977 they won the Grand Slam. The little corporal was translated this side of the Channel as Le Petit General. Fouroux was not a great player. He had neither the pass nor the pace of Edwards. What he did possess was extraordinary leadership skills. Here was French rugby's very own Mike Brearley. Both these men captained their respective countries in 1977. Neither were lauded for their playing ability, both for their contrasting styles of leadership. Where the Middlesex man was cerebral, the little corporal from Auch was dictatorial. He mastered his pack and in doing so served his country well.

INJURIES

IN THE autumn of 2018 I commentated on a game of rugby which broke the two-hour barrier. An eternity behind the microphone. Forty minutes each half with a fifteen minute break for injuries. That's an hour and thirty-five minutes. Allow ten minutes for the tyranny of the television match officiating; there was still a good quarter of an hour of missing time. Missing in action. At the highest levels, rugby union is a battleground. Yes, time for George Orwell's famous description of the Olympics and international sport as 'war minus the shooting' to be rammed into the text. Invariably someone is escorted from the field within the first five minutes, a few stitches, a broken nose. The team doctor leads them off, blood drenching through the ooze of the bandage, nose held, head back. So it begins.

The ubiquitous HIA (head injury assessment) has become as much a part of the game as scrums and lineouts. Players slump with regularity as the games goes on its bloody way all around them. Archipelagos of prone players and kneeling medics. Giants thunder around them, referee loath to blow until the doctor feels the hot breath of the game's flow; quite something, the way the sport plays through others' pain. Compare and contrast with football. Not so long ago the Premier League realised cynical players – doubtless under the tutelage of their far more cynical managers – were collapsing onto the turf with timely consistency. Whenever the other team were on the attack. Whistle blows. Game stops. Yet all that was required to resurrect the agony-stricken player was the magic sponge. The team who were a man down kick the dropped ball back to the previously attacking side's goalkeeper, seventy metres downfield. Everyone applauds the sportsmanship. Aren't we a sporting nation?

Sharp-minded football administrators cottoned on. After a few decades. They ordered referees to keep playing unless the injury looked serious enough to merit a pause in play. But in the face of the furious paying mob, booing in righteous and stupid indignation, soon we were back to writhing cheats rolling around before hobbling to the touchline and sprinting back on. The earlier imprecations seem long since forgotten. Rugby, if anything, appears too macho. There are occasions when the medical team have a hold on the neck of an inert player. Ninety-nine out of one hundred occasions, thank the rugby gods, these are purely precautionary. But hey, a forward is lying inert and a dozen men are sprinting around within ten square metres . . . so far we have avoided the awful moment when the vertical and horizontal collide – to my knowledge. But it's hard not to respect rugby for its willingness to keep the game moving. And just as well. If the match was halted every time a player crashed to the pitch in pain, the game's duration would stretch towards three hours. As it is, I am persistently frustrated when the TV screen on which a match I have recorded turns an ennui shade of blue, the timing for the programme ended with the match no further than the sixty-five-minute mark. Orwell was writing about the nature of propaganda – and to stand back during the Olympics and observe our obsession with medals and anything British, I reckon he made a fair point – but the words, though unintended, are equally applicable to the ferocity of the professional game.

Ten years ago, nearly all rugby commentators would have a few stock phrases for the wobbling warriors. Punch drunk. Most of the words light-hearted, especially when the stagger took on Saturday-night-on-the-town proportions. Beer and battering. One and the same. Not so much heartless as uneducated. Few knew anything about concussion, didn't know that it wasn't just boxers who risked brain damage in pursuit of fame, glory and (eventually from a rugby perspective) money. By the end of my career, I was suffering from increasing bouts of double vision. Balance problems, slurring and a few other malfunctioning mental faculties led me to the Lister Hospital in London and Mr Angus Kennedy. I was tentatively diagnosed with exertion induced ataxia. It can be hereditary, so I dismissed it. I forget the thumping few knockouts . . . what's wrong with the odd concussion? Buy the bloke who punched your lights out a pint post-match . . . the beauty of the game. Game for thugs played by gentlemen. That smug charm remains for those of us fortunate to have played the sport at any level.

It took American football's high-profile injury issues, a film starring Will Smith, and a host of headlines for the doctors queuing up to warn rugby of its own Trojan Horse, to be believed. Even then there remained coaches who paid as much heed to their warnings as Donald Trump does to the threat of global warming. How did we get to the stage where the door to the changing rooms for HIA was nothing less than a revolving one with player after player being escorted from the field? Neanderthal coaching is one answer. The day of the schoolteacher/chief executive coaching clubs as an aside died the day the game went professional (although strictly speaking there was no single 'day' in England as the RFU did their best to bury their heads in the sand; the clubs rose to the challenge and the club versus country conflict was born). In their places were men – sometimes the self-same men – but men who had to answer to a board, to employers. Freedom from the nine to five enslavement, the joy of being their own boss, floundered against the forces of rugby's primitive professionalism. The new full-time coach had to impress the new owner class as well as win games. A director of rugby couldn't explain to the new owner breed how his wonderful five-year plan would work. Five-year plans are a rarity in professional club sport of any sort. Results are tyrants. When they dip, as they inevitably do, how does the coaching team convince the boardroom it is doing a good job? The easiest way to achieve an obvious change with immediate improvement was to analyse the weaknesses of the old game. Zero in on them. One such flaw was fitness and physique. At Bath we trained three times a week. Most of us did our own individual sessions. Yet with another job required to pay the bills we lacked time to do it all. Hence backs were often scrawny, their natural selves, spending pockets of free time practising skills rather than bench pressing. All that changed. Almost overnight backs became bigger. Forwards ran further, lost their trademark rugby rolls of fat, became palpably fitter, faster. An owner could look at the altered state of the team and recognise improvement between amateur and professional. As for improving players' capacity to make good decisions, to implement skills under pressure . . . alas it takes more of an expert eye to spot such subtle changes. Subtlety bade farewell to club rugby. Size counted.

In particular the new athleticism of the forwards represented a seismic shift in the history of the sport. More athletic, more dynamic, more explosive. The game revolutionised into a brave new world of perpetual battle. These are some of the root reasons for the alarming increase in injuries. Injuries the sport has struggled to address this century. The weaponry used in this modern version of muscular chess was substantially upscaled but this alone doesn't explain the surge in casualties. For this we need to spend a few minutes thinking about the death of the ruck. Such a term – technically – still exists, but barely in anything but name. Here is rugby's law 16: 'A ruck is a phase of play where one or more players from each team, who are on their feet, in physical contact, close around the ball on the ground. Open play has ended. Players are rucking when they are in a ruck and using their feet to try to win or keep possession of the ball, without being guilty of foul play.'

Now, the ball on the ground is there because there is a tackler and a tackled man, one from each side. A couple of players in 'physical contact', in other words 'bound', can try and drive over the ball, to ensure possession either remains with the attacking team or is turned over by the defending team. The ruck is a matter of decision-making, dynamism and technique; when to risk numbers, the matter of the body angle and the power, or lack of it, from those trying to drive over the ball and ruck it back. These component parts constitute a ruck. As the tackled player, you tended to place the ball backwards, away from opposition, before adopting the foetus position, hands over head, as the battle raged above you. If you were the tackler, and the opposing attackers won the physical contest of the ruck, you could expect to feel several sets of studs raking your back. I can still feel the skin-deep scars that healed quicker than the memories of your back sticking to the bed sheets the day after the game. Badges of honour. Like gout. The vast majority of ruck victims were raked above the knees, below the neck. All part of the game. Unacceptable, however, was the forward (or occasional back) who did not use his studs with the backwards motion to clear a body. Rather the kick or worse yet, the sickening downward stamp on the head. It's in stark violation of sporting civilisation. You'd be laughed at by your own team for taking a 'good shoeing' but if 'the claret' spouted from the head it was the precursor, more often than not, to an almighty punch-up.

I can't remember the last time I saw a punch-up like the one I described in this book's first chapter, in Wellington, 1985. These days there is little opportunity for the old-fashioned stamp. The frequent 'all in' reaction is more cold than actual war. In fact, it is considerably closer to the 'propaganda' Orwell disparagingly described. The team whose man is tackled in the air, or hit slightly late, do not react in instinctive defence of their own herd but as a calculated act to maximise the punishment for the opposing transgressor. A 50/50 decision becomes a penalty, a penalty a yellow card, yellow metamorphoses into red. It is grubby. We use the phrase 'handbags' in commentary. The feminist within me thinks it's time to start calling it 'man bags' although mine is solely used for books and CDs. The conning is unedifying but surely an improvement on the closed fist and the stamping boot, isn't it? I am not so sure. Remember John Ashworth's stamp on JPR? In Wales every fan over the age of fifty does because such violence was rare but it was also unforgettable – as were the punch-ups. There were a few psychopathic players but the damage done in the overall scheme of the game was limited. Players understood where the line was drawn. Fighting was a sure sign everyone knew that line had been overstepped. So did referees and – by and large – they did not act hysterically when fists flailed. A red card for the agent of the incident would do. Any referee who refuses to send off someone for punching rather than trading man bags would be quickly out of a job today.

Violence is an intrinsic element of the game, and of life in general. There are people who like nothing more than a punch-up. The problem is that few admit as much. The overriding voice has long been that of 'little Johnny's mother'. She is the target of the media and the representative of a scared, sometimes silly society. She gives vent when pictures of bleeding and bandaged heads are all over the back pages, the internet and television screens. She knows little more than the hysterical headlines. She scares people. She loves her little Johnny. To argue otherwise is to be outcast. She is a creation of our scared society. She frightened those in authority so much, the game decided in its early days of professionalism to eradicate the risk of the bleeding head. All for the bleeding heart.

Footwork disappeared and the ruck became an eccentricity from a former age. The odd incident has been replaced not with blood but continual concussion. With internal bleeding. With liver and kidney damage. Strong arms and shoulders found an outlet for rugby's innate violence. But this violence was not berated. This violence was heralded as a new stage in the game. 'Big hits' replaced tackling in commentary terminology. Super slow-motion replays of juddering impacts, 'big hit' sequences, give the crowd what they want – and it wasn't soft hands, not unless the BBC, ITV, Sky and BT Sport were all wrong over the years. An ex-player who says 'hits' are not even mentioned within the law book is a prudish wimp. But there is no such term. And this is where we find our way back to what was once the ruck. Now the players never bind. Now they rarely stay on their feet – or if they do, only just. Binding requires bodily readjustment. This strips the shoulder charge of the impact which sends the opposing player standing near the tackle into another groggy kingdom. Replacing the ruckers are the jackals, a species new to the fields of rugby this century. They evolved from rucklessness. Men who were first to the tackle and formed a wide base with their legs, straddling the tackled man and lifting the ball from its claustrophobic confines. Or ensured the tackled man could not release. The result: a penalty for the jackal against the tackled man. Flankers with broad beams, big arses, massive thighs. The ball was played on the ground, redefining the game. In the 2015 World Cup, David Pocock, the greatest jackal exponent of them all, was the most influential player in the competition until Dan Carter claimed centre stage. No way two bound men could shift a jackal like Pocock. So, bindings were forgotten by players, coaches and most importantly of all, the referees. So the hits at the breakdown intensified. Head on head, shoulder in kidneys, neck rolls . . . the violence hadn't gone away, it had changed shape with the alterations the game made to keep Johnny's mum happy. Our metaphorical mum didn't mind the concussion as long as it wasn't her boy and the damage wasn't there in front of her eyes.

The occasional kick in the head has been replaced with the 'big hit', 'the shot'. The terminology is wrapped up in excitable tones of overt violence like the latest violent computer game. Tackling made the headlines in 2017 because of the 'downgrading' and de-powering acts of World Rugby. The governing body instructed referees to be less tolerant towards the high tackle (anything above the shoulders) in a bid to force players to lower the target area of the tackle. The governing body tried to take a first step back from the abyss into which the legalised violence saw it sinking.

Where once there was the odd ugly stamping incident, then there came numerous clothes-line and spear tackles, body shots. Where one area of violence is eradicated, a new one will rise, especially if the previous law changes were cosmetic rather than properly thought through. Rugby union is more violent than ever. More dangerous than ever. It lacks the brutality of amateur days. Yet its cleanliness is only skin deep. I thought it would be something of a macho boast to claim more than 100 stitches beneath my snowy white hair. Then I heard the Saracens captain, Brad Barritt, saying, all matter of fact, he has more than one thousand stitches. And there was me thinking myself the tough man. Not that anyone else did . . . the most memorable injury of my career occurred at the bottom of the world. Invercargill,

South Island, New Zealand. A quick flight to Stewart Island and thereafter, Antarctica. I was on the bench, midweek before the first Lions Test against the All Blacks. Nobody wants to be selected for the midweek game. Bad news for Test hopes. My Test hopes were high. Most of the guaranteed starters for the first Test were rested or on the bench. Rob Andrew lasted over seventy minutes in a grim, gruelling match against Southland. I replaced the injured fly half with less than ten minutes to stay out of harm's way . . . ten minutes can be a long time. Lying on the floor, pondering the smell of South Island mud . . . *whoosh.* The sudden split in the skull, the immediate spill of blood, the instinctive, brief, panic. Then despair. Being led from the field, head wrapped in a towel that was as red as my Lions replacement shirt. The hair didn't grow back on the right side of the forehead. Rotten memories. And the best laid plans of mice and men once more.

At the beginning of the tour I had been stunned to see how much time Ian McGeechan worked our backs at the breakdown. I thought it was something only forwards did. Dirty work. McGeechan's theory was New Zealand rucked better and more ferociously than any side in the world. To match them would give us a chance of winning (as well as keeping our heads on our shoulders). Oh well, sometimes shit just happens. The only man on the 1993 Lions tour with shorter legs than mine was the Welsh scrum half, Robert Jones. Rob saw me on the floor. Attempted to step over me. Protect his pal. Another couple of inches of leg length and who knows, I may have fulfilled a childhood dream and played against the All Blacks for the Lions. It wasn't the worst injury of my career by any distance but it took a psychological toll. The management asked Doctor James Robson about the extent of the injury. They asked me as I lay on the table being stitched up in a medical room that resembled a cow shed in both style and hygiene. I should have said, 'I'll be fine, bring on the All Blacks.' Even if the truth was that the scar would have been a red rag to an All Black, I should have said, 'I'm ready.' Instead I told them what I believed to be the truth. That I didn't think I'd be right for Saturday and took myself out of the equation. A week later I played my game of the tour against Taranaki. Chances don't come along often. Was I scared when the possible moment of my career arrived? Did I lack the courage of a Lion? The courage to lie. The moment of my greatness flickered and in short, was I afraid?

If that was the most damaging and disappointing injury of my career, the worst was a depressed fracture of the cheekbone in Coventry, 1987. A stray and accidental elbow caught me. The whole bone structure on the right side of my face collapsed. Consciousness lost. One of at least three occasions in my career. Nobody considered concussion back then. Richard Hill stopped for a look. Saw half a face looking a little too Picasso-like and dropped me in distaste. To Coventry General. In my kit, on a bed. The doctor saying, 'Ah, you must be the man in the motorbike accident.' Coventry General. Where my wife brought me (it was my birthday) Richard Ellman's tome of an Oscar Wilde biography. One eye temporarily rendered blind and the other blurred by swelling. Coventry Fucking General.

Bad to worse; I didn't play for three months, didn't go to work for a fortnight. Didn't want to do anything. After I had wallowed for a self-pitying week on the sofa, Lesley suggested I might like to take our golden retriever, Sally, for a walk on the Bristol Downs. Get some fresh air. Sally liked walking no more than me. Two lazy bones. We were halfway to the Downs when the local William Hill beckoned . . . well, a quick detour. A couple of bets. Sally broke the bad luck. Brought me good luck, not to mention the regulars. A couple of visits and a couple more winners. Some cheer to clear my gloom. Fast forward to Saturday morning. Matthew and Kate, the kids, are instructed to walk the walk with Sally. They get to William Hill. The dog veers violently left. Off the pavement. In through the curtained door. The punters are delighted to see their good luck charm once more as they plot their 10p Yankees. They feed her biscuits, this greediest of retrievers, refusing at the first obstacle en route to the Downs. Back home the tale is recounted with childish amazement. Deny, deny, Stuart. 'But mum, we walked in and they all said, "Hello Sally."' I blamed the dog's gambling habit on the cold wind that whipped through this part of Bristol . . . what was wrong with one quick visit? Bad times can be turned into good memories. We all loved that dog. One of my worst memories, lifting her onto the vet's table. I still feel the heft of her tummy, the sense I had of our dog frozen in fear. Dog knowledge that this was the end. She was in pain, that's what the vet said, that's what we confirmed . . . but had she been able to speak would she have said, 'I'm old, of course I ache, but while I can eat there's still pleasure to be had in life.' Humans, animals, we only have the one crack at it. Take it while you can.

JUDAS

'JUDAS!'

The shout pricked rugby's bubble of respectful silence for kickers. An English club game lacks the cathedral hush of a Munster match but the calm would be eerie for someone who has only ever watched football. Especially when the occasion was a derby brim-full of bitterness. This 'occasion' was a Bath versus Bristol West Country affair. The team I left against the team I joined. The bigger city of Bristol with its slowly shrinking club and the tiny tourist spa city of Bath whose club had the fastest growing reputation in the land. I was lining up a penalty kick at goal, for Bath. Against Bristol. At the Memorial Ground, Bristol. Bristol, the club I had helped to what remains their one and only national trophy in 1983. Victory against Leicester in the John Player Cup final. The cigarette lobby-controlled sports advertising in those distant days . . . but are they really that distant? Thirty-five years ago, as I write. Me, twenty years of age in 1983. Thirty-five years prior to my first cap for England, make it 1950. The Second World War hanging in the impoverished thick air of

England. My father and mother haven't yet had the courtesy to consider their entitled son's future existence – there are to be two sisters first. Come on, come on, I can't wait around forever, what with the odds against being born . . . anyway, 1950 . . . where to begin? England losing to the USA in the World Cup. Something I have long known about the year 1950, even as a kid. As a history student I knew Clement Attlee was re-elected with the smallest majority of five seats. The first sign that we future consumers were beginning to tire of the selfless unity that saw us through the dark days from 1939–45 and the poverty that followed. As a racing fan, it would be remiss not to mention Cottage Rake's third consecutive Gold Cup win. He has a bar at Cheltenham Racecourse named in his honour . . . no greater honour for a horse etc. But in those tentative first years of my twenties, it was all Ancient Greek to me. Do today's professional twenty-year-old rugby players dismiss the events of thirty-five years ago as I once did? Deaf and blind to history. For the 2018 twenty-year-olds, 1983 might be remembered as the year of Thatcher's landslide re-election. The year of American cruise missiles arriving at Greenham Common. The year Tony Blair was first elected an MP and, what else but Bristol's solitary triumph in the John Player Cup? I fear none of these events cast shadows across minds. Even the Twickenham triumph. Are these events gone for good? I wonder, when do previous facts become locked irretrievably into the past, without bridges to the present? Perhaps, in this age of mass communication, the answer is when it cannot be seen on a screen of some sort. Then and not until then shall history wear its trousers rolled . . .

Aural history. Blistering bootlegs. Blistering as Hill's passing. 16 May 1966. It is Manchester, the famous Free Trade Hall concert and someone shouts out, 'Judas'. It is the epic Bob Dylan tour, when Bob goes electric. The folkies don't like it one little bit. *Like A Rolling Stone* is set to assault their eardrums when the name Judas finds its way to the stage. Bob – I never tire of the recording – retorts, 'I don't believe you . . . [the longest stress on the second syllable of 'believe'] . . . you're a liar,' and then, 'Play fucking loud.' What am I getting at here? This. Some moron who confused me with the man who betrayed Christ, has – and I am going an awfully long way around the block admittedly – inadvertently linked me with Dylan. Whoever that man was, I'd like to buy him a drink. Not so many people have the nickname 'Judas'. Look up famous people named Judas on National Biography.com (a rare foray onto the internet, I promise). There's only one really renowned Judas. I reckon if they expanded the search to include nicknames there would only be an elite handful of us. Bob didn't much like the insult, 'All those evil motherfuckers can rot in hell.' Bob was bemused, renounced as Judas 'for playing an electric guitar', me for leaving one amateur club for another. He switched from acoustic to electric, folk to rock, I went from Wales to West Country, but the Judas moment was the journey down the A4 from Bristol to Bath. History hasn't headlined my own Judas cry. Or whether I kicked the goal or not (I have no idea) but Chris Hewett, then of the *Bristol Evening Post,* was there to record the abuse for posterity and to laughingly label me Judas as and when he saw fit through his long and accomplished period as rugby correspondent for the *Independent*. I have always thought it a trifle harsh on both Bob and myself.

The betrayal of Jesus was even more traitorous than leaving the traditional Bristol powerhouse for the creative destruction Jack Rowell was forging less than twenty miles away. Hard as that might be for Bristol supporters to believe. I did it because Bath were – like me – ambitious. Unlike the disciples' treasurer, Mr Iscariot, I had little to no interest in money. My first job on leaving Oxford remunerated me to the princely sum of £4,500. You can adjust for inflation and it still remains a salary of sweet fuck all. In contrast, the thirty silver coins paid to Judas would be worth a small fortune now. The most I ever received from Bath was twelve-pence-a-mile expenses. Okay, sometimes I claimed expenses via the M4 and not the A4 which added an extra £1.40 per journey. But, I, like Bob, did not betray the Lord, not for remuneration. Jesus would not have called me a devil for what I did, any more than he would have berated Bob for switching from *Blowing In The Wind* to *Leopardskin Pill Box Hat*. He'd have sat Pete Seeger down and had a word.

Jesus reportedly said (although with no YouTube footage who can believe the reportage) to Judas, 'What you are about to do, do quickly.' Me, I took my time. I missed the kick to beat Bath in the 1984 final and made up my mind to move during the 1984/85 season. An entire season in Bristol colours before heading down the not so long highway that was and still is the A4. Maybe I should have just packed and gone. But it wasn't that straightforward. Is anything ever? Bath had an outstanding fly half of their own. John Horton. A 1980 Grand Slam winner, a man at the very centre of the Bath rise. Johnny could not be discarded for some new kid. He played another season as Bath beat London Welsh to retain the Cup I played a hand – or foot – in helping them win in 1984. Horton informed the key men in the Bath set up he planned to retire at the end of the 1984/85 season. This was the catalyst to approach me. The fly half changed his mind midway through the season. It was too late. I was already plotting the next phase of my career. More importantly, so was Rowell. Horton left Bath for Bristol. A swap. Bitter, feeling betrayed by Bath, John was coming to the end of the road. My journey was nearer its beginning. So I was cast Judas. JH the victim. I lodged with Peter Polledri, the Bristol captain. When rumours reached his ear, I denied them. To my Bristol colleagues I was guilty of the grossest betrayal.

There's no complaint on that count. Good teams stay tight. My decision to depart was a breach of rugby etiquette. I didn't take money but I basically denounced one club for the other. What confuses me is how that action back in 1985 was perceived as somehow being a bigger betrayal than the changing of clubs is perceived in the professional game. I didn't take money, let's reiterate the point. I didn't receive anything other than a frosty welcome for accidentally upsetting a brilliant Bath bloke. No silver, nothing. An out-and-out amateur rugby player. Playing the game, supposedly, for the love of it. Definitely not the recompense. To move as often as I did in my early twenties was seen as 'bad form'. To change clubs now is perfectly acceptable. It is what players do. But players move, in the main, for the money. The very essence of the Judas crime. Betraying his team and his Lord for profit. Today, money is so all-consuming an imperative that nobody questions the validity of the justification. It doesn't matter if the club academy has nurtured you from fourteen-year-old callow youth to the first team, the Test team and something approaching greatness. If the money is right, you go. I didn't always swoon along with Middle England at Jonny Wilkinson's game but I hugely respected the length of service he gave Newcastle, his first and formative club. He did more than his dues. He earned his time in Toulon and whatever money was paid into his healthy bank account. He was an exception. Many others are led by their agents. Mammon is the god of the majority. And so we have been blinded by the scale of our small everyday corruption. Now it normalises our selfish behaviour.

That is not to say amateurism has an automatic moral superiority in comparison with the all-weather lucre of professionalism. It is too trite, too smug, to don one's twentieth-century blazer and proclaim that rugby union lost – or sold – its soul with the advent of the professional game. The unleashing of the unstoppable spell of money. There were ways and means around the code on the amateur's road. There was money in boots, here and there, but in England the hypocrisy of the amateur age was to be found in the networking system, where the blazers worked their blithe spells to protect union's smug aura. Play up and play the game. Bath had men like Malcolm Pearce (later to buy Bristol) who did more than his bit for the club, who employed the idle, indolent and excessively entertaining. He allowed them time to train. Time to become as good as they could. Men like Malcolm were beneficial, essential, to the sport in the dying days of amateurism when a club's demands highlighted the absence of any recompense for a player who was professional in all but the PAYE code. However, clubs such as Harlequins operated on a whole other level. They were the established London club. They had excellent City connections. Harlequins players were not paid to play for the club but many of them were parachuted into highly paid jobs. Careers with excessive earnings potential. What club wouldn't utilise connections? Simon Halliday was a Bath player who, I thought at the time, betrayed his team by quitting the best team in England for just such a career opportunity. It made him a lot of money. He wrote a book, called it *City Centre*. Yet when I asked him, as Pete Polledri had me, years earlier, whether there was any truth in the rumour, he denied, denied, denied. Not so much Judas as Peter. Looked me in the eye. If he'd tell anyone it would be his old Oxford chum, blah, blah, blah. I picked up the *Daily Telegraph* the very next day and there it was. The Halliday headline. I was furious; conveniently forgetting how Pete must have felt with me in 1985. Simon was doing what many did. Moving for the money. The 'opportunity'. In a way so was Bob. The money was, after all, in rock and roll. Or whatever he redefined it as.

Dylan changed the game. He was an alchemist. Made so much of modern music his. The same cannot be said for either my or Simon's influence on rugby. I left Wales for England with nothing but a pair of boots and a Celtic influence. Couldn't believe how few people were interested in Welsh conjuring east of the Severn. As for Bob, he played and sang what he wanted. The man was a troubadour, pure and simple. I too sought to avoid any baggage. Other than that of a rugby union player. But that was unacceptable in the 1980s. You had to have a country. Mine was England. A fact. No more than that. It only ever meant anything set against Wales and the contrasts between the Welsh and, to be honest, Home Counties culture that passes globally for 'England'. I have claimed that it was my three-year period of study at Oxford which changed me. The more I stated this the more I believed it, turned it into fact . . . tell yourself something often enough . . . From this distance I am peering as deep as I can into the past (given deteriorating eyesight) but the crystal ball is a murky one, hasn't shown me anything yet. Introduced into the Welsh national squad as a schoolboy for a game to celebrate seventy-five years of the now demolished National Stadium. I spent a few days with the squad, harbouring hopes of a place on the bench. Nothing came of it. That was fine. Even I wasn't that egotistical. But when I didn't get a sniff of action the next season – as a nineteen-year-old, playing most of his rugby in low-grade university levels – was I really so incensed as to throw in the towel with Wales and join the land of *my* father? This personal mining is turning into a murky business.

Having deserted Wales for England, the next stage was more straightforward. I wasn't going to stay in Wales long, wasn't going to be wearing the black and amber of Newport in such a scenario. The trigger, I fear, was another non-selection. This time for a Welsh Cup match against Swansea. In the game before the side was selected for this cup tie I performed, so my memory sketches in vague outline, poorly at Pandy Park. The opposition the unexceptional Cross Keys. I remember the bandstand the players pass as they head for the pitch, cramped next to the Ebbw river. A narrow valley. Not much else. A few miles down the valley from Abertillery.

A few years on, standing above the exposed terracing in Abertillery – giant terrace steps for monstrously big miners I supposed – with Bristol's most capped undertaker, Austin Sheppard. This time I was assisting with the scattering of ashes. A Welshman whose wish was to be returned to the valleys from whence he came. It was to be my last game for Bristol. The wind was blowing, the night was cold, a game was to be played. We didn't stop to think as the ashes blew back into our faces. A tale for the after-dinner circuit? Who can tell? All I know (or think I know) is that those valleys twice proved the end of brief roads taken. I never did go back to Abertillery after bidding my bitter adieu to Bristol. The valleys . . . some garden of Gethsemane. No farewell kiss. Nothing but a bitter taste of ashes.

There I was, lining up just another in the millions of insignificant penalty kicks we forgotten kickers have taken, when a Bristol burr of a voice shouted, 'Judas'. Don't believe him, he was a liar. It's fair to say I found the nickname funnier than Bob did. Then again, I am an atheist. Dylan a Jew who fumbled his way into some strange fundamentalist religious ramblings (none of us are perfect, even Robert Zimmerman). At the risk of offending any readers of a particularly religious bent, I'll use the 'Judas' name one last time. Put myself in the shoes of any proud Australian who has watched his rugby union team lose a home series 3–0 to England. 2016. Pounded by the Pom enemy, the horror of the humiliation. And there, smirking on the sidelines is Eddie Jones. The Australian coach when the Wallabies lost the World Cup final in 2003. Here he was, resurrecting the corpse of English rugby. A Grand Slam and now a whitewash of his own country. An Australian–Englishman. In the world of sport where patriotism plays a major part the 'J' of his surname could stand for a lot more than the common Welsh surname with which he was born.

Eddie began his coaching career with the renowned Sydney suburb side, Randwick. Where he previously played. It was to be quite a journey from the Oval on the ocean in Coogee to Twickenham. Japan, the Brumbies, Australia A (he claimed the Lions scalp as their coach in the New South Wales town of Gosford in 2001) and then the Wallaby post. A Tri-Nations triumph in 2001 and a World Cup final marked the high points of his early international career. But soon came a sequence of international losses. He was prematurely 'forced from his post'. A brief spell at Saracens and a seriously unsuccessful one with the Queensland Reds. Yet the resilient Jones bounced back into the spotlight as a technical advisor to the World Cup-winning 2007 Springbok team. As a non-South African he was not permitted a green Springbok blazer, forced instead to wear a Springbok tracksuit. From winning the World Cup to another career wobble with his second stint at Saracens, thence wound-licking in Japan, once more his bolthole. He worked away at club level until John Kirwan quit the national coach's role. A rumour, no more, in the west, until 2015 and his guiding hand behind the Japanese victory against the Springboks. Surely one of the eighty-minute highlights of his career, arguably any coach's career. It was masterfully minded. Talk about taking revenge for not being handed a Springbok blazer . . . his brilliant effort in the 2015 World Cup ended with his supposed return to Super Rugby and an appointment as manager of the Stormers, the Cape Town-based franchise in the shadow of Table Mountain. In the English press his name was being mentioned as a possible successor to Stuart Lancaster, whose international career ended with two Twickenham World Cup defeats. Jones was asked the question . . . his reply, 'Why would I want to leave this beautiful city?' Play poker against this man at your peril. I'm not sure Eddie ever gave an answer to what, after a mere eight days into his Stormers appointment, was nothing more than his own ingenuous rhetorical question. Money, what else, was one answer. Jones was reputedly offered a salary that dwarfed anything the financially challenged South Africans could summon. It's a professional game. Who wouldn't take it? A few muttered that a person who had signed on the dotted line of a contract, that's who. But in this day and age, only idealists would expect Eddie to keep his word, wouldn't they? He'd only been at his post eight days . . . the team wasn't in his blood. Alas, their plans for the immediate future were disrupted but Eddie, like Auden's Achilles, hadn't heard of too many worlds where promises were kept.

There's no denying a lack of integrity. But with the scale of the post and the size of the salary, who amongst us would not have betrayed the trust of the Stormers? Had I been in the shoes of Mr Jones, I would have bowed my head to the management who had appointed me. More in apology than shame. 'Sorry' cleans the slate, does for ethical behaviour these days. Surely the guiltiest party was an insatiable RFU. Sport has joined politics in that sleazy world where 'might is right'. Sport being sport, isn't often on the front pages; it is a diversion, bread and circuses, fun and games. Eddie knows it and plays the game as well as anyone in rugby union. He's a master of the microphone, a deceiver one minute, so honest no one believes him the next. Chameleon qualities. In the 2017 Six Nations he diverted the media from an awful English performance against Italy with an excessive attack on the Italian tactic, a perfectly legitimate tactic, of non-rucking. The ploy turned the breakdown into a kaleidoscope with Italian defenders in all sorts of unusual but infuriatingly legal positions. It caused mass confusion in the English ranks and the Sunday afternoon Twickenham crowd. The Italian team and management took the brunt of Eddie's feebly concealed frustration. Yet two rounds later, when the Grand Slam dream died in Dublin, he was magnanimous with the media. Outsmarted by Joe Schmidt, he admitted as much, blaming himself for the poor preparation which played such a part in the defeat. Jones is one of the sharpest minds in the sport. Winning, as he did for two years, and losing, which England mastered in the 2018 Six Nations. In defeat he remained great copy. Entertaining, acerbic. Eddie does not do dull. In another era, his desertion of the Stormers would have been seen as an illustration of Judas-like tendencies. In the time of Christ, that betrayal with a kiss, was written up as one of the vilest acts in the history of mankind. The Bible ensures Judas remains remembered as one of a kind. Transport his actions from then to now, Galilee to Cape Town, and it would seem nothing more than a man on the inevitable make – as we nearly all are – deserting 'The Miracle Brand' of Jesus for a safer Roman return elsewhere. In this globalised world the thirty pieces of silver explain and justify all. We live in an age when nearly anything can be bought or sold: coaches, commentators, players, even musical legends, you name it.

KICKING

IN THE interest of editorial balance, it is time to turn the clock back to that ominous year of 1984. You sharp-minded readers may remember being regaled with my glorious drop goal moment against Harlequins. As early as the first chapter there was a sly reference to the author dropping another sneaky goal against none other than the All Blacks in Wellington. Seems like the losers are getting their chance of a rewrite. As Bob Dylan intimated in his own 'autobiography' – *Chronicles* – an autobiography is no place to search for that elusive little thing we quaintly call the truth. As often as not it is the home of the trumpet blowers. Luckily, this book isn't an autobiography. I'll let you decide whether there's a horn section blowing in these pages as I trip through the book as a protagonist, rarely the intended hero, more the fool, awash in the tentative recesses of disturbed memories. Events go round and round like dirty laundry in a washing machine. We lose our bearings. There's a danger of not pausing to position yourself in the place of today's heroes and villains. I was watching a European Challenge Cup semi-final on television, not working, involving my old club Bath, back in the 2016/17 season. I was in Lyon. Snails and Burgundy. I don't remember whether it was George Ford or the French fly half lining up a late kick. My partner in commentary, Miles Harrison, said to me in the intimacy of our 'mikes down' privacy, after the kick sailed through the posts, 'A kicker gets that ten times out of ten.' Miles is a fine broadcaster but here was an instance of fundamental imaginative failing. You need to have been in that kicker's boots. To take the 'ten out of ten' kick is to realise how difficult the easy kick can be. As I get older, those kicks become harder, the pitfalls more dangerous.

Ford or the Frenchmen – whichever – succeeded with the kick and the game continued inexorably towards George Ford's last-second miss, five metres from touch, to take the game into extra time. The ten out of ten kick had been on the twenty-two-metre line, bisecting the fifteen-metre line. 'Bread and butter' is another of the derogatory terms used by those who have never stood there on that rugby cross, to explain the supposedly utterly unexceptional nature of the easy kick. Via some disturbed memories, I'll take you there. To the unmissable bread and butter kick. Big Brother watching me, way back when. Share my misery. The loser writing this tale.

Bristol, the defending champions. Bath, the opponents. The local upstarts. I was still a Bristol player. The same one who kicked most of his goals against Leicester in the previous final. The same Barnes that had kicked Bristol into the semi-finals with his penalties against Waterloo (yes, I did better than Napoleon when it came to the small matter of Waterloo). The same me that struck the ball with power, nerve and precision as we beat a superior Harlequins side who ran us ragged for large parts of the semi-final. There were few opportunities in the final. Bath were the better team. The West Country upstarts led for most of the game but a converted second half Bristol try ratcheted up the pressure. On both sides. There was less than a score between the teams. It was 10–9 to Bath; the West Country held its breath when the referee blew for a Bristol penalty. Last kick of the game . . . from the ashes . . . bisecting the twenty-two and fifteen-metre line. Ten out of ten. Bread and butter. The remaining toothless pensioners who recall the day tend to be diehard Bristol supporters. Miserable, miserly men of a conspiratorial nature. Here is their conspiracy theory. I was already heading to Bath. Had sold my soul to Mephisto, or Jack Rowell as he was more commonly known. Here was part of the pact. Ten years of trophies to follow and then what feels like an eternity talking and writing rugby. As far as conspiracies go it doesn't amount to much of one. No plot to kill a president in these pages. No Oliver Stone film. No astonishing unravelling of plot in the next few paragraphs. Nothing more than an attempt to help you feel what it is like to be a kicker under pressure.

A considerable portion of my younger life was spent practising goal kicking. In my youth I dreamed of kicking the winning penalty or conversion to win against Wales (traitorous little shit that I was) or even better, beat the All Blacks. If you have paid attention to this book, you'll know that in 1984 the latter chance was to escape me in just over a year. In Christchurch . . .

Back to 28 April 1984. It wasn't quite the fulfilment of the dream kick. But it was the John Player Cup final, it was Twickenham, one of the most famous stadiums in the world and 21,000 fans were making the sort of echoing noise in a third filled stadium that gets into your head. So, the conspiracy . . . had I already agreed to switch clubs I would still have been mortified to miss such a kick, for the sake of my current team-mates and my own showman's ego. The ego is an intrinsic part of most reasonably high-profile entertainers.

As soon as the referee blew his whistle I registered this as a penalty I expected to convert. As did everyone watching. A man on a roll. Kicking as well, if not better than I ever had or would again. If I was a professional golfer you would have described my kicking as a streak. With my heel I dug up the turf on four sides until I had an herbaceous tee on which to sit the proud Gilbert ball. A narrow ball, requiring more precision than the current ones which bizarrely encourage more men to kick in an era when running is supposed to be all the rage. Anyway, back to Orwell's year. In those days Twickenham had long, thick bunching grass. Designed to protect the playing surface. I built a mighty mound, a veritable Silbury Hill of a mound. The sweet spot of the ball (a term I had not yet heard) was wiped clean. There was no danger of kicking through the dense Twickenham grass and mishitting. In fact, there was no danger of anything, so I initially thought . . . a ten out of ten kick I told myself . . . but this was a cup final. This was Twickenham. This was a bloody important kick. The sort of kick with which I had dreamed away my teens. Imagination floods my penetrable twenty-one-year-old skull . . . the briefest fear, no more than a flicker.

I can't miss it, can I? It's an eyes-shut kick. But it is a bloody important kick . . . for God's sake, Stuart, you can kick this with your useless left foot . . . But what if I miss? Stop thinking. Get a move on. The sooner I kick the goal the fewer of these fucking silly thoughts to unnerve me . . . ah, but it is not a matter of nerves, man, just my imagination, running away with me. Four steps back, two steps to the left . . . I know, I know. Been doing this rugby minuet forever. Breathe deep, pause . . .

You could miss. What will happen if you miss? Imagine missing the winning kick at a final. In Twickenham. I can see it going left of the posts, right of the posts. It could happen. What then?

The language of the demons that find their way into the kicker's mind.

. . . It's so bloody easy, just get on with it. Sod the last pause, the deep breath . . .

And in that rushed moment the left shoulder is too open, the torso tilts backwards and the ball fades away to the inconceivable right-hand side of the posts. I am left the loneliest man on the planet. For a split second. This is what the demon said. This is what happens when you fuck up, Stuart, you fuck up.

And so my ten out of ten kick became a nine out of ten kick and I'll take issue with anyone that hasn't stood alone with the ball and the demon while your mates look to the posts, while the pressure seeps into the mind via the devilish imagination. I'll pity the easiest miss and praise the most straightforward kick until me and the microphone are parted for the final time. You were wrong, Miles, way wrong.

Kicking was the great ambiguity of my playing days. I liked to take the responsibility, be the man but I hated those frozen seconds when it is just you, the ball. Your boot. Your brain. Sometimes the demon. Shit or bust . . . that, I now understand, was not the way to approach the dead ball art of the kick. As a child I imagined the match-winning moment, even commentating to myself while preparing to take the crucial kick with my overinflated pigskin ball on my hidden playing field. Casting myself into the centre of the fairy tale scenario. Aware that the borderline between the hero and the villain is no more than the narrow width of the posts and crossbar. The pressure is nothing on the practice field. Many years later I read something Jonny Wilkinson said. England's greatest ever goal kicker had figured it out in a way the vast majority of normal humans cannot. He flipped it around, imagined all those successful Test match kicks were no more than another kick on the training field. He stripped himself of imagination. Thought himself back onto the years and years of empty training fields when every less dedicated soul had trooped off to the changing rooms and, in the process, turned World Cup-winning drop goals from the sublime to the bog standard. Most of us dreamers use the imagination to inspire. Wilkinson exiled his. In doing so he made himself into a machine, a machine that went through the same hands-clasped, squat-prayer routine with which a generation of twenty-first century schoolboys grew up. While romantic-minded idiots had glorious thoughts forcing their way into their heads, he built an impenetrable wall against the outside. He worked and willed his way to greatness. For most of his playing career, Sale's Charlie Hodgson was in many ways his match. He had an instinct for the game Wilkinson lacked. But whilst the greatest difference between the two men was often cited as their tackling, the contrast in physicality and, yes, the kicking, it was Wilkinson's ability to play the last ten minutes – when the pressure mounts to its maximum – as fearlessly as the other seventy. Charlie's imagination, such a blessing in so many ways, became a curse. He knew the demon by name. Imagined the graffiti on the clubhouse wall. Jonny, he kept on doing the same thing, this human metronome. Poetry gives way to prose in those clutch moments. Wilkinson stripped his game back to the bare essentials for the greater part of his career. A Raymond Carver of the rugby field, little waste to overburden the work. Charlie, he had capacity for the florid, another flawed romantic. The fact that he finished his playing days at Saracens, England's most solidly constructed team of those times, explains the longevity and late flowering of this delicate talent. He was straightened out, toughened up.

Even Wilkinson needed help. He had the right stuff up top but without technical assistance he would not have had the rhythm of the boot to transform the sport's toughest mindset into the game's deadliest kicking predator. Don't panic, I am not about to compare myself with Wilkinson but we shared one aspect of our careers in common. Dave Alred, now famous as a golf coach to 2018 British Open winner, Francesco Molinari. For a brief spell an average full back at Bristol. A rugby league full back of little repute. Most fascinatingly, an American football kicker with the Minnesota Vikings. This set him apart . . . he came back to the West Country with a host of ideas. Nobody was interested. Other than Bath. The genius of Jack Rowell was to see the qualities of people like Brian Ashton and 'Hank the Yank' as we called Dave. We were his trials, the breeding ground for his early days as a specialist kicking coach. The England and Bath full back, Jon Webb and I were his first two charges. He changed the way I thought and not just about the art of kicking. But preparation itself. He would have the pair of us in one of Bristol's private school cricket nets at 6.00 a.m., ready to go. This meant being awake by 4.30 to shower and stretch. To be ready for a full hour's drilling before heading off to our day jobs. He made us think of our body as one continuum. From the position of the head to the swing and follow-through of the foot as we 'threw it after the ball'. Now it is fashionable to 'shunt' it. Then the mantra was, 'Spot, line, follow through.' It sounds primitive now but this was the beginning of an important coaching career, one that steered Wilkinson to his great achievements.

It wasn't just the manner in which Dave mechanised us as kickers that made Alred such an influential force in the last years of the amateur game and the early ones of professionalism. It was the focus he instilled within. Through repetition he made us think like professionals. Prepare like professionals to go with the determination to win at all costs which was the brutal base of Bath's professionalism in the no pay days of the 1980s and 1990s. From Bath he quickly made his way to England. He turned my old nemesis, Rob Andrew, into an outstanding goal kicker rather than the erratic one of the early Andrew years. With Andrew running the Sir John Hall show in Newcastle where Wilkinson first emerged as a precocious teenager, this relationship led straight to the Alred/Wilkinson kicking axis. Barnes/Webb, Andrew, Wilkinson . . . maybe my guinea pig days played a miniscule part in the development of Wilkinson – a tiny, if unpatriotic, part in the evolution of England from blundering amateurs in 1983 to world champions two decades later.

On the subject of world champions . . . during the regular stages of Super Rugby 2017, Beauden Barrett seemed to be busy rewriting the art of the fly half play book. Every week he opened up the opposing defence with his speed of foot, of mind, his rapid ability to read a game. It was doors of perception stuff. Whether cross kicking or accelerating clear of defenders, the Hurricanes fly half was playing like a one-man rugby revolution leaping, quantum-like, away from the rest of the slowly evolving professional game. In New Zealand no one cared that he couldn't kick for goal with any consistency whatsoever. He was scoring and making tries. As if fly halves were being released from the shackles of their more mundane kicking duties. If there is an opposite to Wilkinson, Barrett isn't far from being it. But when the pressure built in the Lions series and again a year later when the All Blacks lost at home to the Springboks for the first time since 2009, the imagination of the man played havoc on the kicking tee. The revolutionaries shot themselves by dismissing the importance of the goal kicker. The last time I saw a fly half revolutionising the face of attacking play it was Mark Ella. The Australian who ushered in the era of the flat midfield. He too had one deficiency to his game . . . you've guessed it. Australia had to convert the far more pragmatic Michael Lynagh from Queensland fly half to Wallaby centre and goal kicker – until Ella retired. Does the excess of imagination that geniuses like these two players have, and had, prevent them from switching onto auto pilot when the concentration of the goal kick is required? Wilkinson was not blessed with the innate gifts of Barrett and Ella. What he possessed was an iron determination and a focus. His goal kicking was genius of sorts, the sort that grew out of extreme dedication.

On a slightly less exulted level, I will fondly reminisce on the Bristol fly half of my playing days, Mark Tainton. The cleanest striker of a ball. When his club were running the tries in 'Taints' rarely missed his mark. But when kicks counted . . . whenever it was tight in a derby game between Bath and Bristol, whenever Bristol's determined pack took the game to us, Mark could be relied upon to fold under pressure. Time after time he was Bath's salvation. He was not temperamentally suited to the savagery of the local derby despite his technical excellence. His mind may have let him down as a player but his technique took him places as a coach. He became Ireland's kicking coach. No small achievement for a player who never threatened to break into the highest echelon of tens in his time. Mark can take a kicker with technical failings and iron the problems out. Whether he can confront his pupil's inner demons and teach him to vanquish them . . . this seems more of a moot point.

Mark's a good guy anyway. What would he have done in Aaron Cruden's boots in November 2013? New Zealand had scored a try to draw level with Ireland. Last play of the game. Close to the left-hand touchline, to win it in the Aviva Stadium. As he prepared to take the potentially match-winning kick (a draw is as good as defeat for New Zealand) four Irishmen charged the conversion. The charge was premature. The fly half saw them rushing, a free shot . . . he scuffed the strike. It wobbled wide and low. Straight out of the Guinness Brewery, nowhere near its intended target. Nigel Owens ordered the kick to be retaken. I was watching the game in a pub in Bewdley, a pretty place on the Shropshire border. Heading to Ludlow for a few days' drinking and racing; general dallying about with the lads. I had a few pounds on the All Blacks. Sometimes you know before the ball is struck, the race begun, call it the gambler's instinct. It wasn't the most authoritative of re-kicks but it found its way through the sticks with its low and heartbreaking (for Irish fans not Kiwi backers) trajectory.

Cruden, like all goal kickers, came at the ball from around the corner. Once New Zealand rugby was strictly toe-end, age of dinosaur, technique. Until 1971 when Barry John serenely conquered their country. By the time the Lions left, the next generation of Kiwis were coming at those kicks from around the corner, any corner. John mania. Yet Barry wasn't the hero of Welsh goal kicking in the Five Nations preceding the 1971 tour. Here it was John Taylor who curled the ball over the posts to beat Scotland in Edinburgh. Deliciously described as the greatest conversion since St Paul. Taylor was a flanker. The thought of a forward kicking nowadays is almost inconceivable. Fly halves are not the exclusive kickers but they bear the burden in the vast majority of sides. There is no reason why a fly half has to kick for goal. I suspect it is part and parcel of the fact that fly halves are expected to be expert kickers. The days of a running ten who cannot kick – from hand or ground – are gone. In France, where forward play of a slower and more grinding variant remains at the heart of the club game, scrum halves are frequently the team's goal kickers. Just as they tend to be the tactical fulcrum of the side. There are British exceptions like Scotland's Greig Laidlaw and Ireland's Conor Murray (from range) but they are few.

Once the full back was the kicker. Men like Bob Hiller for Harlequins and England, Joe Karam and Fergie McCormick for the All Blacks. Full backs expected to do nothing bar catch the ball and kick for goal. Now very few of them are place kickers. They do everything but. As for the fly halves, they must be capable of thinking, farting, kicking and tackling in the space of a few seconds. They are rugby's Everyman. Much as all England loves him, I swear some of the romance went out of the game the day Wilkinson made his first shuddering shoulder charge . . . and followed it up with his perfection from the tee. He changed the game for good. Or not so good for a few fly halves with hands to make Alfred Brendel envious but bodies incapable of piano shifting.

LIONS

ON THE evening before Donald Trump announces his intention to either renegotiate or withdraw from the 2015 Paris Climate Treaty, the Lions PR machine informs the media that the squad will head for Whangarei – the destination of the first match of the 2017 tour – in a fleet of fourteen Land Rovers. Guzzle on. It is a classic collusion. Sport and corporatism. The Lions will argue that the team are heading to all parts, various schools, old persons' homes, the normal 'hearts and minds' photo ops, en route to their destination. I too head north. No old people en route for the Barrel. The rain is washing over the Northern Motorway (the other motorway on the North Island is the Southern one), lapping onto the fringes of the road. The Land Rover convoy will power through the puddles, no matter how deep. The Lions, on the road. The weather is weird. Heavy rain is nothing new to the sub-tropical north but this storm has the savagery of the tropics and the steady persistence of an English November drizzle. In Australia the droughts are getting longer, in California the forest fires fiercer. Remote Pacific islands are being washed away. Names soon to be forgotten. Meanwhile, the Lions' Land Rovers head north. The environment be damned.

The Lions are a twenty-first-century corporate lie, a benign fantasy, an escape from the reality of modern times. How else to explain the presence of 30,000 supporters on an island at the end of the world where the population is not much more than four million? Half that of London. LIONS – LIONS – LIONS! A dream. So many stories of people saving all their lives to follow the Lions just once. As for the players, those born within Britain and Ireland idle their childhood away day-dreaming of the famous red shirt. Gareth, Barry, Gerald for my generation. Drico, Maro and Johnno for the latest one. LIONS – LIONS – LIONS!

Amidst these terrible times, dark hours and 'existential' terrorist threats. Little Stevie straight out of the pages of Conrad's *Secret Agent*. Seduced by the serial screaming of the internet . . . the Lions are not such a bad fantasy. Yet beneath the glorious, antiquated ethos of the tour, the pilgrimage, Santiago de Compostela for the soaks and smilers, there is the other Lion. The capricious one that commences its plotting profit the moment after the final whistle blows on the current tour. Men and women working on the next corporate deal. Handsomely remunerated. Servants to the profit-motive first. And foremost. We pay for their privilege.

It's the opening press conference of the tour and Warren Gatland is talking about this or that. Behind him, on the Lions corporate wall – without which there are neither interviews nor photographs – I note the insignia. The corporate logos. Standard Life Investment, Land Rover, QBE, EY. There's also Canterbury. The New Zealand sports company who lost their rights to the All Black jersey. Now they kit out the Lions. There is no honour amongst sports clothing firms. Qantas, Australia's national airline, are another. At Auckland airport the first advertisement to catch my eye is one that says, 'front row, second row, the aisles, the Lions have all the best seats' or something like that . . . To hell with the Wallabies who they actually sponsor. Back in Heathrow, huge Standard Life Investment pennants float on the air conditioning of Terminal Three. There's something medieval about this twenty-first-century advertising . . . the Lions as a last remnant of a past where money doesn't make the world go round . . . phoney propaganda . . . Even the Sky television 'Fan Van' is sponsored by Standard Life. We are doing the work of others. The Age of Facebook.

The Lions is an amalgamation. What's good is bad, what's bad is good . . . nostalgia snuggles up to bottom lines. The Briar and the Rose. The thorn snags this old Lion. Somewhat unexpectedly. It wipes away my gloom when I walk through the downpour into the Toll Stadium in Whangarei, the day before the opening match of the tour. I had waxed lyrical in *The Times* on the subject of the Lions tour opener back in 1993. For I had been named captain. Some sort of consolation for my suicidal ability to blow international prospects. I conjure print memories. Changing rooms, running out into the sunlight, carrying the cuddly Lion beneath my arm. And a scrap. Between Peter Wright, a Scottish prop who had the unfortunate nickname of Tea Pot bestowed upon him during the course of the 1993 tour, and a Northland player who stamped on our cuddly toy. I was captain. That alone was not vague recollection. The rest hazier than claimed. But I do remember the grassy bank. Tomorrow it will be packed with fans and families spread all over it. Excited by the spectacle of the Lions. A slight lump of indigestible nostalgia in the throat as I see it for the first time in nearly a quarter of a century? Or am I inventing a softer-hearted someone I am not? Hang onto the hill and its happy memories, Stuart. Right or wrong. Make them my memories. Enjoy them. Bend them.

A Kiwi fan of a certain age approaches me as I watch the New Zealand Provincial Barbarians train. 'You played here in 1993, didn't you? I remember a bloody lovely pass you gave that Guscott. He ran clean through from fifty yards, it was a good pass.' I'll take his word. Weave a little Barnes magic into a chapter chock-full of doubt, cynicism, terrorism, even the shadow of global destruction. I am quite the dystopian.

An Italian meal and bed. Wake up at 4.30. Not jetlag but the storm drumming on the town's tyrannous preponderance of tin roofs. Global warming deniers, the planet fighting for its life, the futures of all our children and grandchildren . . . wide awake awash in middle-of-the-night madness. Pondering what, at 5.00 a.m., seems a pointless existence. Why not book a flight to Washington DC? Try and do the world a favour. One impossible, insane deed . . . dead of night thoughts. Nothing dead about what is thundering relentlessly down from the skies.

Twenty-four hours later and for a while the tour is rendered immaterial. Another terrorist attack in London. Six dead, three terrorists killed . . . the figure will rise to seven. CNN are bringing pictures from London Bridge, Borough Market, where my colleagues on *The Times* and *Sunday Times* work. It's been a lockdown. The *Sunday Times* sports desk are holed up on the ninth floor, but their journalistic instincts crave to be on the street, seeking out the story, a story. The ludicrous 4.30 a.m. musings, written before the attack . . . a throwaway provocation. It reads ridiculously, callous now. Or are the innocent victims of this Saturday night attack so utterly irrelevant to Trump – who bestows the blessing of his American God upon us – that the lines should stay? Should I press delete? Erase idle thoughts from the middle of a rain-soaked night? If you don't read any of this there is a parallel piece of the universe, albeit only the Stuart Barnes one, which has drifted into an eternity of nothingness. Should you read it, well, thanks to my wonderful agent and publishers, we are back on track. One that could yet lead to some weird and not so wonderful places. We are in a maze, remember, not a labyrinth. God knows where this leads, but it's at least the original idea.

Between middle-of-the-night madness and the awful imposition of some lunatic fantasy of assassination there's a game of rugby. And a beguiling few pre-match hours when you close the mind to the branding and the business and savour the special nuance the Lions bring to small-town New Zealand. Five hours before the big game, the streets are awash with people. Rain miraculously retreated. The centrepiece is a stage in the middle of the town's pedestrian precinct. As we stroll past, a band of Scottish pipers are blowing their hearts out. From the bar where we watch a Super Rugby match between the Crusaders and the Highlanders, I see a Maori dance group. A young girl who sings country accompanied by her guitar. Children watch, they smile. Diverted from the music by the stilt walkers and the people in fancy dress, Mexicans popping out of bins . . . there are quasi-nuns with cartoon faces. All sorts. It's carnival time. A community coming together. For these few hours the whole idea of the Lions is lovable. In the bar we hover around a table booked in another name. When that name and his friends arrive, they don't usher us away. They open their palms. Offer to share their food. Miles appreciates the cheese. The televised game is an exciting one. The man who has booked the table supports the Crusaders. Shows us a picture on his phone, him and Richie McCaw. Together with the Webb Ellis Trophy. Helicopter in the background. All agree it is a fine photograph. Small-town romance . . .

Monday morning and Miles and I are attending the Blues training session from the long distance of the grandstand that looks onto Alexandra Park, a trotting track that doubles as their training camp and head offices. The players are in a party mood. Sonny Bill Williams is doing tricks. Everyone is having a splendid time on a warm Monday morning. Another deception in the process of being unveiled. The Lions are headline news within the ranks of the British and Irish media. We know about the dedication of their fans too, let alone the players . . . but for the Blues this is the least important game of their season to date. The five New Zealand franchises are judged, and judge themselves, on Super Rugby. The Blues recently beat the Reds (from Queensland) in Samoa. The mood is good, the pressure off. The side's press officer as well as their manager, who just happens to be Tana Umaga, and anyone in blue see the game as a free shot. In print I had previously described the match as one that could bring the Blues' season a special moment. I was wrong. It is a bonus. The rest is bullshit. The facts we have been peddling within the ranks of the British media are exposed as fraudulent. The Lions are simply not that big, not until the Test series . . . not in the big city anyway. Country conservatism welcomes the Lions, one of the great rugby traditions, into their community with outstretched arms. In the city, it's no big deal to the boys used to the brands and the business ethos. But don't worry, we'll paint a different picture in the press. Give you our picture. The one the media, the businessmen and the fans want to hawk. If the Lions lose to the Blues we'll bandy around words like 'crisis'. I'll try not to. Not after the events in London. But life must go on. Heartless nihilists are no match for the Lions hordes.

The Lions lose to the Blues. It is not a crisis.

In 1993 every game seemed to have more significance attached than is the case in 2017. Pre-Super Rugby times. In particular, the little towns took a special pride in welcoming, then trying to bushwhack, the Lions. I was on the wrong end of a shock loss in Napier, home of Hawkes Bay. Inconceivable that this little wine town in the North Island could beat the combined might of four unions, but that is exactly what happened. Delirium for some, despair for others. Not enough of the latter to my mind. Our pack was pathetic. A few forwards had thrown in the towel. As captain, I was expected to deliver a speech in the post-match reception. Geoff Cooke, the Lions manager and a man who never really trusted me any more than I trusted him (as a human being

I like him; as manager and selector we sort of saw things from a different point of view, got our signals crossed . . .), did not want me to speak. I was Lions captain and Geoff should not have tried to stop me speaking. An insult to our conquerors. Someone had to thank the Hawkes Bay boys for reminding our team just how revered the red jersey was and is in some parts of the world. We had forgotten. In their victory, Hawkes Bay reminded us. What was wrong with this little speech? Geoff didn't trust me to say the right words. He wanted to control the agenda with the British and Irish media, didn't want a loose cannon blasting away. Always the battle to enforce the agenda. As authority wants itself to be perceived. Geoff and Ian McGeechan's — but not the captain's. I am not saying my take was right but I was determined to offer another perspective. That's how it remains a quarter of a century on. Control the communication was the message then. Twenty-four years later and the control of communication is the message. It's a business. Bigger than any of us dreamed possible last century. Character killing.

The day of the Maori game. Rotorua. From my hotel room I stare across to the lake. Smell the sulphur from the thermal pools, rising up through the bathroom drainage. In the foreground people are wandering onto the green for quick lessons in the haka, the world's biggest haka. We are promised a war dance ahead of the afternoon's game. A lot of lolling tongues. Maori versus Lions, a clash of cultures. The tradition that has slipped across the border into the land of brand. The men with the tribal tattoos and war dance. The veteran Maori number eight, Liam Messam, explained the haka the previous day at the Maori press conference. 'It's dedicated to the god of war, getting us ready for battle . . . we are worried more about connections with team-mates [than metaphorical throat slitting of visitors from the Old World].' The Maori. The little brother to the All Black, still the genuine cultural artefact, for all the cursed AIG on the shirt. Perceptions . . . the Lions as a romantic band of brothers from the Old World, taking on mighty southern hemisphere opposition on far-flung fields. 'Every rugby playing child's dream in the United Kingdom and Ireland is to play for the Lions.' The words of Colin Cooper, the manager of the Maori side. Here is his perception of the men in red and how they would play: 'A kicking game . . . lineout drives . . . penalties from lineout drives, that is what we are prepared for.' James Lowe, now a star of the Leinster team, playing full back, is asked his expectations: 'We've got a lot of high balls coming.' Cooper again, the Lions 'strong up front, a whole lot of high balls . . . line speed [in defence].' I ask you, since when were ogres so romantic? In the United Kingdom and Ireland the Lions are followed with a blind, almost religious devotion by their flock of fans. Here in New Zealand, specialists see them as little more than a bunch of big bullies. The world has turned 180 degrees since 1971. Then, the All Blacks and their frantic footwork were the villains. The visitors the heroes with Barry the Lancelot of the Lions. Now New Zealand regard themselves the rugby visionaries. The ugly prose belongs to the barely rugby literate men from the other side of the world.

In 1974, the Lions were a beguiling combination of brilliance and bruise. Fine, they were up against the South Africans. Any methods to bring this cultural weapon of Afrikaner racism to its knees. Thereafter romance and reality took off in different directions. It took a tour to Australia in 1989 for the Lions to win their next series. And they won it by beating up the team who would become world champions two years later. The Lions, under the revered Ian McGeechan, had little room for beauty. Pragmatism and lineout pressure was the code of the road in 1993 as New Zealand took the series 2–1. 1997 was a famous tour. South Africa beaten for a second time. The midweek team were delicious to watch. The Test team tightened, played percentages and kicked the goals. Neil Jenkins, the Welsh fly half, was converted into a makeshift full back. To do just that. And nothing more. Jim Telfer produced a master stroke, selecting the smaller Celtic props, Paul Wallace and Tom Smith, to destabilise the massive Springbok scrum. Tactically this was quite a ploy but South Africa played their own self-destructive role, battering away at the Lions line without any variety, ignoring the fact Neil Jenkins had never been placed beneath the fury of an aerial bombardment. Maybe the man from the Rhondda would have stood JPR-rock-like and caught everything that fell from the skies. It was worth the Springboks at least testing the rookie fifteen . . . Good God.

In the time it has taken to write a few Leonine thoughts from 1971 to 1997, the foreground green has filled up. I might witness a world record today. I hope the haka happens before I have to head for the stadium . . . anyway, losses in 2001, 2005 and 2009 before the next series win. Again in Australia. In 2013. The worst Australian team in the professional era. It required some ineptitude for the Lions to be level after two matches. A memorable third Test romp and we headed back to the north. Counting the days and months and years until the big one, New Zealand . . . last night I watched them beat Samoa 78–0. The quality of their play quite sublime. The brand needs a special effort against the cultural Kiwis to convince me we are in for anything but a rout. (You can't get them all right!) No rewrite, no re-sketching of memory. Fences are no places for columnists and analysts to sit out sporting history . . .

Anyway, here we are, on the green, two hours later. The haka roars to life mid-morning; 7,700 people gather to break the record. I join 7,699 enthusiasts. At one with the Maori god of war. On the stage is the great Maori All Black, Buck Shelford. This one, however, is a celebration. Lions fans and Kiwis combined. A sense of togetherness . . . terrific . . . soon the green is empty, the record broken, clocks ticking towards the Maori v Lions clash.

Twenty-four years since I played fly half and we recovered from a 20–0 half-time deficit. More good, if vague, memories. 24–20. That was Wellington then, this is Rotorua now . . .

As the Lions' version of the Barmy Army fill the streets of Hamilton, I walk out of the Waikato Museum. A small and moving First World War exhibition on display – 'the distance between laughter and tears' – a line from a letter written in 1918. A poster calling for young lions to help the Empire. The sun shines along the mighty Waikato river. The entire concept of 30,000 people cheering on a sporting team seems silly, but in a sweet and life-enhancing sort of way . . . fast forward a fortnight. One–nil to the All Blacks. A convincing enough win in Auckland. On to Wellington. The predominantly middle-aged, middle-class army of supporters in their corporate red are filling the streets of the capital city. I don't believe Standard Life Investments have taken up more than a millisecond of my thought processing. Now, slowly, surely, they are implanting themselves into a cosy nook in my brain. The fans fork out a small fortune to do someone else's advertising job for free. The supporters. The mainstay of the Lions. Since the 1997 *Living with Lions* documentary they have toured in ever greater numbers. 1971 and 1974 remain the mythic core for the Welsh contingent. All of them want to say, 'I was there,' when the achievements of Barry and Gareth are eclipsed. It has to happen someday. As I sit here writing, thirty-six hours ahead of the second Test, I'll be surprised if 2017 is the year. Another twelve-year wait beckons. Whether the Lions survive for another crack at the All Blacks, that's a whole other question. But as for this one . . . the fans pour into the restaurants early and leave late. The streets are not yet the bedlam we were led to expect. Something to do with the demographic profile of the supporters staying in the hotels – or the vast number still on the piss in either Fiji or Queenstown. Five weeks into touring, the body aches but the spirit survives.

Is it something to do with the Lions? Some pocket of resistance remaining free of the brand? Old Stuart Barnes wants to tuck himself in nice and early, a cup of tea and a good book and be fresh for the various working assignments the next day. But the ancient shadow of young Stuart Barnes envelops the boring middle-aged version and leads him into late-night bars and red wine restaurant frenzies. The years are being, not so much rolled back, as dismissed in the darkness of my old self. Good. In the morning old Stuart Barnes feels like his face is a dried-up mask. One he would like to rip off. Start life again, pores in perfect shape. At night young Stuart Barnes prowls the environs of Cuba Street. There's a jazz band in Rogue and Vagabonds and blues blasting through the chilly night air around the Hotel Bristol. I wear a black hoodie. The hood is knotted so tightly I can barely see out – and no one can see in. I'm invisible. Watching the couples, the guzzling groups of middle-aged men, the bustling boys from Ireland gagging for a Guinness. Forget Owen Farrell and Johnny Sexton, the Lions would be nothing without the supporters . . . or – on the occasion of the second Test – don't forget them. Farrell and Sexton repay the supporters with some clever stuff and two tries. There's a titanic performance by Maro Itoje. And victory. The series is levelled. The myths of 1971 are being rekindled. Daring to dream. Player, coach, journalist and supporter. We all forget the Standard Life advertising. The branding. All those irritations. Damned fine marketing, that.

Everyone loves the Lions. Everyone except the English clubs and, according to the 2017 tour manager, John Spencer, World Rugby. After the second (or was it third?) Test, the Sunday papers reported on the buffeting being received at a World Rugby meeting in San Francisco. There is no one to defend this august institution. The idea of future eight-game tours isn't exactly vandalism but it is a steady diminution of the concept. To hear a well-remunerated member of the Lions inner cartel complaining, is to intuit self-interest. Yet those 30,000 fans are not all fools. Plenty are aware that their role is to give the four-yearly tour the blast of energy which makes it unique, to help maintain this magical link through history, for all the background corporatism. 2017's squad were within a point of joining the legends of 1971. At no stage in this six-week sojourn was there was a sense of greatness – but greatness grows with age. Glory grows like ivy. It surrounds the victorious. As it was, the series finished with a hollowed-out feel. Fans didn't know what to think of the drawn series, broadcasters uncertain what to say, journalists what to write. One more point for immortality, one less to become a brief footnote in history. As it was, the result was a magnificent success for the Lions against the double world champions. It easily eclipsed the series win of 2013. By Monday morning, players, management, fans and press have gone their separate ways. Only memories are left. And, for the moment, the future Lions. Brand and all.

P.S. It is the middle of 2018. A few days ago I received a Lions cap through the post. I think I was number 640; the number is on the tasselled cap. It charmed all old Lions and doubtless convinced a few of them to fight even harder for the Lions and their future. Extremely smart but, nevertheless, a lovely touch indeed.

MUNSTER

IT IS 2010. We are celebrating fifteen years of the Heineken Cup. Most organisers like any excuse for a jolly and a bit of PR. ERC, or whatever the now-defunct organisation's acronym, is no different. A fifteen-year landmark. The season's finale is set for Paris. It's a good spot for a spring-time party. ERC booked their bash on the eve of the Biarritz versus Toulouse final; an Ancien Régime building, in the middle of the Seine. Here in gilded rooms, steeped in history, the Heineken Player of the First Fifteen Years is to be unveiled. My stepson, Matthew, is drinking in the atmosphere, not to mention the endless flow of Heineken. The greats have agreed to grace the occasion: Jonah and Johnno, big Lol, Brian O'Driscoll. Most of them having themselves a Parisian ball.

'Christ, look at Ronan O'Gara,' says Matt, between excessive slurps of lager, 'he looks like he wants to kill someone.' Here he is, the recipient of the award – the best, most influential player in the fifteen-year history of the Heineken Cup. The hero of the evening. And, yes, his eyes are frozen. These are eyes capable of boring holes into you from ten paces. Eyes that would pin you to the wall. Also eyes that can twinkle with delight. But if there is any delight in the Munster fly half's life tonight, it isn't obvious. Munster missed out on the final. Performed poorly against Biarritz in the San Sebastian semi-final. Their fly half isn't happy to be here.

Ronan was the most frightening of his Munster generation. He had a reputation for shirking the tackle (the mark of a bright fly half) but he was a cold-eyed killer of opposing teams. An exquisite eye for the kick to the corner, the delicate drop behind the onrushing midfield. He had what Jack Rowell used to call 'an in-built computer'. And what a competitor. He excelled for Ireland, playing a defining part in their first Grand Slam since 1948. There was the small matter of that seventy-sixth minute dropped goal in Cardiff. But he saved his finest hours for the red of Munster. Clocks ticked slow when 'ROG' was on watch in Limerick. In Thomond Park, O'Gara was the anything-but-blind watchmaker. The guiding hand and boot. The creative force. He always seemed the most secular of sportsmen, utterly rational whenever he wore the Munster shirt. Yet one of his and Munster's great days has gone down in European rugby history as the miracle match. It was a pool match but one made into a knock-out occasion by the earlier comprehensive beating Gloucester had administered to the men in red at Kingsholm. Munster had to score four tries and win by a certain margin – what exactly, I can't remember and it doesn't matter . . . this is about the feeling within the stadium, the cool head of the pilot in the team . . . what counts is that Munster hit the front like a high-class stayer who times its late run to perfection. Seconds left and the fourth try. Met with daunting delirium. But the points margin was still inadequate. They needed the conversion. O'Gara struck the ball through the nerve-racking silence of the situation and bisected the posts. Full time. The miracle. It's still known as the miracle match, many years later.

For many a Munster fan, Munster rugby is an act of faith. Outside Limerick and Cork there's a lot of British and Irish Lions fans who primarily remember O'Gara for kicking an up and under rather than booting it into touch in the second Test against South Africa in 2009. He conceded a penalty, Morne Steyn kicked it from fifty metres. The series was over. Two–nil. Had the Munster man kicked it dead the game would have been drawn. The series could have been saved. But where is the glory in the drawn series? Think back to the strange atmosphere of the 2017 third Lions Test. The Lions drew with the All Blacks and there was no celebrating this astounding series result. No, O'Gara was right. He went for it . . . and went down, deep down in the estimation of a lot of good judges. But not in mine. Quite the opposite. He soared. The same guy who missed from the mud, forty-eight metres out against Leicester in a Heineken tie at Welford Road. Minutes later the Tigers conceded a penalty. This time on the halfway line. Two metres further away than the miss. The mud even thicker. No way the kick was possible but O'Gara forced it through the posts for yet another mystifying Munster European victory.

The assassin. The general. The maestro. The fly half. He was all these things and more to Munster but it was to be his schoolboy half back partner, the unassuming Peter Stringer, who produced the most magical of all Munster European moments. The scrum half had spent an entire career serving the needs of his fly half. The grit to Ronan's glamour. It is 2006. Munster are in their third final, having lost the other two. Stringer puts the ball into the scrum. He will pass to his fly half because that is what he has religiously done throughout his career. Biarritz shift their concentration towards his partner . . . but Stringer, waiting the length of his days, takes off towards the touchline. An unmarked area. The French are caught flat-footed. He scampers. Scores. The try that sets them up for their belated European day of destiny. Anthony Foley, who will die only eleven years later, lifts the cup. He is immortal. Along with all his mates. This day in Cardiff, this day of culmination.

A few years earlier. Munster are red hot favourites against Wasps. A European semi-final. It's not in Limerick, but Dublin is the next best option. Munster are in fantastic form. This is going to be their year. But they cannot overcome the cussed quality of Wasps, the force of nature that was so often Lawrence Dallaglio. Wasps hit back late. An epic win, a heartbreaking loss. In a bar near the ground, I stop to pee. A supporter sways, slurring *The Fields of Athenry*. 'You're the Barnes fella, aren't you?' In the sort of clipped conversational tone that men have mastered in public conveniences, I confirm my identity and commiserate. He shakes his . . . head, looks me in the eye and says, 'It's probably for the best we lost. What will this tournament have to talk about when we finally win the fucking thing?' He was right. Toulouse have won it four times to Munster's two, Toulon three times and Leinster four, while Saracens and Leicester are with Munster on two victories. Yet it is Munster who defined the tournament. Made it something more than a bright and shiny new competition. Munster made it holy.

In those early days, France was so often the scene of battle. Mighty wins against the odds. Defeats that drove the Munster hordes to the French bars with intent. Drinking, dreaming of the next time. The media dubbed the Heineken Cup Munster's Holy Grail . . . for the players and the fans. Their supporters merge the working-class tribalism of football with the more refined culture with which rugby is supposedly linked. Where else in world sport can an opera written by Bizet be sung as the touchpaper for a team? It was originally adopted by the team, taken onto the terraces much as Hammerstein adapted it to Carmen Jones some time in the twentieth century . . . the 1950s?

Stand up and fight until you hear the bell,
Stand toe to toe, trade blow for blow,
Keep punching hard until you hear the bell,
That final bell, until you hear the bell.
Stand up and fight,
Stand up and fight like HELL.

There have been times when opponents looked at the devilish glint in O'Gara's eyes, the Stygian gloom that was once the breakdown against Munster and thought, 'Why, this is hell.' And then there is *The Fields of Athenry*. A song from Connacht but one stolen and made into the Munster anthem some time around the beginning of the Heineken Cup. From Limerick it has crossed the Irish Sea and is a central song in the Anfield repertoire. Football borrowing from its little cousin. Rugby flattered by football. Those dreams and songs to sing . . . semi-final stage and Munster are up against it. Lansdowne Road, an away game in what is effectively the heartland of their great rivals and opponents on the day, Leinster. Where taxi drivers tell you the cost of houses, the price rises in the last decade. Celtic Tigers. Cool. But the 'pretty boys' of Leinster do not roar. Instead Munster produce yet another of those European performances, defying expectation . . . Ronan O'Gara intercepts, sprints beneath the posts and hurdles the advertising hoarding, frozen eyes burning with gleeful malice. It was supposed to be Felipe Contepomi's day after the quarter-final and Leinster's stunning success in Toulouse. O'Driscoll picking perfect angles off the Argentine fly half. Shane Horgan, one day to be a colleague of mine at Sky, scores in the corner. I roar over the words of Will Chignell. He doesn't do the significance of the try justice. I utter a growl of pure emotion. Part acting, part passion. Yes, this was the Dublin side's day. It was going to be their year. But O'Gara glared and picked the favourites to pieces. The fly half touched down in front of the demented/delirious Munster crowd, you decide which. Conducting a crazed upstart opera . . . I'll pause here for two days. A break in the writing as I prepare for the Pro 12 final involving Munster. In Dublin again. And the flight to New Zealand.

There's a glass of Bordeaux in my hand, UAE business class. Little sleep the night before, the night Munster's defence melts against the Scarlets' red-hot attack. Dashed dreams, a desperate day. And now I conjure an even more ignominious afternoon. Croke Park, the home of GAA, the northern part of Dublin. The less salubrious side of the city where Leinster players are not buying up restaurants and bars. Just Belvedere School in a sea of union apathy. Class consciousness is central to the union traditions in Dublin. The doctors; Munster, the self-styled dockers . . . city versus country; Dublin, yes, but the wrong side of the tracks. Munster have hammered Leinster a few weeks earlier in the Celtic League . . . it's 2009. I know because Alan Quinlan has been selected for the Lions. To the horror of the English press who have a soft spot for the athleticism of Leicester's Tom Croft. The Tiger will tour, Quinlan will not. One gouge and another rugby dream flipped over into the realm of its brother, Nightmare. So too for Munster. It is O'Driscoll intercepting this time. Running away, chest out, legs pumping, the tide finally turning against Munster. It isn't meant to be this way but it is. Johnny Sexton enters the fray early for Contepomi . . . a star is not so much born as given a name. O'Gara has a rival and Munster collapse, their dignity in tatters. Not since Leicester took the Thomond Park home record and the leonine Martin Castrogiovanni played the part of prop forward and operatic hero rolled into one have Munster been so subdued. Television turns its back on the beaten boys. Losing to Leicester at home hurt enough but this Croke Park defeat is on another scale. The doctors have dissected them. Probed for pain, hurt and humiliation. All in front of 82,000 people. No doubt this is a major moment in European club rugby history. The changing of the guard – or else your hearts must have the courage . . . mountains have moved within the Irish rugby landscape, cards marked. Elimination, rise and fall, the toppled giant, the expensive boots of the glittering boys who will win their first Heineken Cup against Leicester in the final. Bob Dylan's *Changing Of The Guard*.

The urban elite have replaced the earthy men of the rich farming Munster soil. The poet, Paddy Kavanagh, lived in Pembroke Road, not far from the Herbert Park hotel where I stay in Dublin. Literary echoes. I tend to think the poets would desert their Dublin for Munster. There is something irresistibly Irish about Munster . . . or maybe they are an English idea of an Irish cliché. The Americans who flock to Bunratty Castle are worse but perhaps there is something condescending in my admiration for Munster. I write regularly of Munster men rising from the roots of their province. In my mind there is much that is mythic. Strong silent men. John Hayes types. As the Airbus thrums I am feeling the first fleeting niggle, along with the gout that has popped up and said, 'Guess who?' as it did on the 2013 Lions tour. One bloody glass of wine, that's all. Badge of honour. Anyway, back to the Irish Big Two. It's the Leinster style, particularly under the New Zealand-born coach, Joe Schmidt, that enthralled me. They played with panache. Cyrano de Bergerac. As for Munster, my mighty men of myth . . . in the 2008 final I awarded Quinlan the Man of the Match accolade. All I remember is his provocative stamp on the foot of Fabien Pelous, the Toulouse and France lock. The Munster back rower cunning, drawing a reaction. Nobody thought the French international would lose his temper to the extent he kicked Quinlan up the arse. Yellow carded. To some hilarity from the Sky commentary box but nothing funny for Toulouse, frustrated by Munster and their interminable plodding pick-and-drive-by-the-inch technique which made it all but impossible for Toulouse to get their hands on the ball. It was a master class in complete cynicism. Toulouse barely touched the ball in the last twenty minutes. The ugliest twenty minutes of finals rugby . . . unless you were a Munster man. They played the rules to perfection. So well that the laws of the game were amended to stop teams adopting the Munster keep-ball style. And here am I, a rugby romantic, writing a eulogising chapter. Muttering on with my grand pretensions . . . is this a case of images and distorted facts . . . a book of delusions, the hall of mirrors?

My foot throbs, my head hurts. While everyone else is sleeping or cocooned in the glow of the plane's vast entertainment packages, I listen to Dylan's *Blood On The Tracks* before I open the laptop. Can it be true, this nightmare niggle . . . that after all these years I don't even know myself. This Munster chapter is causing turbulence, consternation. Someone said writing is cathartic, not right now. There is no reverie, no internal peace and quiet as I write on . . . Munster were no lone soldier winning games after losing battles. They won the incremental contests, eked it out up front. There was so much more than the undeniable O'Gara glint. Tactics that, had any English club adopted them, I would have loathed. I hate the word 'incremental', such a downsizing of the sporting spirit . . . an English summer is turning rapidly into winter as this aeroplane cuts through the night sky bound for Auckland. I can't read my own mind right now; is any of what I have been thinking, or the acts with which I have associated myself remotely close to what most people would perceive as 'truth'? Is this book, these sketches from my memory and this Munster chapter one giant distortion?

Is 'my' Munster only an envious English image? John Hayes, Mick Galway, Quinnie and the lads having the craic, is that it? A bunch of men who came together and willed their way to a few European titles? Munster. A vision of how my ideal life as a professional might have played out, or some subconscious attempt to cover 'truth' with feelings . . . is that why I came up with the whole concept of writing for the feeling? All I tell you is I didn't plan to tell a 100,000-word lie. No intentional deceit set out, not a single word. Though I might not have told the full tale, whatever it is, whoever's it is . . . Munster is where I should have guessed the ongoing argument between considered truth and romantic fiction might just run amok. The book's mythic core. And M comes halfway through the alphabet, halfway through the book. Black and white, heads and tails, truth, fiction or this hybrid I call 'feelings'? Your call. I need a break. Need a drink but my foot . . .

THREE HOURS LATER – Much calmer. I read the last three paragraphs as another digression. The transatlantic twitch of a fifty-four-year-old man. Flying all day, too much time to think, to wonder whether this is about rugby or some esoteric nonsense . . . I need to give myself a good talking to. Back to the main theme of the book. Let's search for some solid ground. That season, 2016/17 and the heartbreak of Anthony Foley's death. Munster's darkest hour. Out of the blue, into the dust. In his early forties with a wife and family. Undeniably tragic, there's no line walked between fact and fiction here. The man that captained Munster and grasped the Holy Grail against Biarritz. 'Axel'. He died alone in his bedroom the night before a European clash with Racing 92 in Paris. The game inevitably postponed. The Munster fans arriving at the ground, stunned into silence as the news filters out. One of the great Munster men. Strong and silent . . . wouldn't have had any time for a philosophical discussion on the subject of fact and fiction. Munster fans were fantastic in France. Gathered themselves and sang songs in honour of their prematurely taken warrior. I talked to Irish journalists, trying to avoid the trite, trying not to claim him as a friend. He was no more than an acquaintance. A brief pre-match chat when he was Munster's Director of Rugby the previous season. 'How's it going?' 'All right . . .' 'Good luck . . .' 'Yeah, thanks.' I was a journalist, watching from the sides, no protagonist, no right to speak on a personal level. Foley was their captain in 2006. In death, their captain again. He didn't play in the Toulouse 2008 final, time was against him at this stage of his career. He was benched but that didn't matter. He was Axel and he had been there every step of the way. The last of the old guard who set out on Munster's epic journey. There to get his big mitts on the trophy. I struggled to suppress tears when he lifted the Heineken Cup. Don't doubt the emotion. That truly was from the heart. I am just questioning why I was so taken in by a team who played it clever. Rarely beautifully.

It was no easy task to hold back the tears eleven years later when Glasgow turned up at Thomond Park. The day after the Foley funeral. Half an hour ahead of kick-off, Gregor Townsend told me he didn't know what to expect. What we got was exactly what Munster watchers should have expected. An incredible performance. Tactics irrelevant, they poured forward, driven by the purest of emotional injections. Keith Earls out of control. Emotion overwhelmed him. Red card for a tip tackle. Munster didn't break stride. Fourteen men or not. This was a fearsome tribute. The crowd played their part to perfect pitch. Applauding the Glasgow bus into the car park, their players into the changing rooms . . . what was to follow had nothing to do with Glasgow. They wanted the Scots to know what was about to ensue was nothing personal. Post-match, Foley's two boys joined the team in a lap of honour. I was filing a hurried piece for the *Sunday Times*. Thank God, I didn't witness the scenes. I would have bawled like a baby.

2016/17 was quite some season. The muse stayed with an improving but far from vintage Munster team. In Paris they were awe-inspiring, picking and driving, now with dynamism. The French champions, Racing 92, were crushed . . . a third European title was whispered. A hushed possibility. But emotion isn't an efficient fuel. After a while it runs out. The tank was empty by the time Saracens played them in the Champions Cup semi-final. They were reduced to a splutter by the highly revved-up Scarlets in the Guinness Pro12 final, again in Dublin. One team of myth beating another. These sides shared the honour of downing the All Blacks in the 1970s, songs and plays written either side of the Irish Sea. By 27 May, I don't think even the most religious of us believed Anthony Foley was looking down on his men. The surge Munster derived from their awful grief disappeared as a quite good team was beaten by a far superior one. No more myths on this day.

The final took place slap-bang in the middle of my writing this Munster chapter. It was not the denouement the chapter required. Not when I was writing in present tense, anyway. Looking back from a year on, maybe the magnitude of the Foley loss forced me to think again, made me question what right an Englishman ever had to jump on one of rugby's most famous bandwagons. After the embarrassment of conceding forty-six points in the final, a few Munster fans stopped me as I was about to get in the hotel lift. One o'clock in the morning. Considering I had enjoyed a couple post-match, the answers were relatively lucid. As the lads left and the lift door closed, I heard one of them sneer the word, 'Wanker.' Guessed where it was aimed. So much for me and the bandwagon. I recall the year Sky Sports gained exclusive rights to the then Heineken Cup. RTE lost their coverage and George Hook, an outspoken pundit, was none too pleased . . . 'What do Stuart Barnes and Dewi Morris know of Thomond Park?' said the rhetorician. I couldn't speak for Dewi but I had represented Wales Under 19s there, not long after the famous win against the All Blacks, I think. It was a scruffy old place . . . at least I played on the hallowed pitch, something I doubt George managed, although I may be wrong . . . but he had a point. He was talking of the history, the culture, the essence of the place. Does it belong to only Munster men, or more broadly the Irish? Or does the Munster rugby community say, 'The great traditions belong to us all, everyone should be considered part of the community. We saw where obsessions with bloodlines led us in the 1930s. We should open our arms, even to the English "wankers".' It's for others to judge.

The chapter is winding to its end and I am well aware that Paul O'Connell has not yet been mentioned. The man who cannot walk through Limerick without being stopped in the street. Reduced by an English wanker to a literal nothing. There's a reason. O'Connell's autobiography was published in 2016 . . . a good read. I would say that, the man who wrote the 'autobiography' is Alan English, a mate from his days as an outstanding deputy editor of the *Sunday Times* sports section. He edits the *Limerick Leader* now. And he wrote O'Connell's autobiography. If you want to read about the second row colossus, this book is the place to start. *The Battle*. It is absorbing. But is it an autobiography? The thoughts are those of the big red man, so too many of the words but not the shape of the book, the prompts, the delving into the subconscious. It is a collaboration and a good one but it is not the untrammelled truth. Ghosts spook flesh and blood. Between them, Alan and Paul gave us a fascinating account, an excellent insight into a magnificent rugby player but the truth, the whole truth and nothing but the truth? As good a moment as any to leave any last lingering for Limerick and head towards the next chapter . . . N. For newspapers.

NEWSPAPERS

TIME FOR some truth and reconciliation. If not now, whilst in confessional mode, then when? In 1994 I became a columnist. Balancing the simultaneous demands of playing rugby and writing about it in pretty much the same breath. It wasn't the ideal entry into unbiased journalism. I blew the balanced bit early on, in 1994, in Bloemfontein. South Africa's seat of justice, sort of . . . anyway, I had a contract, a column a week for the *Daily Telegraph*. It wasn't a natural home for me. I chose the old adage, the old excuse. Sport and politics should not mix. Never mind a quiet refusal to tour South Africa a full decade earlier . . . apartheid and the *Telegraph* were not quite one and the same. I didn't beat myself up over it.

The night before the opening game of the England tour in South Africa. As a newcomer to the media ranks I really should have attended an Afrikaner welcome function, ahead of the opening match of the tour. But Jack Rowell insisted – quite rightly – only those not involved in the next day's game should attend. Not all players could be trusted to behave in moderation, even twenty-four hours ahead of a match. Like a lot of the other lads I was keen enough to have my preconceived notions about what we still knew as the Orange Free State confirmed. I was grounded in our team hotel. Doubtless playing a casual few hands of cards. The usual time-wasting behaviour. The first team returned with tales of Afrikaner arrogance, stupidity and outright racism. A not unexpected extreme. Too good an opportunity for an aspiring hack to overlook. My first tour column was filled with florid descriptions . . . 'the sun will never rise on this home-grown fourth Reich'. . . John Mason, the *Telegraph*'s steady rugby correspondent tried to warn me. But I was not one for heeding a warning. Not surprisingly, it achieved what any good column should. It got people talking. Only I wasn't there.

The day after the column was published back in the United Kingdom, the local paper was courteously slid halfway beneath my bedroom door. From my bed I could see the bottom half of the front page. It seemed another Englishman had launched an attack in print on Bloemfontein. I had no idea what syndication was until I saw my smiling face attached to the article. Wind forwards three weeks or so. On the final night of the tour in Cape Town the fearsome players' court found me not guilty. Of what I can't remember. A rare acquittal. Indeed, the generous judgement went further. 'Fearing' for the safety of their intrepid journalist, I was 'obliged' to don a full flak jacket on our final night out in Cape Town. My last evening as a rugby player. Any thought of graduating to war correspondent disappeared beneath the weight of body armour. I would stick with rugby writing, if anyone would have me. On the field the tour was no great personal success. I had not been particularly sharp, while Andrew played one of the games of his life as England beat South Africa in Pretoria. Prior to kick-off, both sides were introduced to Nelson Mandela. I suspect the Springboks were more diverted by the presence of the former prisoner turned president. I probably wrote as much. Words and deeds. It was easier to speak and spell than it was to get out there and do. I was more interested in the country and the politics than the rugby. A recurrent adductor injury flared up against South Africa B on the hard grounds of Kimberley. Another period of fairly intense rehabilitation awaited me (this entailed daily physiotherapy rather than lunch at the Beaujolais restaurant in Bath) and the long tedious slog back towards full fitness. A World Cup year – in South Africa – was the case for continuing playing. An opportunity to cement a columnist's position before the 'big names' like Carling, Moore and Andrew hung up their boots, the case for quitting. I gambled on my wits. Twenty-three years on from the hysteria of the 'home-grown fourth Reich', here is my apology to Bloemfontein. Sorry.

I soon discovered my contrariness was more naturally suited to print than the international pitch. Or life as a building society manager. Since quitting the mortgage industry on return from South Africa I have 'earned' an income from nothing but talking and writing. I quit my day job to write. Sky was an unforeseen opportunity when I threw my salary away for £15,000 per annum . . . plus any other freelance work. Rugby has filled most of my life for over forty years. I have not done anything to save the planet through the course of what seems a pretty pointless existence. My life has been mostly play. Yet I have tried to live by a few of my own rules of the road. I have endeavoured to be – in print – as honest as possible. Such an attitude is not a panacea for popularity. But what is the point in writing about overgrown children (a fair description of all sportsmen, especially ones involved in team sports where there is someone to do everything for you bar play the game) if the work lacks any integrity? To any future player with an eye on the media, I would suggest that self-respect is more important than money. In fact, why not, for a few years, stay off this goddamned patch. There isn't room here for too many Cassandra types.

If someone with seventy caps is reading this and thinking, 'Hmm, by the look of his picture in the paper, Barnes has aged well, this writing malarkey cannot be too taxing,' ponder this. Are you prepared to be provocative, to piss people off for a living? To lose any affection the rugby public holds for you? If the answer is no, get a job with the building society. Anything but write to fill space and give the public what it thinks it wants. If a columnist does not make people think twice, it's not all right. My critics, of whom there are a couple, are a confused crew. They don't know the difference between provocative and controversial. It is not that I set out to shock for its own effect (although that was certainly the over-enthusiastic case in Bloemfontein). I just can't resist going toe to toe with anything I consider an ill-conceived truism. Some call this public opinion. Whether the reader agrees is irrelevant. That misses the point. A column should make a person reassess. That is the duty of any columnist. We live in an age where that is not a given. Now the prerogative is click bait, anything to get the advertisers online. Lists of lists, the top ten lists of lists of lists. Fuck that. Provoke. When I first started tapping away, we were on the verge of going online. The World Wide Web was lovingly about to unleash itself upon the world in 1995. 1994 was, literally, the end of an era. The print world was on the brink. Few foresaw the plummeting print circulation, the imperative and the fall of advertising revenues and the manner in which 'austerity' would shrink the newspaper industry. Expenses were a given in 1994. Lunches lovingly lingering, an easy transition for someone with a penchant for a long lunch. That landscape is broken. 'Fleet Street' is dead. Its replacement not as green and pleasant a land. Although it still beats the hell out of most occupations . . . don't get me wrong. I wake up and count my blessings.

For any ageing player with a yearning to avoid the rigours of going to work, here are a few useful pieces of advice. Win as many caps as you can. Preferably a World Cup, if not a Lions tour. Get yourself a television contract too. The profile helps. Celebrity is something to be cherished. The greater the celebrity the more chance of making a living without even having to write your own copy . . . this is a pathetic way to make some money on the side but the celebrity will have all sorts of entrepreneurial sidelines. Newspapers mean profile. His agent will drum the point home. This is advice for someone I would rather not meet.

To the good guys. Read a lot. It is resolutely depressing to think how many retired sports stars covet a career within the print media without the vaguest interest in how to construct a sentence. There's also the benefit for a bibliophile of finding a fresh rugby idea buried deep in the realms of a novel or, safer still, an obscure poet's work. We are not talking plagiarism. Rather the 'liberation' of a well-crafted thought from the realm of the arts to the rowdy world of sport. Such evolution, such transience, is what enables folk and the blues to survive and thrive through the years. What did Bob Dylan sing in *Brownsville Girl*? Something like, 'If there's an original thought out there I could use it right now.' I know what you mean, Bob. There is only so much originality, but there are myriad ways to think afresh from one subject to another. I read a review of a film on the subject of, say, James Baldwin and maybe find a way to berate the modern game's obsession with data and statistics. Don't ever steal a sentence but an idea . . . place it in another context. *Your* context. Improve it. Ideas belong to all of us. Go out and immerse yourself in areas where interesting ideas abound.

Some more advice that relates less to the realm of the mind. Have the courage to lose a few friends. This is vital. Especially if you are writing for the words and not the bank balance. Nobody likes being criticised in print but from a former team-mate it tends to hurt a lot more. In my fledgling days, I typed things about former Bath colleagues that were more commonly saved for the training field where disagreements are settled one way or another. In privacy. To step out of the shadows of the training field into the spotlight of newsprint is, for some, to cross a line. This is understandable. I wrote columns about mates like Mike Catt and Jeremy Guscott that would have infuriated me had the boot been on my foot. But I always believed what I wrote. To have written if for effect would have been an unpardonable sin. And I am not religious.

Your skin must be thick. Especially when the sights are trained upon England. Sports fans are a patriotic bunch and England supporters are not afraid to offer their own opinions. We are a steely nation. Hence the long historical tie-up between sport and the armed forces. Twickenham is a second home for the military when it comes to pre-match 'entertainment'. On a match day, an opera singer performing from the 'Now that's what I call opera' catalogue and an army presence thrills middle England. What they don't want is Cassandra Barnes telling them that beating this second-rate set of Six Nations opposition means nothing. Not if England wants to be and beat the best. Close your eyes and pretend the world ends at Dover . . . Eddie Jones got it from day one but he was entitled to say it. He was the boss. Much of Rugby England think me bitter. Based around something that happened or didn't more than two decades ago. Unfortunately, we don't 'do' context. It's this game and then the next one. So it goes. The idea of plotting four years ahead is unusual. Alien. Idiotic even. Maybe you can't expect fans who have paid significant sums of money for a ticket to worry about what lies over the horizon, but managers and writers . . . that's another matter entirely. To clarify, I neither love nor hate England. My country is Kiltartan Cross, no, wait . . . don't let yourself be pinned with patriotism because of an illustrious playing past. That last comment is for the next generation of player/journalists, God, not me . . .

Think fast as opposed to deep if you are writing to a deadline. Time is an enemy when the deadline is five minutes before the end of a game. But it can be a friend too. Managers and players can bury themselves beneath the mountainous minutiae of match details. A broad-brushstroke report or column can cut through the spurious word-speak that rugby, like all other sport, uses to disguise fault lines. My friend Stephen Jones, the *Sunday Times* rugby correspondent, causes great debate with his assessment of individuals but more often than not his overriding vision is accurate. Such was the case in his four-year criticism of the Stuart Lancaster regime. He saw through the flaws. Beginning to end. It's a rare ability to cut through the crap.

If you are writing for a Monday edition think, not fast, but deep and slow, search within the currents for something no one else has seen. On joining the *Sunday Times* in 2005 Stephen offered me this piece of advice. 'Write a column that leaves the dailies nowhere to go.' Writing for a daily as well these days, I find myself in a world Kafka would have recognised. Scribbling on a Saturday night to make my own professional life as difficult as possible when I write my *Times* column for Monday on a Sunday morning. I await the inevitable impending signs of schizophrenia.

Write for the whisper of the words and the sound of the sentence as much as the love of the game. A lifetime of rugby is a sentence of another type if there is nothing but the next ruck, the next breakdown, the next young star to turn your white computer screen black with eulogy. Write so you check the printed copy not just to admire the picture byline you haven't had changed in ten years but to see sentences that scan, a piece with which you can feel pleased. Content irrelevant. There is no absolute right or wrong. There's the result of the game and the rest is subjective, all opinion. Not so much a case of 'provide, provide' as 'provoke, provoke'. Provocation is a great word. The world is one bloody great big corporate dictatorship of the uniform. Away from the masked opinions on social media, people unwilling to take another position from the accepted norm and provoke. 'THINK FOR YOURSELF'. Players who provoke are sentenced to life in the Contrary Squad. Coaches and managers don't like players who think, let alone for themselves. Such players are a challenge. Challenges should be relished. Instead they are feared. Isolated like a virus. There have been times when Danny Cipriani has been considered rugby bacteria. THINK FOR YOURSELF. If you are fortunate enough to board the ex-player gravy train, remember that apart from your looks, your caps and the awe in which the rugby population hold you, it is your interior knowledge that counts. The only difference between being a celebrity or a decent rugby writer. Plough your own furrow (there are tractors going up and down the lanes in north Wiltshire as I type; it justifies the dated rustic cliché). Don't fall into the rut. The press pack decides its own agenda. Luckily, I have outstanding editors (hope you are reading, gentlemen) who expect my field of vision to emerge unforeseen. I see from the left, Steve from what I think of as the right. But that is fine. Just don't get caught in the middle of the main roads. Travel solo if you can.

New Zealand has an odd approach to its rugby coverage. Kiwis don't love rugby, they love their beloved All Blacks. Defeat or a poor performance, as I discovered first hand after a narrow defeat in Christchurch 1985, and the press is unforgiving. The national team are burdened with such colossal expectations. Defeat is a disgrace. Yet when an overseas writer has the temerity to criticise, watch out. In Queenstown there was a toilet embellished with the face of Stephen Jones, notorious New Zealand-basher. In this instance, it was New Zealand and its insular attitude to life that is full of shit. There are similarities with Wales. There was once a decent national paper known as the *Western Mail*. Now there is Wales Online. Full of lists, five things we learned and always space for stealing an article from over the border; like cattle raiding. I have suffered many such thefts. Often named as former Welsh schools captain, either 'respected broadcaster for Sky TV' if the article is pro-Wales or 'controversial commentator' if the online edition disagrees with either my comments or words. If it's a pro piece, the photo of me might be a pensive shot of a grey-haired man ruminating behind a microphone. Not too bad. Anti-Wales and there's a classic shot of me pissed, a case of public school rugby twit, dinner jacket, Barbarians bow tie, head tilted foolishly, more than a hint of another chin . . . a drunken toff, bugger his Welsh comprehensive roots . . . there are a few 'comments' from people who claim they went to school with me, none of whose names I recognise (could it be the boy who jumped me in the car park?), men who played against me in our distant youths . . . everything can be remembered online where there is no truth, mainly a tirade of abuse. Yet I occasionally read this salacious shit, the same as I might read the reams of rubbish on various newspapers' comments sections. Readers are in their rugby heaven. The experts are there to be reduced to rubble. To create a platform from which the readers celebrate their own importance at no cost to themselves. The gate keepers are gone and all voices are welcome. Not necessarily their real names. Not their pictures. Not their identities . . . not in the majority of cases. Meanwhile, in the print industry, the number of skilled workers shrink. Ranting lunatics scream from behind screens. Although I have been pleasantly surprised with the interaction since I belatedly joined Twitter and *The Times*/*Sunday Times* below-the-line comments in 2018, there's no question the internet amplifies opinions of idiots. Chimes of Freedom have been replaced with a cacophony of cocksure craven-hearted bullies. Their criticism isn't confined to the four white lines of the rectangle that surround the pitch. Nor do they understand the art of deletion. Sorry, a more ranting than usual digression . . . always did like the ranters, turning worlds upside down in seventeenth-century England.

Back to the advice for the retiring player/aspiring writer . . . don't take yourself too seriously. It is only a game we are covering after all. Personal advice I have not taken as readily as I occasionally might have. 1999 and the World Cup. I wrote an 'astute tactical piece' on how Stephen Bachop, fly half for Western Samoa, could mastermind a shock victory against Wales in the National Stadium . . . so it came to pass. My profound piece? Dropped for a colourful article on a Namibian lion tamer. I was not amused. The rest of the press box were . . . eighteen years on and I can finally laugh at this abso-fucking-lutely dia-bloody-bolical edi-sodding-torial decision. It happens. So much for the past . . . what about the future of sports journalism? In the face of much opinion I think it could yet defy the sly avarice of Silicon Valley. We cannot bottom out and compete with the hysteria of the online world. What the written papers can do is upgrade their quality. Make a newspaper something you like the feel of, something of real value and craft. The race for the bottom opens space at the top end. I don't believe mass hysteria can forever remain the overriding emotion. Don't believe the mob will always mistrust those who have knowledge, expertise and the skills to communicate. The superior newspapers will remain worth reading. There will be sufficiently discerning readers who trust in those whose professional lives are built around a knowledge of their field, not a five-minute fan-flurry of words. A fair few of the selfie set do not like me. Nor many of the players. Even the new-generation fans of my old club, Bath, are less than impressed with an ageing man's criticisms. Good, then I am doing my job. I don't crave followers. I have sufficient friends who know me, not people who think they do. People who drink and laugh with me. Nothing virtual about these relationships. Away from rugby, best take up a hobby where no one has a clue as to your identity. Few stop and berate me at the Royal Shakespeare Company or any music festival.

Don't look for friends. Look for the pleasure of being paid for doing something so many others envy. Being paid to write, being paid to watch rugby . . . it's not a bad way to make a living. It's also a way to hang onto the adrenaline rush that once flowed through the youthful body. It's nothing like the pressure of playing. But for a middle-aged man there's enough of a jolt to keep you alive. The first 'live' piece I ever scrambled out for the *Sunday Times* was an international in Paris, France versus Wales. 1,300 words on full time . . . fuck. Fortunately, five minutes before the interval, the French giants strode over and through those lightweight Williamses, Shane and Martyn. France were clear by half-time. Clichéd? Yep. Sure. But this was a first live report, 'A good big one will always beat a good little one.' Five hundred words on the theme during the half-time interval. Eight hundred remaining in the second half. No problem, home and hosed . . . until Shane danced around and between the legs of the mammoth French. And Martyn put Wales in front with an inspired piece of quick thinking. Big ones, little ones, the whole game turned inside out. Upside down. This was scary. This was frantic. You grow to love and hate those moments.

In the 2011 World Cup in New Zealand, the time difference enabled us to write through the night. The first column would be dutifully delivered, then the second. It was three a.m. by now and 'Thanks for being so prompt, Stuart, could you do something for the Irish edition?' Get it done, get to bed. There are matches the next day . . . 'Brilliant, I don't suppose . . .' Bed at six. Up at seven for a Sky Sports News interview and then to work. By the end of the tournament my psoriasis had erupted, Etna-like. The mouth was a crater of ulcers. The back sciatic and the final, well, it wasn't even up to much. But I wouldn't want it any other way. Hang onto that adrenaline as long as you can. It keeps you living, that and a decent glass of red.

OXFORD UNIVERSITY

OURS WAS not an academic family. 'Camelot'. A three-story town house on the edge of Newport. On the other side of the main road was a park, a wood and a cemetery. All good spots in which to while away some daydreaming hours. In the main I fantasised about becoming a great rugby player, although the identity of the lucky country was somewhat problematic in those rootless teenage days. Other daydreams? The hours spent singing Bob Dylan. All the way back in the canon from *Freewheelin'* through to *Street Legal*. The adenoidal agony. For all and sundry along with my brief flurry into the 'Fuck You' world of punk. Evidence enough. I was not destined to become the British Bob or a brooding Bruce. All I was left with, my daydreams of escape. From Newport, from all those nobodies without a nihilistic thought in their heads. Oh, I was an arsehole, humming along to The Animals, 'We gotta get out of this place.'

I don't recall for sure when the Oxbridge entrance exams were sat (pre-Christmas, yes, must have been) or when the letter from Oxford made it through the letter box to the modern day Arthurian town house. But there it was. A letter from Oxford University on the floor, daring me to open it. I was excited, uncomfortable. Was this fear, these tremors palpitations? Excited because Oxford was as far removed from Newport as Earth is from Mars. As for 'uncomfortable'. I had tasted the world of the quads when I quaked through a sequence of interviews after the entrance examinations. Petrified, the place was indeed another planet. The scent of otherworldly intellectualism . . . I wanted out of Newport but this, this . . . I feared I would drown in the formidable social exclusivity of it all. I stared at people I thought were dons, waiting for their names to be called for interviews. Why would an intellectual be sitting next to me, a comprehensive kid from Newport? It didn't cross my mind that these fellows in their green corduroy trousers and tweed jackets with leather patches on the elbows were no more than potential undergraduates. Eton boys, as prepared as I was scared. Eighteen years old. No longer composed. This was when the social discrepancy hit home. The recognition of being a big fish in, not so much a small pond, as a roadside puddle. I couldn't breathe. That was how Oxford was, a sequence of going under and coming up for air. I can't rewrite history and say I hated those three years but there's no point pretending they were anything other than wasted.

There's the letter, lying on the porch floor, let's say December 1980, daring someone to open it. A sheet of paper spelling social and intellectual success in the eyes of my family, escape in the eyes of their little monster child. That and the kudos of 'Oxford University'. Baize-leg had a pretty reasonable record for getting their pupils into Oxbridge. Not so good that another acceptance wasn't a cause for some celebration. Teachers congratulated me. Praised me. Told me how well I had done. I liked people telling me what a tremendous credit I was to someone or other although all I ever thought about was ME. Buoyed by the back-slapping, the fear was forgotten for a few more months – obviously the news in the letter had been good. I was in – I was on my way OUT! The head boy, the captain of Wales schools, the Welsh squad member while still at school . . . oh joy and rapture . . . now the unaddressed confession. St Edmund Hall. The best rugby college in Oxford. I don't know when I did the sums and came up with the answer but for many years I regaled strangers with the tale of my exceptional examination papers. I suspect the truth is Oxford needed a few comprehensive undergraduates, and if they were good rugger players as well, all the better. Fifty-five years of age and I have finally come clean (although the essays I wrote really, as remembered, were amongst my more original academic efforts). I was never a rocket scientist. It was post-Oxford I was to learn more about the life of the mind. In my twenties, in the Hare on the Hill in Bristol. The late David Green. A former swashbuckling batsman for Lancashire and Gloucestershire. He would recite Auden's 'Shield of Achilles'. Poem after poem from the collected works of John Crowe Ransom over pints of Bath Ale. Those years were boozy but far from wasted.'

As for the dreaming spires . . . the end of my first term in Oxford. It is a Tuesday morning. Silence in St Edmund Hall. The silence that can only be summoned into daylight existence by a heavy fall of snow. That and the fact it is five o' fucking clock. In the morning. One hour until my preliminary exams. History preliminaries, the greatest test of my life to date. Fail the prelims and you are out. Fear of failure, my old friend, gripped me. So tight that I actually deserted the 'Teddy' Hall Buttery Bar for some rare revision during this initial term. A three-hour examination. Testing my French with a question on Alexis de Tocqueville. L'Ancien Régime et la Revolution. My awful A level Latin under the microscope. An essay on the subject of the Venerable Bede. And a general history paper.

In Oxford's famous Examination Halls. Opposite the walls of St Edmund Hall on Oxford High Street. A walk through the snow, the silence, the six o'clock confusion. I was all but alone in the Examination Halls, just myself and an invigilator. He must have resented me. This jumped-up nineteen-year-old, depriving him of his sleep. Hollow pacing steps. Like a ghost. Me, my thoughts and the echoes of footsteps. I concentrated as well as could be expected. As I left this haunted chamber, the rest of the first year history undergraduates arrived for the nine a.m. start. My academic tools stuffed into the bottom of the kit bag. Along with my boots, jock strap and anything else needed for the Centenary Varsity match. This was the reason I was in Oxford. Why I was forced to sit an exam at six a.m. Why I did my best not to stare at the snow falling outside, wondering whether the match would be postponed. This was the first Tuesday in December. The start of the Christmas season for the city. Oxford versus Cambridge and my first taste of Twickenham. The Centenary Varsity match.

I passed the exams. Flunked the rugby. Well, maybe not 'flunked'. But we didn't win and I didn't dominate. Playing for Cambridge were the current England internationals, Huw Davies at fly half and Marcus Rose at full back. Both postgraduates. Neither any better than me. Neither any worse. 9–6 to Cambridge. Was it 9–6? No tries. Just a gigantic snowball fight. Twickenham was white. The ball orange. Our fingers and feet frozen. The one and only time in my career that I teed the ball up with a tower of snow. The terraces were cleared. Reasons of safety. The field was left covered. The groundsman, all authoritarian, saying the snow would protect the pitch from the sub-zero temperatures ahead of the England trial the coming Saturday. He didn't want a bunch of students endangering the trial. And so we laboured through the snow, slipping and sliding to defeat in what was a narrow non-event of a game.

I never did get the hang of the Varsity match. Never played badly, but never did what I was brought to Oxford to do. In my second year I encountered Rob Andrew. In his first year. In his final year at Cambridge, and my first back in the outside world, he deposed me as England fly half. I didn't see how the Varsity match was a stepping stone to an international team back then. Still don't now. There were some pretty good players during my three years as an Oxbridge rugby player but the average-to-awful contingent eclipsed the few decent players.

Can you imagine a few youngsters making the step from Varsity match to England international now? A few old Commonwealth pros come over for the experience but the majority of men taking part are . . . boys . . . so it was then. In 2016 I turned up at Twickenham for an RFU Christmas drinks party. The walkways around the ground were awash with the stumble and stagger of bodies. Casualties of upper-class excess. It's terribly amusing to totter and tumble with a mouth full of marbles. Watch out if you are wearing a replica football shirt though. Anyway, it didn't take much sleuthing to figure the drinks party coincided with the Varsity match. Parking up in the north car park, I made my way towards the function. The light blue blazers of the Cambridge team headed past me, the Bowl (no plug for the sponsors – whoever they are) being passed amongst them. As if they were Dean Richards kicking the Calcutta Cup down Princes Street in Edinburgh so long and irreverently ago.

I don't resent anyone having a bit of fun but what the hell have they/we been doing, playing out this glorified public school game at the home of English rugby? The answer is unfortunately all too obvious. Rugby was born of and is steeped in elitism. Oxford and Cambridge are great seats of learning, but also an extension of the public school system. Universities that confirm to the ruling classes, which is exactly who they are – our future leaders. The Varsity match has always attracted busloads of schoolchildren from all over the country. They grow up to vote for men and women from these universities. The bus trip. A first attempt to train some deference into our system. A homage to this unspoken yet blindingly obvious class system. A homage and a glorification. In the days leading up to the match, Oxford and Cambridge's sporting clubs, Vincent's and Hawks, have dinners where grown men revert to childhood. The one and only Vincent's dinner I attended – maybe there was another, the booze damages the mind – was memorable for the manner in which bankers dipped their napkins in red wine. Tightened them up into a ball. Unleashed them in the direction of the guest speaker. All good fun and jolly good company.

The misery of the Museum Tavern . . . the day after losing. The team hotel is in Russell Square. One of the most majestic of all British institutions is open. The tavern opposite the entrance is stubbornly shut until eleven a.m. Scenes of solace, scenes of tears, but tears of laughter. The day after the end of our world and we are growling our way through as much beer as we can take whilst the Mummies mysteriously sleep a few hundred metres away. We were good at taking defeat with grace and good humour. Oxford tried to teach me about stiff upper lips. Well, I did stop sobbing when I lost . . . that was something. And Tony Abbott didn't win a rugby blue during my three-year tenure. That is a retrospective relief. The atrociously antediluvian Aussie was an Oxford prop forward. I was sure we played in the same side at Twickenham. I told the tale of how the man whose name was abbreviated to 'Abo' (few thought of the cultural implications of calling an Australian by such a nickname) shared the same HQ changing rooms with me. It made defeat slightly more appeasing. Recently Dermot Coleman (a friend, Oxford Blue centre and George Eliot expert) informed me the right-wing politician didn't make the team. Like the first time I saw the All Blacks, time and mind busy tricking me. That or the ataxia is taking its toll.

The bastion of privilege. Bath, one of the greatest English club teams of any era, certainly the greatest of the amateur age, didn't once get the opportunity to play against a touring international team. Within a month of my first term in Oxford I was wearing the navy blue of Oxford against the green and gold of Australia. Oxford, Cambridge and the Combined Forces all played the touring teams . . . incredible fixtures. Incredible too that we only lost 19–12. True, Mark Ella missed a lot of kicks at goal, but, for God's sake, it was Mark Ella! We played above ourselves. A first indication that the English have a capacity to rise to an occasion. Maybe as a nation we have a history of putting ourselves where we shouldn't be in the first place, but when we get there, it's hard to deny the determination of the English. Whatever the rights or wrongs. Myself and Richard Luddington, our scrum half, covered acres of Iffley Road that afternoon, making cover tackle after cover tackle as our veteran winger, Derek Wyatt – veteran one-cap wonder – ceaselessly sought the intercept. Eventually the oldest winger in town managed the intercept and scored the try. We half backs prevented three or four. Guess who grabbed the headlines? Derek was to become an MP. A cunning man. He even got me a book deal more than twenty years ago . . . cunning and resourceful.

Playing against the Wallabies as a teenager was probably the highlight of my Oxford rugby career. However, there was a soft spot for the lower-grade inter-collegiate competition. Quaintly known as 'Cuppers'. I probably enjoyed it because I was captain. Able to demand a commitment unusual amongst average Oxford undergraduates. I put as much into the Teddy Hall team as I did the university side. Didn't win a Varsity match, didn't lose in Cuppers. When power came my way, I rarely wondered what to do with it. I flourished. Growing confident from its terrible corrupting soil. Given the opportunity I could have been a benevolent dictator. Not so good a subject.

One of the most fascinating of all Englishmen has to be Oliver Cromwell. Myself a republican from an early age, I liked the cut of Cromwell. Maybe as early as seeing Richard Harris playing the protector one lazy Sunday afternoon. 'Don't start,' my mother would say when I praised the man who effectively signed himself into history as England's great regicide. 'Don't start,' was the retort when I criticised Margaret Thatcher. Supported the unions, defended communism. A lot of far cleverer people than me were even more stupid when it came to Uncle Joe . . . I hear you asking, what has Cromwell to do with rugby union as seen through the prism of a would-be dictator? The answer is Sir Keith Thomas. One of the country's most esteemed historians. Then a reader of modern history at St John's College. The author of *Religion and The Decline of Magic* – one of the great history books in my extremely humble and reasonably ignorant opinion. *The Ends of Life* is another good read. The man the *New York Review of Books* come to when the constitutional impact of Brexit needs addressing. Academically he was the Barry John of my student life. I was awestruck in that rarefied Oxford orbit. In awe of him still. Sir Keith Vivian Thomas, another great Welshman. Keith Thomas had the desperately bad fortune to be in charge of the undergraduate class of about half a dozen whose choice of specialist subject was to be the Commonwealth and Protectorate. Keith Thomas and Cromwell . . . for a second I thought I could get serious about academia . . . but only a second.

In the term I was expected to focus on my specialist subject, the All Blacks arrived in England. I was selected as a replacement for the South and South West Counties, due to face them in Bristol, in 1983. Training sessions were Tuesday afternoons. At the Memorial Ground, Bristol. Classes with Thomas were early evening. A mad rush to Bristol Parkway. Change at Didcot and taxi to the class, a fare for which I lacked the funds. Straight into the exclusive gatherings where we sat metaphorically at the great man's feet. Five students dressed in their most academic tweed garb. Some wearing a gown as a mark of respect . . . and one lad with a Welsh moustache, a tracksuit, stinking from the training session from which he had rushed away without a shower. An injury in the week before the game and suddenly I was selected to start. At inside centre. My last game at twelve had been my first ever game for Baize-leg against Queens. Circles being completed. Thomas didn't seem to have a great deal of interest in the All Blacks. While my fascination with this period of British and Irish history was inevitably overshadowed by the impending rugby occasion, I wanted to write the best essays of my life for Thomas. Sounds silly but I wanted to honour Cromwell too. In the end everything was half-cocked. Bowed to the All Blacks. Rugby dominated my life. Deprived me of a microcosmic relationship with one of the great historians. We played New Zealand on 15 November between Tests and lost 15–6. I kicked our goals. Points against New Zealand. Out of position, I did well. I was heading towards the 'inevitable' first cap but away from Commonwealth, Protectorate and Keith Thomas.

Oxford was my halfway house. My academic lifestyle didn't get out of first gear and my rugby career stalled. Spiralled into an excess of alcohol. Fine for lads destined for the city and networking. Not so good for someone with serious sporting intentions. Hide behind the drink. When rugby was at the forefront, all was fine. I was a star. People liked me for my rugby. But there was a dark side to me which periodically enveloped the boozy Barnes rugby playing persona. The drowning in his own beer Barnes. The deceitful Stuart who mocked other state school kids along with their 'funny voices' as they hid in the bowels of the Junior Common Rooms. Breaking Space Invader records. Me, with my South Wales accent, sharing in the laughter of the privileged. At night I would lie in bed, wholly cut, hiding the misery of who I was, or wasn't. Ashamed of what I was. And what I was not. My escape had taken me to an exotic world in which I could not be comfortable. The Gate of India was my bank. I laughed as fellow students did the 'waterfall' (pissing under the table), got stuck into six pints of 'Pink Panthers' . . . six gins and a splash of grenadine as you ask . . . fell down stairs, bounced back up and played some pretty good rugby the next day. If I played poorly I had a ready-made excuse; the same for academia. Excuses could always be sought in the bottom of the barrel. Such was the social and sporting life for the first year. In the second I pretty much refused to play for Oxford. Other than in the build-up to the Varsity match. I knew this world of Evelyn Waugh was all wrong for me. I had joined Bristol and was climbing the English pecking order with rather more success than I had in Oxford, slithering haplessly away from academic respectability. Again, I deserted my team, this time Oxford, for the greater good of my own career. Judas? Second term was full of fixtures against other universities and touring teams. I did play and meet Michael Lynagh when Oxford and Queensland University drew 12–12. (Why does my memory recall this game, let alone the score . . . and is it to be trusted?) Neither one thing nor the other. Not quite the earthy rooted rugby player in Bristol. Nor the fortuitous Oxford student where I drink deep. Do anything except think.

I walked away from my three 'fantastic' years at Oxford (don't be weak and confess to disappointment) with a third in Modern History. Received a letter from an eminent St Edmund Hall historian, Blair Worden, reminding me of my many other contributions to college life. Blair was a decent, gentle man. I walked away with three Varsity match defeats. Walked away with an entrenched drinking habit. Such were my networking skills, I found a job in Bristol paying me £4,500 per annum. Too immature to maximise the intellectual opportunities. Intimidated by my lack of class . . . read that any way you want . . . Oxford intimidated me as much as English rugby and its undercurrent of upper-class sanctimony off the field and conservatism on it was to irritate me. I needed professionalism when all around was the old amateur ways. I would find it in the end.

PROFESSIONALISM

ENGLAND'S WORLD Cup-winning team in 2003 were – in some ways – a bunch of amateurs. And all the better for it. Eight years later, Martin Johnson managed his pride of English international professionals to a shambolic quarter-final elimination against a French team fuelled by the recent humiliation of their own loss to Tonga. There's something amiss here; I think it may be our preconceptions of those words, 'amateur' and 'professional'. The latter tend to treat the former like an ageing aunt, old and musty, an embarrassing whiff in the parlour.

Yet it took a group of musty old Englishmen, imbued with the amateur ethos and the sheer love of the game, to lift the Webb Ellis trophy, a name as far removed from professionalism as black is from white. Men like Johnson and Lawrence Dallaglio, Matt Dawson and Neil Back all fought their formative rugby years as unpaid performers. These were men who thought for themselves. Made decisions. Something beyond the Johnson managed/mismanaged side of 2011. The game was getting deeper into professionalism yet the rugby thinking was more shallow than ever. Six years later, Eddie Jones's so-called savvy England team were bemused by the Italian policy of not committing to breakdowns in a memorable muddle of a Test match at Twickenham. They asked the referee, Romain Poite, what to do. Twenty-two years since the game turned professional, the players didn't have the rugby intellect to think for themselves. 'You know something is happening but you don't know what it is, do you Mr Jones?' His charges were clueless.

Johnson himself pinpointed the problem. A rare 2017 interview in his capacity as ambassador for some corporation or other linked to the Lions. Full steam ahead for the Lions Gravy Train . . . to paraphrase the great leader, his 2011 team could not think on the field. He made the contrast with his 2003 team. Yet in typical Johnson style I don't believe he went to the next stage of thinking. He identified the problem, he did not diagnose it. It's why he was a great captain but a failed manager. He could fix what was bang in front of his eyes but managers need broader vision, a set of binoculars.

The problem was rugby stupidity. I have touched elsewhere on the dawning days of the professional game when anything obvious, like gym work, was good and anything more cerebral was cast aside. Johnson evolved from the end of the amateur era when players were encouraged to think for themselves. Because England's traditional rugby education levels were not far above remedial (Welsh state eclipsing the English public rugby schooling) few players relished the responsibility, but Johnson was an exception in a team of exceptions in 2003.

What he didn't seem to comprehend was the inexplicable reversion to wooden thought processes sixteen years into the professional game. The players have to take their share of responsibility but coaches and managers were the real villains of the piece. A game of rugby is like life. It is random, chaotic and will not lend itself to cold-blooded analysis. Yet managers and coaches have been determined to map out the next eighty minutes as if they were Crick and Watson, about to crack DNA. Players are spoon fed game plans as if there is only the one side participating, as if there is no one there to make a mess of the strategy. It takes the numbing lack of rugby thinking in most of pre-professional England to undreamed of levels. Words like 'process' have taken on biblical-like importance to the priests of the training paddocks. Players reiterate phrases like 'going through the phases' as if brainwashed by the cult of coaching. Commentators say it too . . . going through the phrases.

There are a number of reasons. Coaches, on becoming 'professional', had more time on their hands. Living and breathing the game. Aeons in which to think. Managers determined to show the owner how hard they were working, how dominating their presence. I remember an old Bath colleague transformed from player to coach in the late 1990s being asked how Bath would transform a poor run of form. 'We'll work harder.' Just do the same things that have got the team into the mire with even more commitment. Nearly the definition of madness. Work hard and stress the mantras with fiercer commitment. This was the answer for many a club in the formative professional years. These were the late years of the twentieth century and the first few of the twenty-first. Any expectation of more sophisticated thinking was – paradoxically – destroyed with the next generation of technology as the hi-tech industry invaded rugby, bringing an unchecked combination of computers and statistics. Statistics took rugby out of its boozy clubhouse culture for good (or bad), into the conference and meeting rooms and, always of course, online. Statistics and the speed with which these mind-boggling numbers could be analysed and crunched was the new oil of the professional coaching age.

The head coach, the forwards coach, backs coach and fitness coach were joined not just by the eminently sensible and imperative appointment of the defence coach but a veritable army of tracksuited young men. Through the course of a game they will have their heads focused on the screen as ever-changing numbers flash up. The senior management will have access to the same information. Metres made, tackles, tackles missed, passes, metres run, whatever you want . . . as much anaerobic information as the latest computer technology will allow is in front of their eyes. These screens are the windows to their souls. Everything a coach needs to know is there for him, everything bar the context of the events. I bumped into Eddie O'Sullivan, the former coach of Ireland, in the press box at a Munster versus Ulster Easter Saturday clash. Eddie didn't like me much when we were on different sides of the line. Now he makes money from the media he's pleased enough to see me. Time can heal the horrid headlines. He's not so pleased with what he describes as the thoughtlessness of the modern player. 'You want to know the problem, Stuart?' I know what is coming. 'Coaches with their heads buried in laptops instead of the field. Everything is programmed, there's no thinking.' Divided by vocations, united now by frustration. For the first time I notice O'Sullivan is no taller than me. Another little corporal.

Our Irish Napoleon is working with the BBC Ulster veteran, Jim Neilly. Jim gets in on the act, 'I was sitting near the England management in an England versus Ireland game and Andy Robinson and his team of analysts had their eyes trained on their computer screens. Syd Millar [a legend of the Irish game] leaned forwards, poked Andy in the back and said, "You'll get more out of watching what they do on the field than on a screen."'

I'll take my stand with the ageing stinkers. I may be wrong but there's no software that, at least to my scant knowledge, analyses the quality of a player's passing. The GPS systems help management measure miles run and impacts made but the sheer quality – or not – that is something else. They lose the game in the vastness of processed information, become blinded to the complexity of the game. Behind the abundance of numerical information, the broad scenario is lost. But with such a wealth of information, a manager must impart his knowledge. The best coaches and managers ask the players questions, the majority tell them what they did wrong. Watch what happens when an important penalty is given. Many teams will instinctively turn their heads, waiting to see the sign from the touchline where a Neil Jenkins-type figure is the go-between from the big boss with the walkie-talkies.

In open play, moves are prefigured several phases ahead. To be able to see what's in front of you and remember a five-phase play takes some doing. Gary Kasparov was once asked how many moves he could see ahead. Look too far ahead, said the Russian, and you'll not see what happens in front of your eyes. Bingo. Rugby's professional problem in the proverbial nutshell. There should be a tension between the game plan and the half back's capacity to call it like Kasparov. It's what the All Blacks and Beauden Barrett do so wonderfully well. Too many managers have started to think rugby is a game of chess. I often call it 'muscular chess'. A lovely phrase but it's dumb. Chess pieces can't think for themselves. Technology helps players and managers work out lineout moves, defensive shifts, attacking moves, but when the whistle blows it only takes the one unexpected event to blow the best laid plans to pieces. Stuart Lancaster's England were a well-drilled team. They could perform with clockwork precision. In the year before the World Cup I was so impressed I placed a substantial wager on them to make the final. Fool of a Barnes. It's fine when you are on the front foot. But when the game did not go as England's management planned – these pesky others – England lost their way. Chris Robshaw was a captain who failed to think on the hoof, his team-leaders likewise. Prepared for the perfect game is no preparation at all. Left in the lurch, without a thought of their own, the failure was alas, all too easy to identify.

Eddie Jones didn't make half as many changes to personnel as people expected when he replaced Lancaster. He restored Dylan Hartley as hooker and made him captain. Created almost a cipher for the former Australian hooker. Jones ran the game through his skipper. And the skipper, with the help of these previous failed thinkers, played and thought their way out of problems that would have overwhelmed them twelve months before. Yet the Italian ruck fiasco was a searing reminder that the overall culture of the professional age in England remains staunchly non-thinking. As far as utilising the bench goes, thinking has completely fallen from favour. Spectators often wonder why mass substitutions occur at the same time, around the fifty- to sixty-five-minute mark. Because it is what coaches do. The fact that team A are screwing team B at the scrum is irrelevant. Decision made pre-game, decision stuck to. How can a coach expect his players to think when he doesn't? As for the GPS tracking system, it's a smart piece of kit. It enables management to see when a certain player's body is tiring. Take him off, even if he has been magnificent. Even if the kit is limited in its applications.

What sports science has not managed yet is a device to measure the sporting intelligence of a player. A smart player might be three per cent more tired than a team-mate but he's ten per cent smarter. It gives him more chance of making a good play, running a shorter support line. Because he's smart. But nobody is interested in smart measurement. The same applies to will power. Anyone able to take a reading of man's determination? I played with people who were fine specimens, fabulously fit. But they lacked the will to run ten metres through the hurt to make a try-saving tackle. I also played with lazy oafs who cheated their way through the dreaded fitness sessions. But come the moment, they would blast through the burning lungs and all the pain, ignore the messages their aching limbs sent to the brain. Those players would probably struggle for a professional contract.

They were too amateur. Professionalism, proud of its advances, remembers nothing of the amateur game's virtues – at its peril.

The old and the new are not as far apart as the die-hard supporters on either side of the amateur/professional divide believe. When the old amateur train was chugging into the station for its final resting place, the professional train wasn't travelling at such a rate to prevent many jumping from one to the other. We travel somewhere in between. The game is intrinsically the same one, same rules. When it comes to conditioning however, we are in the realms of the revolutionary. Players are much bigger, much faster and much fitter than those of us who plodded through the fag end days of amateur rugby ever were. Or most of them are. The interesting exception on the size scale is New Zealand. Aaron Smith would have been a small scrum half in my day while Nehe Milner-Skudder is another shorty. The brilliant Ben Smith is long but lean – you wouldn't stop to admire his physique were he to pass you wearing a t-shirt. The All Blacks have evolved into a faster and fitter team, not a bigger one. Nor did they obsess quite as much as most Test countries on the subject of defence. 'Defences win titles.' Shaun Edwards' mantra became a touchstone for professional thinking in Europe while John Muggleton delivered NRL-style defensive drills to the Wallabies. Winners of the last two World Cups, the All Blacks continue to head in another direction to the rest of the world. They are a long way ahead. Imitation is a losing game. Something revolutionary is now required to catch the team that continued to seamlessly evolve from amateur to professional.

Back to the condition of the average professional rugby player in the British Isles and Ireland. Here we are triumphant. In the realms of the unprecedented. Forwards are fast, backs beastly big. Rugby is less a game than a product. A product in which collision has been enthroned as king. The first generation of professional fans fawn over the thumping hits. Why run into space when you can smash straight into an opponent? Dewi Morris once disparagingly described these monsters as 'gym monkeys'. Bloody big monkeys.

Collision and condition as king of the jungle. Would a fading memory from the amateur era have liked the chance to play in today's professional age? It is a much-asked question. The answer is yes and no. Yes – who wouldn't have relished the opportunity to be as good as he (or she) could be? I didn't get paid to play the game but everything else was professional, for that time. In Stephen Jones's autobiography – the Welsh fly half, not the journalist – he describes the pressure of the professional game as being focused on 'win, win and win'. If that defines professional, I was a pro throughout the Bath years and back to those lunatic schooldays. I was psychotic for the win. The endless hours in which a man might become as strong as you could be, as fast as you could be and as technically accomplished as possible . . . what an opportunity.

But these opportunities – strength, speed, skill, I name them in the wrong order. I believe that sorting out my left side, enabling me to pass and kick off both left and right would be my pre-eminent requirement. Speed and size would come second. Rugby players are athletes that are trained, converted, into rugby professionals. It takes time to master technique and game understanding. The priority is all wrong. Back to front. To place the gym ahead of the training field would have infuriated me. Fuming without an outlet. Don't challenge the system. Still, even the gym is one hell of a lot better than working nine to five. Imagine a medical team that could have diagnosed my groin injury for the sciatic problem it was for all those years of agonising cortisone injections into the groin. Imagine the ice bath after being battered blue, black and white. Imagine all that lovely pampering . . . sounds pretty good but I'd need an entire medical team to myself. I bruise just watching rugby matches from the commentary box.

I loved trying to think my way through a game, especially when the fields were thick with mud as the Recreation Ground invariably was from October to April. Impossible to run and pass for more than ten minutes before the pitch was ploughed up. I relished the freedom to think. Someone instructing from the stands with his head in a computer screen and his mouth wired to a walkie-talkie. That wasn't rugby as I knew it. If what we were doing was amateur, then I loved amateurism all the way back to its Latin roots. Ah, but today's pitches. I might even have enjoyed the exquisite mental torture of the goal kicker if we had played on these perfect pitches of today. All the debate surrounding natural or artificial; come on, that's nothing compared to grass or mud.

Bigger stadiums, larger crowds and the growth of localised support from Newcastle to Exeter. This is good for the game, its popularity and its future playing potential. The clubs have short-term financial problems but professional club rugby has played a fair game. They were midwife to the professional game in England. The RFU ought not to have committed itself to the impersonation of an ostrich as the amateur rules of rugby lay in tatters. Everywhere bar England and France, the national ruling bodies took overriding responsibility for the elite end of the sport. The international teams gained control of the finest players; everywhere except England and France. Since then there has been an almost constant low-grade niggle between federation, union and clubs. As I write we are enjoying cordial relations, but an impasse is always waiting around the next unforeseen corner.

The clubs appear crassly commercial (I accept my dislike of the commercial runs deeper than many a rugby fan's) but when the game has been amateur ever since the old wives' tale of Willie Webb Ellis picking up the ball and legging it, that is bound to be the case. The argument exists that rugby lost its soul by selling out to money. There is something in this but the tide will not turn back. Best to make peace and work within the system. But there remains one essential question, one which determines the degree to which sport remains the essence or the justification for money-making: is the business sport or sport the business? Alarm bells ring with the latter. Maybe it explained the vast divide between Arsenal's supporters and their board on what became the soap opera subject of the departed Arsene Wenger. The priority of the business has to be the sport, the performance on the field. What else is the product if not performance and results related? Fans follow their teams for the tournaments they win – the best way to make the business successful is to win trophies, gain new followers – not the performance of the profit and loss account. I'm not suggesting bankrupting a club to win 'silverware' (vile word) but a well-run club which lacks the ambition to splash out on behalf of the team – it can be facilities, not just players – will surely fade from our hearts and minds sooner rather than later.

The sport has retained some of its roots, even as it has laid down new ones. It has not evolved into the destructive form of rugby capitalism some feared. The clubs' monopolistic tendencies are awful but the clubs themselves have been relatively conservative. There has been no terror in the wake of the professional enlightenment. Indeed, if anything, it is shifting too much the other way, into that brand new shiny smiley business which appeals to the vacant online acolytes. Players are trained in the art of media relations as my generation never was. Trained to say nothing whatsoever. It will rebound against them. I was always willing and ready with a quote. I figured the friendlier I was with the media, the kinder they might be with me. In the end you would have to say the policy of loud-mouthed independent thinking paid off. There's still no sign of a nine to five existence.

I fear a pleasant sporting world of predominantly middle-class equivalents of football players. Say something in those post-match press conferences, boys, say anything but make it interesting. Rugby players are in danger of becoming professional bores with their non-answer answers. Fitter than ever, happy enough, economically comfortable . . . not drinking too much. Regular exercises at the gym, at ease with themselves. They put my generation to shame. No microwave dinners, a diet of six salads, white meats and not a saturated fat in sight. As healthy as we were not. Rugby players are pragmatists. Idealism is for idiots. Sporting politicians in their bright yellow boots with their perfect white teeth. Staying out of trouble.

When Bath lose they shake hands, congratulate the winners, take it in their stride. I would shake hands and sprint for the changing rooms where I would sob in fury, the little thirteen-year-old from Baize-leg whispering, 'You're a failure.' How can these men chat away so amiably in defeat? Is it because they have the safety net which no rugby player in the dying days of amateurism possessed, a wage packet? Is a salary enough to take the sting out of defeat (or is it that Bath are simply used to losing)? The two are incestuously entwined.

A few years ago I read an interview with the England flanker, Tom Wood. He was talking about the drink culture that surrounded the sport. Saying that once he got away from it, that past seemed a waste, leaving him out of condition come the next Monday. Aged fifty-five, I tend to agree with Tom. It is fantastic to awaken fresh and raring to greet the day. But these were rites. They bound men in a manner Monday to Friday existence could not. There was excess and, too often, shameful behaviour, yet in the main, the Bath drinking days were productive. They bonded forwards and backs together, the first, second and third teams and the supporters who stayed around late into the clubhouse night. Drink knitted the fabric of the club together. A dietician would properly dismiss this paragraph as the nostalgic nonsense it might well be. The damage done to the body and the brain was possibly substantial . . . but you know, when I was writing about the lazy slob who cheated training but made the match-saving tackle as much with his will as his body . . . well, he and his like were always the last one out the bar. Some people are measured in units.

I played for the most professional team of my era. We were not as fit or as fast as our West Country equivalents today. But mentally we were tough. A lot of body fat on a few of us but even more steel. If we were to be pitched into action twenty or so years forward with the same training pattern as this Bath team and they were burdened with our shameful booze habits of old, we would thrash them. The difference being the immeasurable mental strength locked silently through the spine of the amateur side. If we were to head towards North London and Saracens I reckon we would need six to twelve months off the sauce before daring to even walk out of the changing rooms. They are a timeless operation, one that plays it hard and is not afraid to have a few pints when the mood is with them. If you are looking for an English rugby definition of professionalism, settle for Saracens. It run deep through this squad of players. In many ways they too are a bunch of amateurs. Watch their glee when they win, their dismay when they lose. The rest of England loves Exeter but my heart was lost to one of England's least-loved clubs. Beauty, my friend, is in the eye of the beholder.

QUITTENTON

ROGER QUITTENTON, 1940–2013, RIP. International referee, 1977–1989. Infamous in Wales for all eternity. Cast your mind back to the very first chapter of this book. Andy Haden and his sideburns in 1978, the Wales versus New Zealand match I undoubtedly attended. The dive . . . Brian McKechnie puts the boot into Wales . . . yes, the man with the whistle was Quittenton. An Englishman, a gentleman and a professional in the sense of his detailed preparation, a man ahead of his time.

He and Clive Norling were the officiating headline acts through most of the 1980s. Tight shorts, keen eyes. Keener than legend would have it. 'The penalty was for Geoff Wheel jumping off the shoulder of Frank Oliver . . . Haden's perception is that the dive secured the penalty. That is a load of rubbish.' So Andy not only cheated a nation but has made a living off a lie. Is there no end to the man's calumnies? Enough on the sordid subject of the second row. This chapter belongs to the men in the middle. The whistle-blowers. The late Roger Quittenton, one of the most famous in his day. Our point of entry. According to

Norling, the Sussex schoolmaster was a fitness fanatic. Although the Welshman admitted, 'I was never a big one for fitness . . . training sessions could cause injury . . . I walked a lot.' I hear you, Clive. I heard Roger too, in the late eighties, whispering in my ear, sweet something . . . it was a club blockbuster. Bath versus Neath. England's finest against Wales' fearsome storm troopers. At the Recreation Ground. They had either beaten us already that season in west Wales or the scars from the previous campaign remained. We were to kick off, I was either digging my tower or placing my plastic kicking tee on some firm island of grass in the Bath sea of mud. Taking my time. Close to the ground. Roger leaned down and said, quietly, 'We're not going to lose to the bloody Welsh, are we?' A schoolteacher on the side of the pupils. A posh and more reverent Mr Hamlet, my Latin teacher . . . Chris Hamlet, our classically educated beatnik. There wasn't a more archetypal Englishman than the softly spoken Sussex referee. 'We're not going to lose to the bloody Welsh, are we?' Still hear the gentle cadence, the slightest of chides in the use of the word 'bloody'. Had Jonathan Davies, the dervish who had previously run me ragged at The Gnoll, heard a whisper intended for my ear alone, the famous high pitch squeal would have echoed through the nearby Roman Baths.

Boot on the other foot, JD. Anglo-Welsh club games were ferocious affairs. Until the advent of the leagues there were few English clubs capable of competing with the Celts. Welsh club rugby was magnificent. Nationalist animosity. If the hard men from the mines and steel industry with their raw rugby ability didn't make life tough enough for travelling English teams, there were the referees. In the amateur days there were insufficient funds for an Irish or Scottish referee to take charge of a Wales versus West Country derby. You crossed the Severn Bridge. You had the referee as well as the team to beat. In theory, the games were friendlies; rugby uses the strangest of terms. As for the

Welsh sides, they suffered the same officiating issue in reverse. It gave the English hope at home. It gave them nothing across the Severn.

One of my favourite wins in the blue, black and white of Bath was an away win at Cardiff on New Year's Day. At the tail end of my career. Good as we were and had been for a decade, we could not win in Cardiff. Never. Literally. I'll not name the referee who sent Ben Clarke off the day we finally dropped the 'never' from frustrated descriptions of our trips to the capital city. He had previously refereed me at schoolboy level, making his way up the greasy pole of referees. But it didn't stop him sending me off for persistent abuse, post the Clarke red card. Was there actually a card in those carefree days of corruption and violence? I took a bit of a punt. Wondered if I could get away with ignoring the referee's dismissal. I brazenly walked towards the middle of the pitch. Away from the touchlines . . . 'Like I said, next time I hear you talking to me like that, Stuart, you are off.' First name terms. After the game he was sharing a pint with Ben in the Cardiff clubhouse. That's how it was in those days. Not so much cheating as protecting your own. I'll admit you have to view the sport from a distance before you can shrug your shoulders and grin.

Referees have greater affection for the game than players. Never the winning aphrodisiac. Just an urge to participate. Maybe most were frustrated fans, incapable of playing to a decent level. There are not many Glen Jacksons (former Super Rugby and Premiership fly half, now leading international ref) on the circuit. Now there is an interesting phrase, when you stop and think about it – we talk of referees being 'on the circuit'. As if they are judges. And like judges they receive little love from the masses. Old, out of touch, Establishment, these are the criticisms you will read in a tabloid newspaper . . . on the subject of judges. In the people's dock, the stands of the stadiums, referees are regularly vilified with the epithet 'Homer', one of the longest-standing standard rugby terms of abuse. It is a fine harangue for a fan. It can mean the referee is overly loquacious, a teller of epic tales, although, for all the link between rugby and the public schools, Homer is probably an infrequent read on the terraces of Franklin Gardens or the Stoop. Could be a reference to Bart's dad. Last and most frequently applied is the 'Homer' that accuses the referee of excessive bias towards the home side. There is something in the last accusation. It applies to all team sports. Something subconscious slips into the mind of a rugby or football referee just as confidence for a home team comes with familiarity and vocal support. Referees do not intend to be Homers. Most of them cannot help it. You have to recognise the symptoms before addressing the problem. In this instance referees are indeed Blind Homers . . . actually, when I typed 'Blind Homers' for the first time, I mistakenly tapped 'g' instead of 'd' and hey presto, Bling Homers were born. Now there's a thought.

Nothing Homer-like about the final refereeing decision of the 2017 Lions tour. Romain Poite instinctively signalled a New Zealand penalty from a restart. The ball ricocheted off Liam Williams. Ken Owens caught the ball. Had time to avoid it but chose to catch it. A split second later he panicked. Flapped his arms and released the ball. Too late. Penalty All Blacks. The game was level, a chance now for New Zealand to win the game, and the series, with the last kick. Biggest decision of Poite's life. He got it wrong. Eventually. But for all the right reasons. He had the TMO to assist but only if there has been foul play. He uses the airborne presence of Kieran Read from the kick-off to 'seek' out an infringement. In doing so he can compose himself. Biggest decision of his rugby life. Be smart. Don't rush it. Jerome Garces was talking him through the permutations, his friend and colleague running the line. Two of the world's leading referees. Working together. Yet somehow the wrong decision is reached. Poite gives the decision Marius Joubert should have conjured in the controversial 2015 Scotland versus Australia World Cup quarter-final. There, a Scotland forward was also in an offside position as it deflected onto him from the Scottish restart catcher. In this instance it was a clear case of accidental offside in the rain. Should have been a scrum, Australia's put-in. Instead Joubert gave the full arm penalty – the one Poite initially and correctly gave against the Lions. The Frenchman, unlike his South African colleague, was sharp-witted enough to buy some time for himself in the moment. Bottom line though, Poite's instincts were right. Joubert's wrong. Both fucked up. Steve Hansen wasn't happy when I saw him after the match. Who can blame him? He went into the press conference and refused to criticise the referee. That was classy.

Poite, Jaco Peyper and Garces are three of the world's best referees. Between them, they blew it. I suspect Nigel Owens would have come up with the right decision. Owens would have penalised Owens. His confidence, his certainty and his showbusiness instincts allow the Welshman to back himself in the microsecond of the here and now in a way few others do. The French duo, notwithstanding the error, are two of the best. Wayne Barnes is another outstanding official but there's none better than Owens. What defines Nigel is one word: empathy. It is the most important word in the mindset of any referee. Trawl through the interminably badly written Laws of Rugby Union. The word will not appear once. Have I read it through? No, Nigel Owens told me so on the way back from a South Africa versus New Zealand encounter in Johannesburg. It may have been the finest game of attacking rugby I have ever seen. In his Wales Online column, Owens described the game as such in the August of 2018. Kieran Read was extraordinary. The performance of the referee wasn't far behind. Of course, the best referees get the best games. It accentuates their qualities. This match was two years before the 2015 World Cup. I had no qualms about describing him in print as a certainty for the Twickenham final two years hence. It did not cross my mind that Wales might make the final.

Empathy – the power of identifying oneself with another – or something like that. Referees have to be capable of imagining what a player is thinking to identify why he acts as he does. There are too many laws to live by the book. Rugby is a complex game. Much minutiae. Many technicalities. Rugby league is so much more straightforward. League fans prefer their code for that reason. Union followers have an affection for the complexities of the fifteen-a-side code. The trick to being a great referee isn't getting every technical decision spot on through the course of eighty minutes. More a matter of missing nothing of major match-defining importance. I don't much like the phrase, 'manage the game'. This suggests a referee is an intrinsic part of the process when he is actually the arbiter. He stands apart but he understands. That is what the great referees can do in a way their contemporaries cannot. Nor their overseers.

The bloody assessors. Assessors used to watch a game of rugby with a clipboard. They have been analysing referees long before analysts, stupid with statistics, were losing the larger coaching picture. I remember giving Norling a lift to Bristol Parkway from Gatwick after the Hong Kong Sevens. A long time back. Doubtless we were both downplaying the importance of fitness as we headed west along the M4. He was shocking me with an assessors' tale. A Cardiff versus Swansea game. East versus west, spiky contest in a packed Cardiff Arms Park . . . a classic game, fast, furious, frenetic. Cardiff edged it. Just about deserved their win, said Clive. The crowd were content, the players applauded each other from the field, shared beers . . . the referee was asked what he thought of his own performance by the assessors. Norling assumed he had played his part in an excellent afternoon of rugby and told them so. The assessors shook their heads, showed him the tick list (or should that be cross list) of his manifold errors. By the letter of the book, they adjudged his performance a poor one. Nobody else noticed. Such assessors are still frightening upcoming referees. The ones that can't referee, with their book full of pedantry. These shadowy forces linger within sections of stands where the sun refuses to shine. That was the day Roger Quittenton's mate lost his faith in officialdom.

Refereeing for the assessors is not dissimilar to your local MP working for his leaders instead of you and your constituency. Only the very best evade the box-ticking legions. In the bruising world of professional rugby, the road to the World Cup final is long and fraught with bureaucracy. And more and more law amendments. The law book is in a constant state of tinkering, trials and experiments. The fact that Super Rugby is a fast-evolving version of super fast rugby while France is a grind of scrums and mauls makes it even more difficult. Interpretations in one hemisphere are utterly foreign in the other. In the north the scrum is almost sacred. In the south many see it as nothing more than an outdated mode of restart. In the north it is an essential attacking weapon. In the south it is the price you pay for knocking on. Andre Watson's interpretation of scrum laws nearly cost an infinitely superior England the 2003 World Cup. We empathise in entirely opposite directions as far as it goes either side of the Equator. But unless the much-debated global season has the effect of globalising the game – have the world all playing at being a poor man's New Zealand – the sport will continually find itself lost in translation. A referee has to adore this sport to go through this hemispheric confusion. The best are silk purses put through the wringer . . . and they end up being called sows' ears or much worse . . . Homer!

The referee who misses nothing, who blows at every misdemeanour or error, will not go down in history as the first perfect referee. More the man who destroyed rugby union. Every breakdown is such an unruly coming together of bodies, at ever greater pace, that each collision has an incident where the whistle could feasibly be blown. Nothing would happen. Nothing comes from nothing. An endless screech, another scrum, a penalty kick for touch or goal. The terror of tinnitus on the field of play. On the terrace. Now the referee has assistance should he so choose the vain pursuit of the assessors' idea of the perfect performance. A utopia of officiating leads only to a dystopia of staccato rugby. Flick over to the football for three minutes and find no one has moved when you click back to the rugby inaction. The impact of the assistant referees (once the lowly touch judge but these gentler times demand a more respectful name) and the television match official is stringing out games. When a match kicks off late and you have a report to write after the microphone is laid aside, every delay for every innocuous incident that an assistant referee might (or as its very wording suggests 'might not' have seen) seems to slow not so much the match clock as time itself. In the 2016/17 season the two-hour match mark began to be passed with regularity on many a maudlin afternoon. We need editors.

There are remedies. For a start, assistant referees must be reminded never to communicate with the referee using the words, 'potential foul play'. Have you seen it? Yes . . . then stick your flag out and bring the villain to justice. If it 'might' have happened, what were you watching? Let the game flow. Allow the authorities to analyse any incidents post-match and have justice enacted that way . . . yes, but what if someone gets away with something which might have impacted upon the match? It goes round in circles. The pursuit of perfect justice is another inane utopia turning our old friend, time, that slips right through our fingers, into a dystopic delay.

If the play is foul it had better be filthy. Otherwise keep the flag by your side, sir. But television match officiating is most famous/infamous when it comes to 'Try, yes or no?' or 'Is there any reason why the try cannot be awarded/why I cannot award the try?' Firstly, television cannot 'prove' anything. Television is only the enabler. Thereafter the television match official and the referee between them have to make the decision. He sees the same picture as me, the same as Will Greenwood, the same as Miles Harrison, the same as you and your fellow supporters. The same picture but often a difference of opinion. Technology helps humans make a better decision but it cannot deliver God's Verdict. It is subjective. The elite officials are more likely than most to make their own mind up. Owens in particular prefers the evidence of his eagle eyes. If a referee is in the ideal position, his view is superior to that of the priciest piece of broadcast kit. He'll call what he sees. But what happens on the one in twenty occasions he is wrong? Broadcasters and writers point the finger. Fine. If the 'expert' expects maximum accuracy he has to live with the torture of the two-hour game. Yet the same critic will be writing his savage indictment on the unendurable length of a game, at the same time expecting an end to 'mistakes' from the man in the middle. Take your pick. But you cannot have it both ways.

The TMO when he is asked, 'Try, yes or no?' is being asked to give an independent opinion. The third eye. This makes sense. I think it is the only element of the TMO try-scoring process that does. If you are going 'upstairs' as commentary claims (although the TMO is in a booth within the broadcast compound in the car park) it should not be for clarification but a subjective opinion. When the referee asks, 'Is there any reason not to award the try?' he seeks back-up. If the try has been scored – in the referee's mind at least – he should back himself. If there is doubt, for example the ball is over the line but without proof of being grounded – he really should not give a try on the assumption of a hunch that somewhere in the mass of bodies the ball touched the try line. But what do we get? 'I see no reason not to award the try.'

Without evidence of grounding . . . it's not so much teamwork as officials sticking together. Two different things. If the decision is instinctive, call the try . . . but we all know that will rarely happen. The system is all too often covering the referee's back with the support of the system. Often an inexperienced referee will go to the TMO to check his laces are tied and his shorts are looking good. Another interesting use of the technology is the referee's more and more regular decision to view the incident on the 'big screen'. He might run ninety metres to the other end of the field to see the evidence with his own eyes. I am all for full employment but at this stage one has to wonder whether the sport is getting as much as it could from the TMO who has been turned into a glorified assistant producer, asking for the footage to be 'rock and rolled' as TV would say. Forwards and back, backwards and forwards. From the corner camera, from the touchline camera, from the camera behind the goals . . . two hours, five minutes and counting . . . had the referee been in the sort of position Owens, Wayne Barnes and the likes of Norling and Quittenton before them took, we wouldn't suffer the 'excitement' of the try-scoring – or not – minutes. Keep an eye out for the younger referees. More and more of them do not bother to chase around the side of a lineout drive as it nears the line. Nor do they get into the sort of crouch position where the glimpse of the briefest contact between grass and ball may be had. The wrong side of the ruck. Standing upright. So what, let's go 'upstairs'. It is hard not to come to the conclusion that the advent of enhanced technology is serving to damage the profession of the rugby referee.

Consistency is a key word. The laws are multiple and confusing enough without inconsistent interpretation. You are nominally supposed to bind on a player when you take part in a ruck over the tackled player and tackler. But with the opposing 'jackal' (the predatory player preying on the tackled player with both hands on the ball and supporting his body weight) shaped like a neat letter 'n' over the ball, there are few options but to neck-roll him. This throw has now been outlawed. It is an automatic ten minutes in the sin bin . . . so a player takes the other option and dives off his feet. Flattens the opposition. It isn't legal but everyone does it . . . a new unwritten rule which is allowed despite its illegality according to the game's law book. But keep it consistent. The same with neck- and head-high tackles. When zero policy was brought in to eliminate high tackles at the beginning of 2017, all referees should have – for once – followed the 'protocols'. Players had to understand there was nothing but a card for any perceived foul play. The whole point was to keep everyone's heads on their bodies. Coaches as bright as Exeter's Rob Baxter bewailed the mid-season introduction of a law change. Yet the season finished with tackling more controlled, less reckless, Exeter 2017 Premiership champions and flying, as opposed to tackling high. One of the rare times Baxter got it wrong.

World Rugby's mid-season intervention created a few rare examples when empathy became error. Commentators criticised radical referees who gave no leeway. Even as men slipped into the unlucky tackler's shoulders. Mireas Mitrea, a Romanian who referees out of Italy, didn't budge from his orders. Television pundits moaned about 'what comes next . . . and what is the game coming to?' How we moaned and groaned as we forgot the rationale of the thinking. What seems to be coming next is a sport where clothes-line tackles are not the order of the day. Where we discover that head-high straight-armed tackling is not an intrinsic part of the Samoan and Tongan DNA. So here's an opportunity to praise World Rugby for taking immediate action in the face of professional protests. By the time this book is published, I am sure we will be living through an era of new trial laws. The era of the eternal tinker.

Yet still, referees praised . . . what next? Wayne Barnes to be made welcome in New Zealand? Well, Romain Poite has finally taken some of the heat off his English mate while Jerome Garces had the temerity to send off an All Black – Sonny Bill Williams – and whistled them to defeat on home soil in the same Lions series. As for Wayne, ten years' fatwa is sufficient. Let's end the Kiwi feud with my namesake. Even if it is at the expense of two delightful Frenchmen. Hopefully the mob will forget the Lions series error rather quicker than the French forward pass in the 2007 World Cup quarter-final, Barnes waving play on. 'You are asking for too much now, Stuart.' I can hear Roger whispering those words in my ear even now. Am I getting sensitive? Sharpen up, Stuart.

THE RECREATION GROUND, BATH

IT HAS been a struggle to formulate these thoughts, commit them to the page . . . some inner warning telling me to let good things stay where they are, tucked deep in the recesses? Where will the tapped memory take me? The old battered Recreation Ground, the changing rooms . . . ground floor. Beneath the clubhouse. Beneath the members' bar. Stone steps lead up into the changing room area, turn right if you are a Bath player. Left for losers. The external steps give way to what I remember as internal tiling, brown? The home door and a room with barely space enough to squeeze the team and replacements. The senior players have their own pegs. It took me a while to claim mine. Once in possession I never let it go. Proprietorial. An important word. That's exactly what the Bath boys were; proprietorial. Our Recreation Ground. No matter what the official deeds suggested. Walk the dogs all you want in the green heart of the city beyond the temporary stand. Opposite the old wooden Grand Stand. Once you stepped inside the fenced perimeters of our domain, it was at your peril. In a decade at the club I lost one cup game.

Leicester of all teams. Threw my lucky red socks in the Avon. Never worn a pair of red socks since. I should have billed Dean Richards. His fault. He was monumental that day.

The ground didn't belong to the club. This might have changed by the time the book goes to print. At the time of writing it did not. It was a gift from the city. A gift which, in truth, the club has repaid a thousand times over. There are the Roman Baths, the Royal Crescent, the Assembly Rooms, some fancy Georgian streets and there is the Recreation Ground. A World Heritage city proud of its past. A few councillors envied the prestige of the present which Jack Rowell's team once brought the city. The Japanese and American tourists have now been joined by the weekend travellers from Leicester, from Toulouse, from Edinburgh and Dublin. Wives are welcome. The corporate collusion between club and shopping a snug fit. The club has its own shop. On Pulteney Bridge. Bringing the past and present together. The Recreation Ground is in the heart of the city. Low lying. Alongside the Avon and the architecturally wonderful weir. You can drop down some steps from Pulteney Street, no more than a couple of dozen, and you are off the street and gazing into the rough waters of the weir. Past a little coffee shop, some bars and restaurants, and you'll come to the gates. The main entrance to the Recreation Ground. People have been pouring in for thirty years or more. So too the waters of the Avon. They used to seep in after a five-minute shower. No private security kept the water out. Not then. The pitch we played on was porous. Always inundated. November to the beginning of April. In September and April it was firm. We scored a lot of points, had a lot of fun in those months. Envy is an ugly trait, I know, but that emotion bubbles away when I think of today's Bath players. Playing on a pitch where only the far corner dead ball area, near the Sports Centre, puddles up any more.

Most of the season we were bog warriors. It blunted our backs. We didn't seem to care. Defeat was rare, catastrophic. Two decades on, I know better than to use words like 'catastrophe' and 'tragic'. But that was how it felt. Beyond contemplation. Shake the hands of your conquerors. Mutter something that sounded sincere. Retreat to the tile-floored changing room. Abuse, recriminations, self-loathing, loathing, full stop. Rowell's silence the worst of it all . . . pain . . . then the beer. And more beer.

The opposing teams were always made welcome. Afterwards. During my three-year tenure as captain, my hospitality forte were trays of gins, a few tonics poured randomly . . . a £100 kitty which the late Lang Jones, deputy head of King Edward's School and head of bars at Bath, ensured went further than it really should. A friend to the players. Drink in despair, drink with the heads held high. We poured drinks for our infrequent conquerors. Having poured our souls into a pledge to beat them into an unrecognisable state the next time . . . smirking shits. The trick to handling defeat well? Take it terribly. Act the part. There's a whole generation of amateur Bath players who scream in anger when Bath lose at home and the television director zooms in on the players sharing a joke seconds after full time, moments before it dawns. Some of these guys don't give much of a damn . . . I have touched on the subject elsewhere; a pet hate. I saw Van Morrison at the Cambridge Folk Festival a few years back. Big band sound. Soaring notes. Clean voice. The polite festival audience that will cheer the famous songs and clap hands overhead in that 'Hey, I know that one' sort of shallow way. There was no soul, nothing authentic, Van was going through the motions, doing it for the money. 'Give it up, Van,' we said. But he can't. There's the music and the corruption of the money. We had no money, we had no perks bar 12p a mile. We had nothing but an insane dedication to success. If we were sacrificing four nights a week to training, what was the *raison d'etre* other than to win? To wallop the next set of bastards with the temerity to trample over our turf, or rather our bog? Winning was all there was. Here I was, at home, at last, amongst other people with a similar fear of failure. This was to be bliss . . . even the fights in training, the bitter recriminations when a man was dropped, the acid tongue of our Svengali, Rowell, and the never subdued fear that played havoc with my mind for most of a decade . . . apart from that it was gravy, all the way.

The showers and bath were through the changing room. The bath. Or were there two? Memory rust . . . the one bath at least was on the left-hand side of the room. The echoing clip, clip of long studs over the tiles. Overused toilet cubicles at the far end. Stank with nervous shits. To the right as you entered were the showers, only a few and never that powerful. The forwards, pre-kick-off, would retreat to the shower area. Shouting 'One, two, three, four,' (could they count to five?) as they ran up and down on the spot. Laughable from another century. Nigel Redman, pumped up before one game, accidentally hit the shower handle with his elbow. The pack dripping wet as they emerged from the changing rooms. Backs trying not to laugh . . . Rosslyn Park one afternoon. Their manager was a mate of mine. Hugh McCardy. I am having a rub on the physiotherapist's couch when 'The Park' walk into the ground. Heading, not surprisingly, straight for the changing rooms. No other players in our makeshift 'rub room', I give Hugh a wave from the couch, located off the changing room itself, an inadequate cluttered space looking onto the concourse where fans mill before the match. He waves back. Hughie grins . . . I am not alone by now. 'Look at that London wanker, laughing at us, thinks we are a bunch of cider heads, who the fuck does he think he is?' Hugh is Scottish. A couple of the forwards nod in a nasty silence, unimpressed with this typical piece of Metropolitan arrogance. Five minutes into the game, one of their forwards is laid out on the floor. Nose, jaw, something damaged, Bath forward flexing his fist, 'That'll teach you fuckers . . .' Was I insidious evil? Never trust the short ones.

Out of the changing rooms. Watch out, you can slip on the tiles. Not the right sort of psychological mark to make, the away team watching you. You, all steamed up and falling on your face or arse . . . negotiate the tiles, the stone steps, a few more feet of concrete walkway for the fans and then the grass, or mud, that welcomes you onto the Recreation Ground. An adrenaline explosion. A release from mundane everyday life. It is an eighty-minute spell in which law and order is all but suspended. Emotions heightened. Something well done seems great, something poorly executed is terrible. And fear, always fear to drive you on. 'Bath, Bath, Bath!' The same chant . . . and there's Doreen, good old Doreen, same place same time, every fortnight. Are you still with us, Doreen? I hope so. 'Come on, my lovers.' The West Country in its wild days.

Pre-match in a hotel – Dukes – near the ground. Brunch. Before it was called brunch. Jack, in the nicest possible way, saying, 'In the nicest possible way, we need to deal with him . . .' Fingers pointing straight at one of many assassins for the day. Lawless, an eighty-minute escape. Beautifully dressed local residents of the architectural wonder that is Pulteney Street, as we stroll the street, 'Go on Barrrth . . .' The link between players and fans a real one in a city of no more than 80,000-odd people. The clubhouse was divided along these lines: committee room nearest the Avon. Public bar in the middle. Members' bar at the other end of the building. Behind the members' bar a converted skittles alley. That was the players' canteen. Don't recall the food, only the lovely ladies that gave their time for nothing. Their version of dedication to the cause. The public bar was where most of the players drank. The committee came up with an idea. Cordon off a section of the members' bar for players and wives. We raged against it. Yet the intent was good. A little space for the participants and family. But the men mingled, players, fans, even committee men. This was a republic of rugby players and their partners. Saturday night was big in the Recreation Ground. Drinking ourselves senseless . . . why? I suspect relief. Didn't bother to give a name to it in those days . . . just drank. Binge drinking didn't exist: relief drinking, ah, now this was another thing.

So much for match day. In the mid-1980s we still used the Recreation Ground for training. Monday, Wednesday, sometimes a Tuesday . . . or did that come later? Did it come at all? Have I lied so long about the dedication of a talented group of amateurs that I have reinvented who and what we were? Maybe. Cold nights, they are the ones that lodge in what is either a memory or fictitious past. The night dark, the leaking pools of light from the old floodlights, a stage on which we were able to rehearse, to run around, to leave the rest of life behind. The president swimming naked on a Sunday morning in a Robert Lowell poem . . . that's how it felt to me. 'Waking Early Sunday Morning'. 'O to break loose' and something about salmon swimming upstream, alive enough to spawn and die . . . was that it for us? To be free, if a little bit afraid. Beneath the lights, over the fence, above the Avon, the floodlit Abbey, the stillness of a September night. The joy of a perfectly struck drop kick in practice. If there was a God he was with us on the Recreation Ground, not in the Abbey. The Abbey was old, we were young. Alive and without an owner, an agent, an anything but each other . . . or for some of us, ourselves. Was the Recreation Ground my sporting home from home, as I have always insisted, or a personal stage? One where the fear of failure helped me learn my lines? Discard those thoughts. In a dark nook my thoughts form.

Now Bruce Craig sits imperious in his corporate box. The television director cuts to him more than any other owner in England. Why not? This is, after all, Aquae Sulis, the Roman Spa town and here is its twenty-first century emperor. Garlanded with the glory of all his millions and ownership of the club. Andrew Brownsword, the first man to buy Bath, claimed his role was one of stewardship. To keep the traditions going. The club fell from its heights as the ambition of other clubs like Saracens loomed on the professional horizon. But Craig was rumoured to be ready to spend. He would buy back the club's glory days, days when the old lags rolled around in the filth of mud not lucre, fighting for nothing but the win, the win, the win. Alongside him sits James Dyson, an even mightier entrepreneur. Powerful men. The senator . . . showing everyone his gun, but no free tickets . . . no trophies, nothing of any note.

Bread and circus. The Roman Amphitheatre that is the Recreation Ground gives the good people of Bath and the west their weekly entertainment. The little 8,000 ground of the amateur days replaced with 14,000 or more. The temporary stand is grander, the bars beneath the stands provide promise of relief should the team fail to provide the entertainment and euphoria in the event of victory. Corporate logos everywhere. Cider, ale, Dyson's brand . . . billboards, shorts, shirts, everything up for sale. Do you detect a cynical note? Indeed you do . . . but where did the evolution (or regression dependent on point of view) begin? I'll tell you where . . . back in the late 1980s. I was club captain and part of the club's negotiating team that struck Bath's first ever corporate sponsorship. Triumphalism at the deal done. South West Electricity Board. Look back at the photographs. Blue, black and white jerseys with the SWEB logo splashed on our breasts. Further deals followed, a small one with Puma telling much about the mentality of those Recreation Ground days. It was not the kit and money that interested us. More the match balls that came with the contract. The fat balls with the unmissable sweet spot used throughout England replaced with a narrow missile of a ball. Flew miles if you caught the small sweet spot, went nowhere, or nowhere a kicker wanted it to go, if the ball was mishit. As it often was. We played and trained with Puma balls. No other club even knew we used them. Not until they arrived at the Recreation Ground. How the RFU allowed us to use our own choice of ball tells a great deal about the amateurism of the union in those days. And our determination to obtain any edge. We didn't have a salary and we didn't have a dietician but we had a ferocity, a fear and a fury that made a trip to Roman Bath unpleasant, on a good day.

When the game went professional, the clubhouse portraits of Bath's England players were temporarily taken down. It was a new age. History was being eradicated. The testimony to Jack Rowell was not only the roll call of trophies over the years but the displays of recent internationals. I was a fading magenta portrait replete with 1970s Welsh moustache. Pleased to hear it had been removed. They were reinstalled. The fans didn't want to forget the great days. Even if the new barons of Bath did. Where do they reside now? I haven't a clue. People say to me, 'Do you still get down to the Recreation Ground when you have a chance? Do you have a soft spot for your old team?' The answer is no on both counts. The ground, glorious as its setting may be, is what you make it. We made it into the clichéd sporting fortress. It was our home. We didn't own the turf, the mud, but we owned the aura. That was then, this is now. Kit Marlowe would have enjoyed the three-card brag sessions, the binge drinking, the violence that permeated the place. The playwright wouldn't have cared so much for a world where post-match the players have their official duties to fulfil. First to the corporate overlords who must not be offended. Family can wait, unless they manage a quick chat. A hug on the field. A much-welcomed Recreation Ground tradition. This is not a criticism of the modern Bath players so much as recognition of the times in which they play. Moneyed days. Far removed from the muddied days of my youth. We were Shakespeare's band of brothers. We squabbled and fought.

Especially on the training fields but the bond that tied this team for the best part of fifteen years was one from which few wanted to escape. The Recreation Ground, we thought ours in spirit for a decade. But it was never truly anyone's. Not the property of the players that came before, it is not for those who have followed and will continue to do so. We had our time. The Recreation Ground is in the care of others. So, no, I don't miss the ground, I have the memories. Memories that I can bend to my particular will because the plain ledger of results reveal we were so powerful. Yet my fear of failure was never expunged. Even the Recreation Ground's magic was not that powerful.

As for the team, there is no continuity between then and now. A team is about people. I can understand a fan following the name. The badge. The ever-changing kit (closing the mind to the commercial cynicism of the bewildering new colour combinations). But to have been a player is to have been in the metaphorical trenches with friends . . . not always friends off the field but soulmates on it. If one person creaked the edifice could crumble, even something with as strong a set of foundations as our team. Bath is Cooch, Dawesy, Oafie, Dadda Vic, Ollie, Morph, Del Boy, Spudsy, Simmo, Robbo, Egdy, Clarkey, Withey, Hally and Hilly. Knighty, Bammers, Hallers (pronounced Hal-urz), Jerry, De G, JP, Catty, Swifty, Mofield, Barry, Tricky, Oiker, JC, Webby, Jim, Mas, Robbie, Chalkie, Lil, Bob Hoskins, Reader, Jimmy Deane and so many more unmentioned. They are my Bath. And, of course, the coaches, Tom, Dave, Brian, Hank the Yank and above all, Jack Rowell.

If R represents the Recreation Ground, it has to be bracketed with R for Rowell. Jack was not a 'nice' man. He'll take that, I hope, as the compliment it is earnestly intended. He wanted to win. End of story. And he would go close to whatever lengths were necessary, 'In the nicest possible way, Chilcott.' That pointed finger, the loaded gun . . . the promise of something, anything, but nice for the intended victim. He saw something in a young Gareth Chilcott where few others did. Jack grasped the importance of violence, of intimidation and made Roger Spurrell an early club captain. A defining statement. Over My Body for those who would beat Bath. Jack was a rugby gangster. Our Capo. He does business in the Ukraine to this day. He loved a certain frisson.

Jack called us a rock group. Didn't care that we combined club blazers with scruffy jeans and straggly club tie, or bow tie. This was his backhanded idea of a compliment. He was our Phil Spector as well as Al Capone, rolled into one. He was Bath. The cup final was the highlight of the amateur club season. Under Jack, Bath did not lose a final. The closest they came was when some stupid cocky kid missed a kick to win in 1984 . . . thereafter it was all Bath until Harlequins took us to extra time and I brought my kicking career full circle, both times to the benefit of Bath. The night of the final, an orgy of alcohol in a Bath hotel. The next day . . . round to the Rowell residence for a party before the open-top bus tour of the city. Eternally grateful to the enthusiastic teenage fans who sprinted from one viewing spot to the next, short cuts keeping them ahead of the bus and we bleary-eyed drunks. At the end of the evening Jack would still be there, his wife, Sue, smiling at the alcohol-fuelled antics. A captain of industry with a fixed grin that was set in stone on cup final Sunday. Unbreakable.

We were not the best behaved. Jack as bad as any of us. His humour could be cruel. Cutting. Yet it was the essence of who and what this generation of Recreation Ground players were. Jack was a man of vision in an age of blinkers. He plotted long term and encouraged us to think the moment through. His coaching sessions were a series of questions when so many coaches did and continue to live by statements, not confident enough to let others work out the strategy. Jack opened our eyes. Taught us to think for ourselves, utterly anti-English. We went to Wales where we were encouraged to fight as hard as we thought. Year by year this man from the north east who had coached Gosforth to the cup, made Bath into a steelier side. He knew which buttons to press. He would speak softly to me. Tell me I was the brains of the side, that I was the most crucial component. He probably said it to all those players in need of psychological support. Others, straightforward tough nuts like Richard Hill, he would berate. I remember Richard playing an absolute blinder once, coming back into the changing room, slippery tiles and all, sitting next to me, furiously unwinding the tape that held his fast passing hands firm, saying, 'What's that fucker going to say to me now, Barner?' I think I suppressed the laugh. So the trick would work again.

Rowell was a sports psychologist ahead of his time. When he became England manager it suited him to select Rob Andrew, although I had been his emissary for so long, although he had sat with me and disparaged my rival. But that was Jack, we were all pawns in his game. Not every player trusted him (I suspect some had the same opinion of me) but we danced to his tune. A tune all the better because it was raucous. He encouraged us to write the song as well as play it. There was a period when Jack as manager and Brian Ashton as attack coach soared higher than any English management team has before. Maybe since. Our Lennon and McCartney.

Abbey Road, the Abbey on a training night, Spurrell fighting with Robinson. Rowell – gummy grin exposed to the cold floodlit West Country night – pointing and peering above the chaos from his great height. This is my Bath, my Recreation Ground. Or should I say my memories. Bath is nobody's. Good luck to those who now inhabit the space. My reality is locked in time. The players of that era, the fans, the coaches and angled above us all, Jack. This past is my truth. A place where fear was never quite conquered but most other teams were. As I write, the

Recreation Ground remains in the same glorious location. By the Avon. All else has changed. It couldn't go on as it did forever.

One final footnote. The happiest day of my broadcasting career. The day Bath beat Brive and won the Heineken Cup. The dying fall of Jack's generation had climbed the heights we surely would have done had this tournament existed in the 1980s and early 1990s. I cried in the Sky Studio. Drank champagne on air. Broke all broadcasting rules. Dashed for the changing room where recent team-mates celebrated. I was a journalist by then. One that had been critical of men in the celebratory changing room. Had broken the rugby code of *omerta* – but fuck that . . . Jerry laughing, the hyena laugh that takes me back to wild days . . . 'Barnesy, the only thing that ruins this day was having to give the try-scoring pass to Callard.' Jon Callard, the Bath full back, scored all the points that day but to Jerry, Callard's lack of . . . panache . . . diminished the moment. Only a Bath man of that generation could have jested so brutally. That is what I loved about Bath, that time, place, truth, beauty and brutality. Who and what we were. Those days are long gone. Lost, except in that endless universe of our private memories.

SCOTLAND, 1993

'YOU'VE GOT a problem now they've picked you, Barner. You are going to have to prove you are as good as you keep telling everyone you are.' Jack Rowell and that gummy grin of his. Twinkle in the eye, challenge in the words, the slight catch in the voice. Pure Bath, pure Jack. Some players need building up, others knocking down. Some of us existed somewhere in between. Jack just cracked the joke, usual Saharan dryness. A Monday night. Six days later I would finally be restored to the England number ten shirt. Scotland, Twickenham, the Calcutta Cup. My opinions on the subject of selection, as Jack half-joked, were hardly kept to themselves. Journalists were polarised on the subject of Andrew and Barnes. Rob had harvested a huge number of caps to my paltry eight but the argument never quite died despite the lopsided statistics. Especially when I made sporadic returns from the self-imposed exiles. Exiles that cost me the opportunity of a few more caps. Exiles that kept me sane.

Outside Bath, this was the game for which I would be remembered. So many people have told me they were there.

Some of them – a little like me and the All Blacks in 1972 – are in thrall to this minor myth. With it comes major memory default. They've seen the try, though. And their dads recall the excessive hype surrounding the day. I'm always grateful for the kind words. There's a lot of fans who don't think a lot of the person they think of as me. Some delight in the dreadful days; days you know they were too young to have seen; say, my shambolic effort at full back in Dublin 1987. Some of the knockers weren't even conceived. That's no bar to any watch they keep. Chronology can confuse. These things happen. Tony Blair in a photo op in St James' Park said he saw Jackie Milburn from the Gallowgate End. The dates didn't add up. Must have been before he was born. Poor advisers/blatant liars. Years and facts tangled up. Unless he was on the terrace as a four-year-old. Otherwise a disregard for the historical process. It happens all the time.

What happened that day at Twickenham changed my life. The bloke with the big gob from the West Country actually could play a bit. He could talk and walk. Definitely talk. One year later I was writing for the *Daily Telegraph*. A few months after finding my way to newsprint, I was the first face of Sky Rugby Union. One jink off the right foot and a decent pass changed my life. Building societies (although my employers were good people), marketing (whatever that was and is) farewell. Best of all, the day after the Scotland game, as I lurched out of the car into an off licence, buying a bottle en route to my mate, Dusty Miller's, for a celebratory slurp and Sunday lunch, the manager waved away my offer to pay. On a roll . . .

This late, brief lunge into the arms of celebrity had its origins long before Dewi Morris – the irony of our long partnership as Sky pundits still induces a smile – wound himself up to throw a pass back to his new half back partner around the England twenty-two. But we are ahead of ourselves. The break that launched a famous try, that would change a life. This began, not with a pass in our own half but an apologetic telephone call to Geoff Cooke in 1991. World Cup year. Cooke wasn't about to welcome the not so prodigal son back into the ranks. I don't blame him. There were dues to be paid. I dug deep into the pockets of my rugby shorts for spare change.

Fortune was the staunchest of allies when I wore the blue, black and white of Bath. We didn't get on so well on the wider rugby stage. I made a mess of my relationship with England, not Lady Luck. But that great big Geordie streak of Bath was to come to my aid. Jack Rowell, mentor, tempter, just about everything but Father Confessor, had been appointed manager of England B. It became England A in 1994 but forget the alphabet, this was the second team. Jack wanted the main job as England's manager, every bit as much as I belatedly yearned for one more crack at the red rose. The days of treating the B/A team as a developmental entity disappeared with Rowell's appointment. Winning was all and to win he demanded old heads to go with the sprinkling of stardust in that B/A squad. I was appointed captain. Fellow Bath scrappers like Graham Dawe babysat the younger forwards.

With captaincy came the trust I relished. The ability to mould a team not into the England way of playing but the Bath one. It was MY team. That's how it felt. Victor Ubogu, Neil Back, Ben Clarke, Tony Underwood, Ian Hunter, Graham Rowntree, even a young second row by the name of Johnson. 'Youngsters' who were part of the second team package for varying periods. Serving time in such ranks was the stuff of dreams. A happy player is more than halfway to being a good one and I, I was ecstatic. The best I would ever feel outside the Recreation Ground. It wasn't just the rugby. We had our own second tier Five Nations (as it then was). I was an American Grand Tourist out of a Henry James novel. Our trials and tribulations took us to London, Madrid,

Paris and Rome en route to the 'B' Grand Slam. Ireland were dispatched in Richmond with Hunter and Underwood, a pair of princes out wide. In Madrid, after an average performance, I didn't travel with the team to a Spanish TV studio to watch the senior England–Scotland game (where Guscott dropped a goal, that's all the lads said; they were deeply unimpressed). The full team was of no interest, not yet. I preferred pounding the floors of the Prado museum. Velazquez and his horses. Rear end too big to jump a fence but quite the sight hanging on a wall. There I bumped into a high dignitary of the RFU who sacrificed the Scottish trip to represent the union in Madrid. With his wife. A cultured lady. She looked at me – imperceptibly down from her nose, quaint in her beautifully mannered confusion, 'And what, Stuart, are you doing here?' We sportsmen should know our place.

A Grand Tour and a Grand Slam. France a filthy game, the rest plain sailing. Another diversion in this maze of digressions, if I may? Ahead of the away game in France, Martin Haag, the Bath second row, picked up an injury. Into the team came a young Leicester lock. By the name of Johnson. He'd only played against Bath once or so. We didn't know much about him. 'Barner,' said Rowell at training, 'see if you can drop a few kick-offs on his head.' Johnson rose, claimed them with disdain. 'Do you think we can get him?' The toothy grin. Johnson didn't leave Leicester. But he left our merry band sooner than the rest of us. Into the England team. On the road to Somewhere. Somewhere BIG. The rest of us travelled to New Zealand for a tour after the Grand Tour/Slam, the summer of 1992. I was refused permission to take time off my job. Showing some spine, for once, I quit. Now determined to not only have one final hurrah for England but to give myself a sniff of a return to rugby's greatest land with the next year's Lions. But to make that Lions tour of New Zealand I had to jemmy my way back into the England set up. I played some confident, slick stuff. Ignored the Test team. The head was kept down, our team was terrific, getting the press talking. We should have won both 'Tests' in New Zealand but my kicking wrecked our hopes in the first of them. It was the most painful defeat since the missed kick for Bristol against Bath in 1984. It hurt me and our team, I failed them when it mattered. Oh, another little scar. Rewriting I see the priority of the pain. Me first.

Next autumn we lost narrowly to the Springboks in Bristol. Defeat was rendered less traumatic. I had played a balanced game, making breaks, mixing it up, running the game under international pressure. The pressure was building on Andrew as the Test team struggled to find the rhythm of the recent Grand Slam teams. Another composed and confident display for the Barbarians against Australia at Twickenham (the younger Underwood was again outstanding). The Barbarians were good to me. My obsession with results and an unpatriotic stance didn't prevent this magnificent testimony to all that was great about amateurism from picking me to play on high profile platforms at various times in my career. They liked to run. Liked to think on the hoof. I enjoyed the Barbarians as much as those Spanish horses.

I think it was in the wake of a poor performance against Wales. That's when the decibel levels became deafening. That's when I thought even Geoff Cooke might be forced to throw me into the fray in a bid to beat away the criticism (most of it deserved) of the wooden nature of the English performances. And there it was one fine Monday morning, my name on CEEFAX, England's team announced, me the fly half. The headline. And there was Jack, baseball cap tilted, teasing some humour out of the headlines, 'You've got a problem now they've picked you Barner . . .'

Indeed I did. The team was dominated by the pack, much as had been the case a decade earlier. Will Carling was captain. The forwards ran the show. Defeat in round three of the tournament dented their iron will long enough for me to prise open a gap with help from a few friends. Games aren't just won on the field. Preparation is everything, or at least quite a lot. Physically, mentally, a team and the individuals comprising the collective have to be primed. Relaxed . . . how to relax with Jack's joke. Too close to the forefront of the mind for a comfortable Friday night's kip ahead of the match? A bottle of wine was the answer. A bloody good bottle, nothing gut-rotting . . . the Petersham, England's long-standing team hotel, had a decent cellar. The management were sympathetic to my plight. They saw the bead of sweat breaking out above the top lip as I headed upstairs to my room after dinner. Away from the tables with buckets of CocaCola available. No alcohol. A book was my usual mode of relaxation. Jerry knocked on my door. He had an infinitely superior idea. It was probably a Pomerol. My choice of red in a crisis. Jerry opened wide the bedroom balcony window, lit up a cigarette, smoked his way through a few while we sipped the wine and talked of tomorrow's match. Staring out on that oxbow of the Thames meandering through meadows on the edge of Richmond. Jerry never doubted his capacity to convert words into deeds. On my part, I was reduced to hoping. The hopes matured with the Bordeaux. What could have been a little sleep ended up a deep one. I woke up as ready as I would ever be. Conditioners and sports psychologists can say all they like. Whilst a little over half a bottle of Pomerol might not be the ideal approach, not in a physical sense, it is a damned sight better for a man than a sleepless night. I felt fantastic. Bring on Robert the Bruce and all of Scotland. Where are you, Macbeth?

I don't recall the actual moment. Every Six Nations or so there's a rerunning of the try. Almost exclusively ahead of Calcutta Cup games. So many fans remember, remember the majesty, the magnificence of the score. But it wasn't like that. The pass to me (I confess to having double-checked on YouTube before writing up the distant recollection) wasn't from the scrum

I thought it was. The move began with a lineout. The forwards did their bit and drove across the gainline. Dewi threw an awful pass. Very high. Not wide. Ugly as sin. A serious stretch for a shorty to pluck. A real rib-breaker. The Scottish open side was Iain Morrison. He couldn't resist the temptation. Envisaged the England number ten crumpled on the turf, in agony, out of the game. The prize scalp of the day. He flew up, too fast. A feint one way and a change of pace the other. Going, going . . . gone . . . the pass off my right hand was thrown a thousand times a month on the Bath training ground – and so was the step practised – yet people still talk of the play. I got to thinking it must have been memorable. Just watched it back, the step was smart, the pass good enough, where it should be. But compared to the pass of Owen Farrell to Elliot Daly for the match-winning England try against Wales in 2017 or Finn Russell to Huw Jones against England in 2018? Let's call it quaint. Nothing nostalgic about my drinking, smoking buddy. Jerry took off. No other phrase will do. Burned his way between a centre and winger, a sublime pass and Rory Underwood was celebrating. Jerry had scored an earlier try running straight onto my usual fade, right to left, lines we cut in our sleep. Jerry and I played bit-parts too in Tony Underwood's try. There's a bit of pace on my part, a certain cockiness, a load of dark hair, bundles of buzzing around. Some sly little passes but come on. Hardly the stuff of history.

There are other aspects to the game I think I remember. Bad restarts. Left to right off my right foot. Far easier for the forwards attacking the kick with their more co-ordinated right side. Much trickier for the man without a left side. In Bath I would have switched direction. In the England set up I simmered and saw one aspect of my game slump some degree below the acceptable. The forwards would have been pining for Rob. There was a lovely kick off my left foot though. I caught the ball in our twenty-two, midfield. Moved it onto my left side and connected. A smooth screw kick, some distance into the Scottish half. Nobody has ever spoken of my left-footed kick but I was proud of that, by this stage of the game Test rugby was easy. We would have run Scotland off their feet. Should have. The backs were sharp. I was a catalyst. A rumble started around Twickenham, 'Roll Out the Barrel', how did they know the nickname? The middle-class mob had made me up. The afternoon was a dream, an imperfect dream but a dream nevertheless. It's a dream with Rory Underwood's mother cavorting in the stands. The BBC director is onto her bouncy celebrations in a flash. Below her my wife, Lesley, and my two stepchildren, Matthew and Kate, look slightly stunned.

It was not a great game of rugby but we produced what the public were told by the press they wanted. Ambition and accuracy. Something a little bit funky. One rugby writer waxed lyrical, I had made my critics eat their words by the libraryful. I like the literary reference well enough but the words didn't ring true. I did for England some of the things I did week on week (in my good periods) at Bath. I had a few tricks and a lot of backs' moves up sleeves of rugby shirts always too long for me. Room to keep them hidden. But some of the basics were blemished – and that is me being kind to myself. Worst of all, when England had Scotland in disarray I allowed the pack to amble around at their own sluggish speed. The match trundled into anonymity. At Bath I would have been the one dictating. Screaming. Demanding. That's one of the crucial roles of a fly half. At Twickenham the crowd grinned at the glitter and missed the fact that the steering was sub-standard. But for once that was all right. I woke up the next day, Prince Hamlet for the only time in an international career of bit-part attendant. Finally, after the entitlement of the school years, this was the Sunday morning I had expected to encounter on so many more occasions. So many more bottles of complimentary wine.

Damned if I was going to confess to the flaws in the performance. It wasn't the fame as much as the glory I wanted.

For as long or as little as it lasted. I was the central story of rugby journalism, at the epicentre of its unthinking hyperbolic worst. I went into the game as the story and had I done nothing else bar make one break I would have come out of it as the headline-maker. Rugby is like football. The minutiae are simply small irrelevancies most of the time. Give the public a hero and if that's impossible, then a villain will have to be hung out. The bloke who scores the three tries, the centre forward who grabs the hat-trick, they are the heroes, that's how it is. I didn't score a try but I fulfilled my designated role. The only angle going into this game was success or failure. For a few days even some of Andrew's fans jumped ship but the fan is a fickle thing. So too is fate. Whatever that means . . . another excuse for another mistake in the maze?

Hero to villain. It took a week. A week where the vast difference between the now and then stands revealed. England met Thursday morning. Training and a trip to Dublin where we were expected to rip Ireland to pieces. Preparation? For me, two days' drinking at Cheltenham on the Tuesday and Wednesday of the National Hunt Festival. Interviewed by Radio Five with Richard Dunwoody in the paddock. Him on his horse, mine a high one. Two days' solid drinking, two too many. An inevitable fall from this privileged position as media darling. Especially when the core of the pack were knocking the Guinness back on the Friday night. A boozer at the back of the Killiney Castle Hotel. An hospitable landlord. An ambush and we walked into it. For once I was not part of the Friday drinking crowd. My internal damage had been done at the races. The tale is one of an Irish steamroller pack. How Mick Galway played himself into legend and a Lions tour. And in my mind how I fucked up. The truth begins and ends with appalling English preparation.

I had no need for a calming drink on the Friday. Not that week. The exact opposite, a reminder of the pitfalls, was overdue. But no, I was going to finish the job of the previous week. Ensure

England started as we should have finished against Scotland. Show the England management what they had been missing all these years.

Fast forward from amateur to professional, twenty-four years later, an England team expected to clinch a consecutive Grand Slam in Dublin. A back line that received rapturous (and merited) reviews against Scotland the previous Saturday. The first time George Ford touched the ball in attack, rhythm replaced with cacophony. The passes dropped where last week they had stuck. An Ireland pack in dominant mood. I was living in the present of the press box and hurtling back to the past where we don't always dream. We suffer nightmares. On the day before the 2017 game I wrote a column (Gold Cup day) warning England that the past is never that distant. Why would they read an old fool from another century? Because history does repeat itself. It was windy wet, a day when the rain made the Dublin turf slippery. Treacherous. A day when you can slide, when the studs and the centre cannot hold. 1993, 2017, the Bath fly half in England's white on both occasions. I willed England to take a backward step, away from the marauding Irish defence. I had stood flat, aggressively so, threatening an opposing back line. Stupid if your pack are winning bad or no ball. Déjà vu.

Stupid is kind, it doesn't begin to describe my eighty minutes. The double Grand Slam seekers were no smarter. Eddie Jones confessed to his tactical sins of omission. I knew I was tiptoeing towards madness but after all these years, damned if I was going to do what I would have done without a moment's thought in Bath. Drop deep. Kick. Regain some composure. Play territory. It was an eighty minutes, no, a week of sporting suicide. Aged twenty-one I would have learned from the bitter experience. Aged thirty I pondered late into the Dublin night how spectacularly I had thrown away all my chips from the previous week. It had been a losing Cheltenham too. The bloody Irish. In 2017, suffering from an insidious bout of insomnia, I stayed off the drink at the races. Ended up in profit. Sober, I watched England follow the 1993 road to despair, *Molly Malone* replaced by *The Fields of Athenry*.

Had I been the summariser a quarter of a century back I would have castigated me, the England fly half. For I was the headline news. What goes up must come down. Unless you are Dan Carter or Jonny Wilkinson. And I would have been right to slam Stuart Barnes. Commentators should cut slack for a kid. For a thirty-year-old there could be no excuse. No mercy. Here's snatches of how me (2018) commentating on myself in Dublin 1993 might have gone. 'Barnes is playing much too flat. England need some territory to temper the early Irish onslaught.'

'We're halfway through the first half and England have to sharpen their game, the Irish pack are all over them. Barnes is playing as if his pack is as dominant as they were a week ago against Scotland. I have to say it, but this is a little naïve.'

'He's clearly trying to force the game. He has been around long enough to know better than this.'

'Full time and a great win for Ireland. Eric Elwood produced a masterly performance at fly half.' (The director, if any good at all, would cut from Irish fist-pumping joy to English misery. CUT TO A CLOSE-UP OF BARNES. 'Great shot guys, look at that bottom lip jutting out,' says the director.) I continue waffling, waiting for the interviewer to get into position. 'As for Barnes, he has travelled from the sublime to, I hate to say it, almost the ridiculous in seven days.' A lingering shot, head slumped . . . maybe one final dagger of a comment to make the 1993 version of Mrs Barnes hate me forever. That's how it goes. Did I receive any mercy from the day's commentators? Don't know, you think I ever watched that shit back? I certainly deserved none. I tried hard. Trying hard is not enough. Any fool can try hard. Did the press spare me? Again, who knows? I had preferable things to do than read the sporting obituary of Stuart Barnes. Former rugby player. Like what? Drink too much Guinness for my good and try not to think about the impending Lions selection. On the basis of one game, Ireland's Eric Elwood deserved a spot. It was my great fortune to be adjudged on the Scotland rather than Ireland game. Eric's bad luck. The great get to do it all over again. The good have to grab their chances when they come along. I don't think I was helped by the England set up but there's no pretending I maximised my own chances. Ha, but that complimentary bottle of wine from the previous week had tasted good.

TELEVISION

NEVER TRUST a television natural . . . any man or woman not unnerved by having to smile and talk directly into the camera at the first time of asking has rather too much regard for their own selves. 'Treat the camera as if it is a friend,' was an early piece of advice. Who of my friends has the silent capacity to demand you reveal all your imperfections, the warts and all, like a TV camera? We non-naturals begin our television days thinking of the blemishes our new friend cruelly highlights, magnifies . . . one thing I quickly learned after joining Sky television in 1994. Be nice to the make-up department. The wild eyebrow, the mole with a few hairs sprouting from it, the bags beneath the eyes, these and many other slight imperfections are lying in wait to be announced to the watching world. The camera is merciless. The person who is pleased with him – or her – self the moment the adulterous affair with the camera rolls? Don't trust them. Smooth and slime. Broadcast bedfellows all too often. The bloke with the blemishes is your man, worried about what he says, not how he moves and looks. As for the blemished women, not many of them make it broadcast side of the camera. Black, white, Asian, transgender, gay, straight, lesbian, bisexual . . . roll up, roll up, but ugly, urgh, forget it.

My narcissistic tendencies were of the intellectual nature. Fed up with being thought of as the English equivalent to the dumb American Jock, I yearned to be taken seriously. If I wasn't going to get the Sky presenter's job for which I was being screen-tested a few months after retiring, it wasn't going to be on grounds of stupidity. Oh, my screen test was magnificent. Me, a man who read *Lord of the Rings* when nine was not going to mess up the autocue. There were nerves, of course there were. It was a new environment and a salary I suspected would ease the pressure of being a thirty-one-year-old freelance writer. Focus on the camera with the red light, my 'friend'. Take a deep pause, the moment before kick-off, don't let the adrenaline send you babbling into a paroxysm of overflowing paragraphs. I took my time. Not a pause was ignored. Full stops were given due deference. Not a stumble, not a stutter . . . superb. The executive producer thanked me for making the journey from Bristol to Sky. He said take the show reel home. Watch it a few times. Damned right I would. And Lesley. The kids, even Sally the dog and Daisy the cat. I was a natural.

The Barnes family sat down to see the beginning of a fledgling career in television . . . there I was, smiling, the smile false as the Joker's, still, I could work on that . . . what about the Richard Burton like delivery of the autocue? 'Hello – and welcome to Sky – Sports – coverage of rugby union.' An assassin's smile and a pause long enough to slip into the *Moonlight Sonata*. I – am – Stuart Barnes . . . and I am bringing you [emphasis here] LIVE COVERAGE [oh, but how furrowed the brows] of the English club scene,' . . . enough, flick the off switch. The silence of the sitting room. The shrill tone of the phone breaks the silence. The executive producer, 'Hi, Stuart, I guess you will have seen the screen test by now. I just wanted to tell you not to be too upset, there is plenty of potential . . .' I interrupted, 'That is kind of you, Piers, but I am used to disappointment. I am a big boy and have been dropped enough times by England to take some negative news. It's good of you to call though . . .' He wanted me back in Sky the following week, for another screen test. Forty odd pounds worth of petrol. Me, earning a guaranteed annual income of less than £20,000. I couldn't afford the luxury of such time-wasting. I said as much. Fear of failure now furiously flapping its wings. Flying around the room. 'I'll think about it.' Easier to stay in the West Country and avoid the 'Sod 'em tomorrer' of a second screen test. If I hadn't changed my mind I might have done something useful in this world, or nothing . . . wonder what else Piers saw . . . no other applicants maybe?

Sky Sports' rugby coverage began in 1994/95. Stuart Barnes, recently retired, high profile, low international mileage on the clock. Every Saturday afternoon we came on air an hour before kick-off, went off forty-five minutes after full time. I was obsessed with the links to and from the break. Being a rookie at the Beeb must be so easy, no bloody ad breaks . . . I learned every single link, 'Now we'll take a break, after the break we'll have etc etc.' All day Friday learning links. Determined not to stumble. I rarely did. The price to pay was a woeful woodenness. I thought I was doing fine as I made my monotone way through game after game. To this day the latest generation of Sky rugby employees laugh when they come across old reels, unbelieving when I explain the problem wasn't the autocue but the absence of one. Beginning to end. I was smart enough to memorise it all . . . forgot that I was only ever cast as an attendant in the school plays . . . now I was filling the lead role. In three months I made the transition from a thirty-one-year-old rugby player who thought he knew it all to TV rookie.

Hired as an outspoken expert, I found myself asking prop forwards like Jeff Probyn questions about fly halves. This was a world turned upside down. I soon worked out a way to answer the question before getting to the part where I pose the dilemma to the guest. It was a world of complex subclauses and delayed question marks. Yet nearly a quarter of a century on from my amateur dabbling, the presenter as font of all knowledge is familiar in all forms of televisual life. Sport especially. Too many presenters have the deep-seated fear of being outed as the charlatan among experts. When his or her role is no more than a conduit . . . or was once. Now every person in front of the camera is a star. Whether they have achieved enough to earn our respect, the very fact of television celebrity makes them into stellar objects themselves. The presenter has a critical role. He or she holds the structure of the programme together while bringing wisdom and words from the experts. But we inhabit an age of closed questions. Not, 'How do you think X is playing', rather 'X is playing well/badly, isn't he?' Presenter, reporter, you name it, they'll leave the recipient of their wisdom as often as not with nothing but a 'yes', 'no' or best of all, 'as you just said . . .' for an answer. 'Wow, those guests are useless, all they do is agree with the presenter.' 'Very much so,' is an old football favourite of mine. So the one expert is brought to ground and the ubiquitous expert revealed. Plenty of these are people who look lovingly into cameras from the first screen test onwards. When Sky scratched the experiment with me as presenter and decided to make me into their regular 'pundit', the presenter's role was handed over to the late David Bobin. Old 'Bobo' knew nothing much about the game and that suited him fine . . . 'Your thoughts, Stuart.' There are younger elements within Sky who mock such a style but three open-ended words brings more out in an expert than a convoluted question which invariably finishes . . . 'isn't it' (with no sign of an elusive question mark). The master sports presenter of my lifetime has been Des Lynam, a shrug of the shoulders or a twitch of the moustache to go with his spare sentences.

In the 2017 European Champions Cup final, we 'lost the pictures' (I love that phrase; as if they have a life of their own and have wandered off in Marks and Spencer's food hall) which were replaced with colourful vertical bars all fizzing in vibrant life. Miles apologised for the temporary loss of picture. I said what came immediately into my head, 'Bridget Riley paintings cropping up in the middle of the European Champions final, that is a first.' It wasn't deliberately smarty-arty, it was merely me. How I am and how I think. Indulgent, possibly. But if we are happy to indulge in the mundane, what's wrong with appealing to the educated? It's condescending to think people are all too stupid to either understand a rarely spoken word (and we are not talking Anglo-Saxon obscurity here) or look it up online/in a dictionary. Broadcasters, talk up, not down to people. Dumb talk leads to stupid people. Think politics, friends.

Last night I had a dream. After an all-night broadcast everyone vacated the dream. Without me. In dreams I never drive. My bag, with all my worldly goods, wallet, passport, everything, left on an unguarded bucket seat, gone. Sitting on a cold terrace step, watching the post-match industrial cleaning. The only person remaining without a high visibility jacket. Ready to be swept up with the rubbish. Well, I have been around for the best part of a quarter century, blowing in the wind, here and there. Who needs Freud? An alternative crazy dream used to haunt me. Hasn't plagued me for a while. Confident I know my way around or maybe I have finally cast off the fear of being discovered as the outsider. I'm standing naked. Outside the stadium walls. No idea how to get in. Nor where to locate the commentary position. Time after time, always naked, always exposed. Kick-off minutes away. Vast concrete bowls where a man can cover the entire circumference with every lift shaft looking the same. No one notices my nakedness except me, no one sees the sense of panic. Except me. Those days are done. The worst that can happen isn't that bad. It's only sport.

In the first years of commentary I feared coming up short of words. I would gut the thesaurus on the Thursday before the match. The day before I would approach the job like I used to ready myself as a player for the game. Think through the eighty minutes. Submerged in a boiling bath . . . every eventuality. You can't know which way a game will go unless every player plays his part to perfection – or imperfection – but given enough permutations, you'll have a good idea as to why the game is going which particular way. As a player that enables you to change it, as a broadcaster to explain it. That is predominantly my job.

How does the two-handed commentary work? The lead commentator and the summariser? Miles Harrison gives the viewer the who and the what. I try to explain the how and the why. Miles takes you through the wood, I explain the journey. He talks over the live action – most of the time – I talk over the replays. If he talks too long into the replay there's the chance I will bleed into the restart and the live action. If I talk too long over replays, he's likely to be talking at the next stoppage when I might have a tactical point to make. Little overruns break the flow. But for any new broadcast teams in any sport, it's a good enough rule to keep you on the right path. When we covered the Pro12 league – now Pro14 with the inclusion of two South African sides – Sky in their managerial wisdom, decided an Englishman from Nottingham and his partner from Essex required something slightly less Saxon and the three-handed commentary with an Irish/Welsh/Scottish influence became part of our act. How should that work? Here is my take. The lead commentator says the most but his words carry the least depth. The second voice – me – says less than the lead but delves deeper into the game. The third voice says the least of the trio but every observation is like an acute shaft of light in a rugby darkness. Illuminating. Which none but this third expert (with the help of a clever assistant producer) can spotlight.

There's more to a commentary than the match, of course. Timings are essential from the moment the presenter 'throws' from the studio to the commentary box. Here the 'lead' is king, this is his domain, those purgatorial minutes before the match kicks off. A scene-setter and a taking of the audience through the teams. It takes time to prepare this. How much, you'll have to wait for Miles' *Art of Commentary* book. I'll tell you about my brief role before the referee blows the whistle. Pick out a player or two from each side, succinctly explain his importance to the proceedings. Twenty to thirty seconds tops. Three words per second; so I was told over two decades ago. Much has changed since then. Not time. It only feels like it is moving faster these days. Sixty words minimum, ninety maximum, work on something in between and rehearse. The difference between a rehearsed top and a lazy read through words scribbled earlier that morning is the difference between being a professional and a bum.

I can't claim that I have treated every game the same. A Lions Test match is not the same as Glasgow versus the Dragons but the art is to think them as much the same as possible. This capacity to maintain the highest standards day after day is what has made this current Bob Dylan even greater than ever, as he and his band hit the highest musical standards night after night. Playing on, into his seventies. It's what made Tony McCoy the great National Hunt jockey he was. From Carlisle to Cheltenham, Newton Abbot to Newbury, he gave every horse he rode the full McCoy treatment. He might not have been the most poetic jockey ever to sit in a saddle but like the protagonist in Dylan's *Tangled Up In Blue*, 'the only thing he knew how to do was keep on keeping on . . .' The magic is indeed to be found within the mundane.

Bill McLaren was lucky. Great voice and lovely turn of phrase but lucky. Lucky to broadcast at a time when there was so little live rugby. Those lovingly compiled commentary charts of his were all well and good when live was nothing more than the Five Nations. Day in, day out, week in week out, commentary is now a more gruelling game. More industry than art. Cliff Morgan was an even more, to my ear, poetic broadcast voice but again, he is forever linked in my mind's eye and ear to the 1973 Barbarians versus New Zealand match in Cardiff . . . or was it 1974 or 1972? Cliff played piano. Head of BBC Sport, an apartment looking over the Thames. A cultured colossus with a lilting melody. Would I worship Cliff's voice if I had heard him twice a week?

I don't have that mellifluous tone. I don't have to hit the high notes for the major moments. This is the job of the lead commentator. I have occasionally worked with leads who didn't understand the significance of the impending score. Never with Miles, he is a master of the try. But the flat note has occurred with others. Just the once or twice. The second voice cannot hijack the lead but he can make the same sort of howling noise a fan might make as it dawns on him, the split second before the try or the goal, what brief ecstasy is coming his way. A human voice as a train thundering past . . . part simulation, part genuine excitement. Which is how I see commentary. You can't allow yourself to become lost in the frenzy of the fan. Yet you need the adrenaline that comes with caring. On a good day, it is more instinct come the kick-off. On a drab day, you have to act the part. Admit it's not a very good game but never one short of interest. And that is not a lie. Some of the most interesting games are the worst ones. How to explain all these professionals playing their part like the rude mechanics of *A Midsummer Night's Dream*?

My voice got a little gravelly in 2013, not quite like sand and glue but too strained for my taste. Constant coughing, soreness, complete loss of voice when pushing the cords. Eventually inevitably, paranoia. A device down the throat. Searching for the Big C. Found nothing but wear and tear. The ears, nose and throat consultant suggested I contact a voice coach. She worked with The Royal Shakespeare Company. For a long time with an outstanding actor by the name of Jonathan Slinger. Good enough for me. A lifetime of inappropriate technique was the problem. Commentating from the chest, throwing the voice. A common phrase. 'Throwing'. An awful way to 'project'. The power of the voice resides somewhere down in the gut. Expand the belly and emit the sound. Ever wondered why so many actresses from America and so many people who grew up with Australian soap operas, finish sentences on that irritating high note? They are running out of air. Holding their breath. Worried about the look, the perfection of their figure. Not enough air can be stored in the chest. The strain, the cords, back of the throat and neck, all take a verbal hammering. Opera singers? There's a lot of large ones in a thin person's world. Pavarotti, it all comes from the belly. My voice coach called my well-established stomach a friend. Be proud of it.

Some find my commentary tone harsh. 'Didn't you ever make a mistake?' is a question I have often been asked. No, I didn't . . . scratch that . . . a joke . . . thousands, of course. I have written about a few of the whoppers. Wandering around the maze. But my many mistakes are nothing to do with my words. It isn't about comparing. It is saying as you see. The eighteen-year-old kid who drops a pass . . . I'll not ignore it but hopefully the audience is reminded he's an eighteen-year-old kid. It's the superstars who receive the tongue lash. There is a need of correction, the big names sometimes get away with a mountain of mistakes because of who they are. It's for that reason they merit criticism. And they should be old and ugly enough to take it. I'm not making fun of their mum, or kidding on the subjects of their kids . . . I couldn't care about what they do with their lives. Other than on the field. They are pretty well paid, people pay to see them . . . if Hamlet forgets his lines, the theatre critic doesn't pretend it didn't happen. In rugby we have too much reverence. It's getting better. Maybe you might see it the other way. That we in the media are getting worse. I'll stay bad until the bitter end.

Television is changing. Not just channels. Social media has – we are told by people of the social media age – redefined viewing. The age of exclusivity appears to be drawing to an end, the era of concentration for more than five minutes dead for all bar those of a certain age. Small sound bites replace considered features. Facebook live feeds the one monster, twittering opinions, another. Or maybe I am becoming conservative in my dotage. Maybe every extra year makes a man more nostalgic as the depth of past glories grows ever deeper . . . and the future becomes shorter by the day. Maybe this is what ageing is. Maybe, but I have plenty of rage remaining inside me. Too old to use the training room buzzwords. Too old. It's someone else's language but it's not the truth. It's the same old adages dressed up in new clothes. Ex-players who enter the media can be tempted to reiterate the words of their coach. Let the public into the deeper insights. Understanding Latin in the Middle Ages entered you into conversation with God. Yet to use nothing but the current player speak (and I can think of some whose language is bereft once they stop 'coming round the corners' or 'getting around the edge') is to limit the time these individuals will remain broadcasters. When their wave of coach talk withdraws they'll be stranded high and dry. Nothing left but their moribund stock of dead phrases. Bar a decent command of language and a knowledge of the game, what makes a good commentator? The answer is simple: a great game.

We are attendants, nothing else, we don't even steal a scene or two. Best to remember that. I was part of the Sky rugby department which won a BAFTA. When England stunned the world and drew 26–26 with the supposedly unstoppable All Blacks. Amongst our rivals for the Best Outside Broadcast was the handover of Hong Kong. It's fair to say the award was a surprise. It should have been awarded to the players. We were good but no better than any of a hundred other games. It is rare for viewers to criticise a broadcast when the game is good. We are barely noticed. That is how it should be. When the match is awful, so are we perceived, our criticisms, our replays, you name it. Television is only as good as its product. Such is the perception and perception is . . . well, you've seen how it goes with politics.

Am I biased? Apparently so . . . the non-English accuse me of being a John Bull patriot. English fans despise my lack of patriotism. I'll take that as a compliment. And reiterate. I am no patriot, a scoundrel in other ways perhaps . . . I never stood proud for England. I did for Bath but these were my brothers. For any ex-player wishing to break into the broadcast game, loads of caps help, ethnicity isn't a hindrance. I once would have said to be any good, being a bit of a bastard is essential. It was for me. The first years as a rookie in television are not always easy. The same criteria as becoming a writer. I criticised former team mates, berated friends, lost a few of those friendships along the way. I had to be – or appear to be – cold. I hope the next generation still need that critical edge but I wonder. Is sport entering an age where it is little more than another branch of light entertainment? Where criticism cannot be accepted in our totalitarian spirit of fun. 'It is only a game.' It is, but the trick of sport is to pretend otherwise . . . in the broader reality it does not matter. In the eighty minutes of the game, it is everything. Television has to tread carefully between these two differing realities.

UP AND UNDER

TUESDAY NIGHTS. Hurry through the history O level essay on Henry VII and ready yourself for the finest forty minutes of the working week – floodlit rugby league. I think that's what the programme was called, *Floodlit Rugby League*. I could navigate my way around maps of England and Europe courtesy of my youthful obsession with the Football League and European Cup, Cup Winners' Cup and Inter-Cities Fairs Cup. Now I was to search the map for Salford and St Helens. A sodden somewhere in the grey drizzle of the industrial north. The programme was introduced by Eddie Waring. The first half had inevitably been a fine forty minutes of rugby. The second half was bound to be even better. Rugby league draped itself in its protective clothing of hype long before my old mates from Sky, Eddie and Stevo, wove their extravagant yet homely spells. Eddie Waring (not Hemmings) wore a pork pie hat . . . well, in my memory that's what sat atop his head, slant angle, a smile to warm a cold night in Wakefield.

We all get a thrill from sport under lights. Football is ten per cent quicker when the lights sparkle, I swear it is. The green of the pitch more verdant. The speed of the pass quicker. Pinball-paced football. With *Floodlit Rugby League*, mainly it was the swirl of rain the lights exaggerated, the loamy hue of the muddy pitch enhanced. But it was sport, a strange form of rugby and it was live on BBC 2. A long way from Lord Reith's vision. Rugby league, as a sport, was a separate identity. In South Wales it was a bit of a bogeyman. Its henchmen arrived at Welsh internationals' houses in the middle of the night. Briefcases full of used tenners. Carried Dai Watkins away from Newport. Malign folk tales. We didn't bother with the BBC's league coverage on a Saturday afternoon. Why would you when you could be watching Aberavon versus Newport, or Newbridge versus Neath? No record button. And it certainly wasn't mentioned in the Saturday rags, not outside Lancashire and Yorkshire anyway. *The South Wales Argus* had all the football and union scores, hot off the press in the pink 'un, even some of the English rugby club results . . . but league? League was an oasis of midweek magic when sport slipped into televisual slots until then designated for *Play for the Day*. Some rerunning of a kitchen sink drama . . . moan, moan, moan . . . who is this Pinter bloke, dad?

You will still search in vain for much in-depth coverage of league in the national papers. League has a home on Sky with the most loyal of family fan bases. *The Guardian* has reasonable coverage. A nod to the *Manchester Guardian*. Left-wing intellectuals taking to the working-class game. David Storey was a former league player. The man who wrote *This Sporting Life*. Another grim tale where the plotline is thick with coal dust and despair. I didn't see the link with Wales back then. A successful professional sportsman whose emotional life is in tatters. Oscar nominations. Awards at Cannes. The world loves to show its sympathies with those less fortunate. Ken Loach. *Billy Elliot*. The film where Welsh miners and metrosexual gays get together for a terrific tear jerker in the Valleys. The title escapes me. Idris Elba starred as a rugby union player with some sort of sorry love life. Set in London. The film went straight to television. Not talking high-budget drama series either. *100 Streets*? I don't know . . . a cosmopolitan version of *This Sporting Life*? No wonder it didn't bust many blocks. Who imagined union players having the tough sort of life Richard Harris portrayed fifty-five or so years ago? Perception. And union is seen as the middle- and upper-middle-class game. No matter that football is more to the Eton taste. 'Ra Ra'. The nickname some league fans have bestowed upon union tells you all you need to know about the perception of the game in league heartlands.

The difference between union and league isn't simply a matter of extra speed (league) or extra complexity (union), it is class. Our politicians tell us that class is dead but contrast a day watching Wigan or Bath and you'll see that ours remains a divided nation. Does union have an air of superiority? Does league have a chip on its Harry Ramsden fish and chip shop shoulder (see, I can't help myself and I am on the side of the working man; whatever that is)? All very silly but true. When the crowd flock to Bath, it is a social gathering. When you watch Wigan it is a communal coming together. 1895 (*Sketches from Memory* making a late dash for the history section of your local bookshop) and the Northern Rugby Football Union break away from the Rugby Football Union. Even then based in the decidedly non-working-class Twickenham. In a nutshell, the northern clubs wanted payment for those players who lost out on income due to rugby commitments. As nobody has ever 'grafted' for a living within ten square miles of an area affectionately known as 'HQ', the RFU were horrified at an outbreak which linked the northern clubs with gathering socialist rumblings. As Europe prepared to tear itself apart in the twenty-first century. And so, at the George Hotel Huddersfield, twenty-two northern clubs broke away. The RFU issued sanctions. Amateurs, as well as professionals, were barred from the RFU if in any way affiliated to, besmirched by, the Northern Union. This was the moment when England lost the services of their best and most competitive sportsman as well as the most decent of all Englishmen. Think Shakespeare's Hotspur; union had that gadabout, Prince Hal. The myth of the mighty northern man.

The game began to evolve in different ways. Because Northern Working Man was obviously innately less intelligent than his public school-educated counterpart, league lost two players per side, league selectors finding it increasingly impossible to remember what numbers came after thirteen. Lineouts have always been union's version of Bletchley Park when it comes to cracking codes. Simply wasted on those northern wooden tops . . . drop the lineouts. As for proper scrums, these lazy unemployed sorts didn't have the pluck to work for a living. Scrums were beyond their limited moral fibre. And so the same game diverged in different directions. Union settled smugly into its amateur ways, sneering from the committee rooms of HQ. League lambasted every man ever to play union as the equivalent to those in the cavalry ranks whose bloody behaviour gave us the Peterloo massacre and a poem by Shelley, or was it Byron? For the best part of a century, battle lines were drawn. We had Nigel Starmer-Smith. They had Eddie Waring and his 'oopunurnder'. Some union commentators and writers of an extremely conservative disposition didn't even use the warm Waring phrase for a high ball. It came tarnished out of those polluted northern skies. 'Garryowen' was the new traditional name. An old club based in Limerick . . . the first place where a ball was kicked high. Yeah, sure. And William Webb Ellis picked up that ball in the grounds of Rugby school and ran like Forrest Gump. At some stage I switched from saying 'up and under' to 'Garryowen', probably when Oxford turned me into the toff most league fans now recognise me as.

1895, 1819, it's all getting a little too fusty. Let us ignore the best part of the twentieth century (including the shameful

1940s when the FFR collaborated with Vichy to get their hands on rugby league's assets) and focus on the last decade of the twentieth century. The last decade of amateurism. The 1990s. Dave Alred is not yet an official England kicking coach but he is building a reputation at the Recreation Ground. An England training session at Twickenham is winding to an end. This is when we do the absolute essentials like restarts . . . when we are all knackered. But that's the way amateurism was, you couldn't do it all. Still, Dick Best, the England coach, had shown some initiative, phoned Dave, asked him to turn up on a Sunday morning. At Twickenham. Work on the kick-off . . . good thinking, except the late Don Rutherford, the secretary of the RFU, sees the former rugby league man stride onto the sacred turf. Into the inner sanctum of HQ. He runs screaming out from wherever he is – puce – demanding the removal of the kicking guru. Who had once and briefly crossed codes before his move to American football. There can be no link between the two codes. Never shall their paths cross. Dave is shown the door and will not return to Twickenham until the game has become professional. It makes me wonder, all these years on, did Bath break the rules by allowing him to coach at the club, even though the then schoolteacher was paid the same rounded sum as the rest of us? Instinct says who gives a shit but maybe we could be stripped of all our titles.

In Brian Ashton, Bath already had a devotee of the Northern Union. A visionary in a union land where visionaries were not trusted, Ashton was one of the most influential coaches in the latter years of the amateur age and the early days of professional rugby union. Brian analysed league's running lines and their decoys, the constant subtlety of the sport's changing ways. He studied defence but only to work out ways to outwit it. In this he was radically different to all that was set to come with the onset of professionalism and the landslide that would be league's influence on union. Ashton was the positive to the negative that travelled south and engulfed union. League was to make defence king with Ashton's attacking voice friendless in the wilderness. It is easier to destroy than create. More the human instinct, for all the popularity of Lego. From the wild northern fastnesses came the men who would change the face of the English game. In terms of professional detail in the latter years of amateurism there was no club in England approaching Bath. Yet to watch our defensive drill was to see something as much an afterthought as an England restart session. Drift today, cut open tomorrow. So it was when we played Wasps in a final in the mid-'80s. We were confident enough in our thinking to change back to the more familiar man-on-man system before the half-time team talk. Just as well. Someone's throwaway thought to drift in defence could have cost us a final . . . but why did we want to spend so much time on defence when we had all these attacking threats? Attacking moves were harder to master. More satisfactory. Making the evening after work seem a sacrifice worthwhile. Especially when a move cut open another hapless defence on the weekend. Running free was part of what being an unpaid player was.

Professionalism brought extra preparation time. Cut down on the smiles. With this arose the oppressive obsession that was defence. Had there not been extra hours to train there would still have been the same diligence due to defence and probably even less attacking preparation time. If that was possible. League had its attack men – like union – but union had never spent long thinking through defence. Here the professional outlook radicalised the way we contemplated rugby. Rugby without the ball. A new concept. Two men led the way: Phil Larder and Shaun Edwards. The one became a World Cup-winning defence coach for England (following in the footsteps of John Muggleton, another league coach who had built an outstanding Australian defence on which they based their 1999 World Cup triumph), the other a cult figure within the English and Welsh game.

Edwards had the slogan 'Defences win titles' plastered on the walls of the Wasps changing room and tunnel complex. The last subliminal message before kick-off. The former Wigan scrum half's union coaching will end unfulfilled, illustrious as it has been with both Wasps and Wales. Because of the reputation built upon his defensive record. He would have been an equally good offensive coach. Full of wiles. His defence was not subtle. It was constant pressure. An attempt to mug time itself. No time to allow opponents time on the ball, to run, catch and pass. No time to think. Ironically, he has always known the game he plays is that of the high-risk bluffer. 'The best teams could cut a system like ours to pieces,' he told me over a decade ago, then paused and added, 'but they'd have to be bloody good.' The club teams tended not to be quite good enough. Wasps went on a trophy-grabbing rampage in England and Europe. New Zealand, however, they have that extra bit of quality and in the Edwards era Wales have yet to beat them as I write. The success of Shaun has convinced every club that defence comes first. It is a fallacy based upon a lack of attacking conviction. Andy Farrell's recent rush defence with the Lions and the Irish Grand Slam side boosted the reputation of league's legion even further. Did he make a genuine breakthrough in 2017? Blunted the All Blacks. Will mid-term redevelopment cost New Zealand? We'll see in Japan. I haven't forsaken my faith in attack.

Larder was a superb defensive coach who didn't want to pick Will Greenwood, whose attacking brain brought out the best in Wilkinson. Larder was a sceptic. He once confided Greenwood's tackling wasn't up to Test standards. I walked away wondering what a coach's job is, if it isn't to improve a man's weaknesses. Fortunately, Clive Woodward came to another point of view. Greenwood knuckled down. Anyone can do it. Defence is more about will power than any innate skill. The gym sets a man up for his defensive chores. Whereas nothing except endless hours of practice, technique and something special can turn you into Dan Carter. There are lots of tremendous tacklers, there are fewer balanced runners. Fewer maestros. The influx of league's professional defensive systems, so new to old amateur union, set offensive play back a decade in the northern hemisphere. We are still getting over this decade-plus of austerity in attack.

Personal memories? 1996. I worked for Sky on the much-hyped cross-code challenge between Wigan and Bath at Maine Road, Manchester. Under league rules. It was awful. There was no austerity in the Wigan approach. They came at my old club from angles union players had rarely, if ever, seen. 82–6, a week after Bath were winning the cup against Leicester at Twickenham to secure a fourth league and cup double. Union and Bath humbled. Under union rules Bath won the rematch 44–15. Where Bath had looked bereft under unfamiliar rules in Manchester, now Wigan were wondering which way the Bath attacks would come next. Initially they came through the middle, around the fringes. Areas where Wigan were not used to the cascading surge of forward after forward. Pick and drive, pick and drive. In the second half Bath loosened up and allowed Wigan to avoid a bloody retribution. My old club went on to win a European cup but the manner in which they failed to subject Wigan to a revenge beating told me the bad old great days were ending. HQ, according to Maurice Lindsay, only agreed to host the rematch when the Millennium Stadium bid for the game. The enemy had hardly been welcomed at the gate . . . except for an unforgivably generous second half from Bath.

Elsewhere the cross-code borders were about to open the other way as the financially stronger game of union seduced the stars of league with what seemed then like staggering sums of money. Bath signed Jason Robinson and Henry Paul for a brief spell. But it was Robinson's return to union with Sale that was to signal the most successful of all league-to-union transfers. He would, and will, always be remembered as a dual code great. He began his union career in confusion. Clever teams would kick the ball to him. Pin him in the corner. He'd always dodge one, maybe two, but then the third and the fourth would collar him. He couldn't get up and wriggle his bottom now, could only concede the penalty for holding onto the ball or face being turned over in the tackle. He had to learn to kick and when to kick. He did that and by 2001 he was a Lions star, by 2003 a World Cup winner. For all his coruscating movement he worked hard at his game. Playing either winger or full back is the ideal position for someone making the transition from league to union. The least problematic switch. The further from the action the less a player has to think. In rugby league, you can 'have a go' and if you are tackled, shovel the ball through the legs. In union, you have no such option. Every step you take brings you nearer the safety of retention or the threat of turnover. When to kick, when to open up. League is quicker but it seems predominantly a preordained game. A hybrid, part American football, part rugby union. This has caused untold problems for the big league lads who fancy a crack at union.

Here I offer you the most stupid fallacy in all of sport. League forwards are more skilful than union forwards. There are NO league forwards. They don't scrum, they don't jump, they don't hit the breakdown, there is no need to endure the pain of a union prop. As soon as the ball is out of the 'scrum' everyone is a back. And here is where the translation gets difficult. It happened in the case of two league legends, Farrell and Sam Burgess. They made the journey from league to union. Two big men but neither of the exceptional bulk to muscle into the pack, neither quick enough to be a back. Farrell played without impact in the 2007 World Cup. The selection enhanced neither coach nor convert's reputation. Farrell was all hype, Burgess mainly hype. People wanted them to succeed or flop. Few bothered to reflect on the reality and the grey existing between black and white.

The reality was sporting insanity. Playing flanker or inside centre (the usual position for both men in union) requires as many small decisions to be made per match as any position on the field. It takes a union-reared flanker a career to understand when and when not to hit a ruck. We were expecting these rookies to master millions of tiny little complexities because of their expertise in another code. Bath got the hang of hubris when Mike Ford started telling the watching (were they?) world that Burgess was set to redefine the positional play of union when all he was about to do was create meltdown in the England 2015 World Cup campaign. It was palpably obvious that Farrell was too far past his prime when he arrived in union. Burgess lacked time to make himself into a top class Premiership player, let alone a rushed international without a defined position.

It didn't help that in 2015 Farrell was a key member of the England management team. When some Bath DIY Salesman of the Week picked Burgess as his man of the match against London Irish at the Recreation Ground, Farrell used the award to justify his high opinion of the league convert. That's how it went. Farrell was always going to back him. The Wigan legend saw too much of himself in Burgess. Given a fresh set of legs I bet Andy still thinks he would have cracked union – maybe he would – well, here was a younger version with Farrell pushing all the way. Stuart Lancaster's biggest error (or one of several when the subject of selection crops up) was to bow to the pressure of the other England coaches in the Burgess debate. Stuart was less convinced about Big Sam than the rest. Those of us who were in disparaging mood, who based judgement on our own eyes, were not warmly received in league heartlands. Political correctness is on the side of league. It's that class divide again.

Subtle but simmering throughout. Never mind if neither of them were remotely worth a single cap on merit. As opposed to being picked on potential. Both were picked on nothing but hot air and wild hope.

Union takes time to figure out tactically in a way league does not. That is a strength and weakness of both games. In an age where entertainment comes with easy to understand explanations, league benefits from the simpler structure. To direct a game of union, the TV director is forever cutting between the tight, wide and the variety of kick. In league, there tend to be four or five runs and then the kick; 'tight, tight, tight, tight, tight, wide'. And so on. Directing by numbers. It's draughts as opposed to chess. That's how I see it.

Union has the advantage of a World Cup that isn't global like, say, the football World Cup, but is another scale of globalisation compared to league and its limited little competition. Australia lose every now and again and that is about it. League fans will say the same about the All Blacks but there is real diversity when the world of rugby union comes together. That is why the TV companies pay the big bucks for the one World Cup and not the other. League fans are limited in number but devoted, loyal to league. Pretty much the same number of viewers tune into Sky's coverage every game. They are a tribe. Outstanding fans but you feel the tide of inevitability is lapping at their feet. Now that the amateurs have finally taken the professional route. If you are reading this in Australia please discount the entire chapter. An exceptional land of league. The exception which only proves the rule.

VILLAINS

ONE MAN'S villain is another's hero. Take Milton Friedman, for example. Hero to the Free Market fundamentalists. Villain to many who have suffered the often savage implementation of his and his disciples' privatisation policies with its ensuing human rights 'hiccups' and austerity. Or worse. The bogeyman to what remains of any coherent global political left. A visionary if you happened to be Ronald Reagan, Margaret Thatcher or part of the elite minority in Chile, Argentina, South Africa and elsewhere from the 1970s onwards. I have been reading my essential Naomi Klein.

I'm glad Milt never turned his beady eye on our little sport. He would have concocted policies for the good of the international game. Business would have either fed the Test match money-making beast or union would have withered on the vine. Now there's a word beginning with 'V' that lifts the spirits. Wish I'd titled this chapter, vines. True, I might have struggled to finish it. Might have worked the spell checker to death. Popping corks and typing away. Another contender was the word 'vandal'. It fits the bill equally well.

The battleground is not Chile. It is Wales at the turn of the millennium. 2002 is a confident guess. My 'villain' is a man called David Moffett. He's a hero to some. Moffett was born in Doncaster, raised in Brisbane, renowned in New Zealand. A lot of people thought him a Kiwi when he came to Wales to save their national game. A little like Friedman and his acolytes, he had the one-stop ideology. Tear the guts out of the small town teams and create 'super teams'. He was amongst the founding thinkers behind Super Rugby. Super 10, Super 12 . . . he left before it stretched to fifteen and the recently over-bloated eighteen. It has stopped being Super any more. The number of teams is set to dwindle. Less is more. Moffett, never a man short of a word, predicted the problems of an eighteen-team tournament well in advance of its implementation. He's no fool. But a villain in many Welsh eyes. And a vandal.

Super franchises seem to work in New Zealand. A small population with a relatively large land mass. Bar Auckland and Wellington there are no substantial cities. The tragedy of the Christchurch earthquake only emphasises the fact. Rugby is about the All Blacks first. And second. Provincial rugby third. Club rugby is junior partner to provincial rugby. Before Super Rugby there was the National Provincial Championship. Still is, but it has been relegated in importance. This was where support was once strongest and passion greatest. The Ranfurly Shield was the stuff of legend. The evolution from province to franchise was an easy one. Teams with player and supporter bases covering substantial chunks of the country. It was hugely beneficial to the national team. Fewer teams. Greater strength in depth. Superior standards. New Zealand began winning more and more.

Wales wanted what Moffett had. A seemingly magic touch. Offered him enough money to lure him from the land of the long white cloud to the Principality. A love of rugby, a lot of sheep. The similarities between countries existed. Skin deep.

Wales doesn't have much of a population either. Not compared to its nemesis neighbour east of the Severn. Unlike New Zealand, however, it has no great land mass. North Wales does not share its southern equivalent's feel for the game. Rugby union is not played in much of Wales. In north and mid Wales it is an afterthought – like league in New Zealand. The sport follows the M4 corridor west from Newport to Llanelli. An hour or so with the foot down. Once there were some good quality diversions. The valleys. Pontypridd in the Rhondda. Newbridge, Abertillery, Cross Keys and Tredegar in the Gwent Valleys. There was also Pontypool. The legendary side through the seventies and eighties. Pontypool Park and a meeting with what was known as Viet Gwent. The Welsh front row of Graham Price, Bobby Windsor and Charlie Faulkner. Charlie, first senior coach in my fledgling Newport days.

Days when we knew an away trip up the valleys would be eighty minutes of unbridled hostility. When the number of doctors in tow doubled for a midweek visit to Pontypool. Newport, a town on its downers, was seen as the city slickers in the minds of valley men. Across the county border in Glamorgan, Pontypridd were waiting to give the capital city Cardiff side an equally good going over. I witnessed a lot more of these matches than I played in. Hard games. Hard men. Good crowds. Swansea versus Llanelli would squeeze 15,000 into St Helens for the west Wales derby game. Pontypool would likewise be packed, the bank throbbing, when Cardiff dared to leave their decadent lair. In the 1970s the best club rugby was played in Wales and France. And the crowds reflected it. France, their club rugby predominantly played in the small towns of the south-west. Wales on the urban stretch of motorway and valleys famed for their coal mining industry. The mines went first. The communities stayed tight. One of the foundations of these economically challenged communities was the rugby club. Secular church for Methodists. To go to a game at Pandy Park in Cross Keys, or Eugene Cross Park in Ebbw Vale, was to see a community represented on the pitch with pride. Passion off it. A visiting team could forgive a good kicking in the interest of local solidarity. As in New Zealand, the national team was the pride of the nation but the local club, I suspect, had a slightly greater role in the social life of the valleys than the more far-flung Kiwi clubs. None of this made a mark on the Doncaster-born businessman. He had his way of doing things. Good enough for the strongest rugby nation in the world? Bound to work in little old Wales . . .

Never mind the impact upon the established clubs and their communities. All that mattered was the elite end of affairs. The national team. If they thrived, the impact would benefit the entire rugby nation. We were experiencing Friedman, Thatcher and Reagan's trickle-down politics. The rugby fields of Wales the testing grounds. And so Moffett, with the help of the WRU, vandalised one of the greatest of all Welsh heritages. Its wonderful club game. Claiming Wales lacked the player depth to sustain the old ways and all those senior clubs, he broke the game apart. Created five professional teams. The supporters are yet to give the decision the seal of approval. Not with their hearts. Heads. Feet. Crowds collapsed and are still nothing like they were in what, I admit, feels suspiciously like nostalgic good old days as I ruminate from the comfort of my office. Whatever they were, the fans supported the game in greater numbers.

Whole swathes of community broke away when the Big Five came into being. Newport Gwent Dragons were one of those five initial franchises, Super Teams, call them what you will. The Gwent Valley teams and Pontypool went from proud community to 'big city' feeder overnight. In the west, Swansea and Neath, near neighbours, historical rivals, were suddenly neither the black of Neath nor the white of Swansea. Neither one club nor the other. The fans were not fooled into following a team devoid of any historical sort of identity. Llanelli and Cardiff initially remained pretty much themselves with the fifth region, the Celtic Warriors, a combination of those belligerent yet warm rugby clubs, Bridgend and Pontypridd. The Warriors folded quickly. Financial woes. The WRU bought and disbanded them. More asset stripping. Leighton Samuel, the initial Warriors owner, claimed he sold his remaining fifty per cent share on a promise that the team would not be disbanded. The WRU settled their dispute with Samuel out of court. Bridgend are now under the wings of the Ospreys while Pontypridd fans have to travel to Cardiff for their Pro14 rugby.

The fans are too often forgotten. Or taken for granted. Without the support, the atmosphere, sport is intrinsically revealed as the trivial game it is. It needs the noise and the colour to convince television watchers this must indeed be an important event. Forget the quality. French rugby has long relied on atmosphere to seduce their television broadcast partners into spending vast sums of money on the Top 14. English club rugby is getting the hang of atmosphere. That atmosphere is absent in South Wales. The great Identity Snatch has done inexorable damage to the Welsh professional game.

Were there any alternatives? Not according to Moffett and his supporters. It's all about the economy, stupid. A Bill Clinton campaign? Anyway, it is not just the dosh. It is about so much more that cannot be valued in spreadsheets, profit and loss . . . but let's consider the case set out by Moffett. The WRU was in the shit when Moffett arrived in 2002. Before his involvement with SANZAR (South Africa, New Zealand, Australia Rugby) he had worked in the waste management sector. He was going to clear Wales up or dump them deeper in it. Here's what his supporters will say. A loss of £3.7 million was turned into a profit of £3.6 million. So much for the business side of it. On the field he has since reminded critics Wales had won nothing in the quarter century before the creation of the Welsh 'super sides'. By 2005 the red dragons were winning the first of their two Grand Slams of the decade. Profitable off and winning on the field. It seems a strong case. In one way it is. From the top down the initial decisions to slash and burn the club game is a tough one to refute. Judged from the grass roots up there are a few more questions in need of answering.

Everything he did was for the benefit of the national side. Wales simply have to do well. In the Six Nations they have been successful. While they have won titles and Grand Slams, beating England a few times in the process, well, all is well. What next, however, when Wales have a bad Six Nations, or a few bad Six Nations? Or to be more exact, what happens to the support base? Forty years ago, a club collision . . . Aberavon versus Maesteg or Llanelli versus Bridgend, would draw the local communities together. Rugby life beyond the national one. A chance to recover from the trauma of losing at Twickenham. Now all that is gone. There is competition of course. But for the big clubs it is downgraded to an insular, lower grade amateurism undreamed of in the 1970s. Too many chips have been placed on the success of the national side. If Wales have two or three bad years, the sport will come crashing down around the ears of faltering Welsh fans.

The echoing emptiness that is Rodney Parade emphasises the decline of the club game. The Blues cannot find a way to fill the famous old Arms Park. The Scarlets – Pro12 champions in 2017 – have only the once rekindled the one-time Llanelli Stradey Park atmosphere in their so far so soulless Parc Y Scarlets. English broadcasters fell briefly in love with the west. But Wales is threatened with rugby stagnation. Outside of the Test team (and they are no longer selling out the Principality Stadium for the autumn internationals) there are too many gaping holes in the terraces, vacant seats in the stands. The roots need sunlight.

Moffett hit the headlines again in 2016. He admitted the Welsh system he put in place was no longer working. The truth is that it never did. But short-term success can mask long-term failure. Super Rugby and New Zealand could yet suffer from their own declining attendances. Products created for the benefits of the national elite and the sport broadcasters confuse the quality of the individual performer with the communal needs of the supporter base. New Zealand are enjoying an outstanding run of success in Super Rugby but the only worthwhile crowds come when they play one another. It's partly the fact these tend to be the best games but also the lack of interest in teams with their made-up marketing names. Rebels, Sunwolves, Sharks. I noticed that during the 2017 Lions tour a few of my Sky colleagues began to refer to the Blues as 'the Auckland Blues' and the Hurricanes as 'Wellington Hurricanes'. Substantial inaccuracies. Mistakes these professionals would not make back in Britain and Ireland. As if the 'traditions' of a Lions tour almost seduced them into talking of a former era. Playing against towns, cities, not franchises.

We had our moments of madness in England. In the last few years before the game went professional, someone came up with the idea of the Divisional Championship. The South West. London. The Midlands and the North. In theory it was fine. The North, with its fewer large-scale clubs, would give some players a good opportunity to press their claims in front of England selectors. The South West comprised Gloucester, Bristol and Bath. A backs coach so bad we had to eject him from a training session the week before one match. The Bath backs were the basis of the back line. We stood flat. Played it the Ashton way. On the gain line. Over it. And used our favourite strike moves. Moves that ripped most opposing defences to shreds. Our backs coach was a decent man. Went onto greater things within the RFU, so I heard. But he was useless. Too nice to name. Perhaps he improved. I don't know. I do know he told us our moves couldn't work if we stood so flat. That we needed to drop deeper. No trick of the memory that we exiled him to the changing rooms, out of the elements, when he wouldn't stop pestering us. Dumped him. This drop in coaching standards. The Bath boys couldn't stand it. We won the bloody thing in my last year as captain. The year before or after I quit the competition. They booed us onto the field in Gloucester. Too few Cherry and Whites in the team. Great club fans that they are, this Divisional tournament didn't fool them. The Shed knew a load of cosmetic crap when they saw it. A crummy little competition. Interesting that in the early years of professionalism, Cliff Brittle, a major player within the RFU for a brief and controversial time, and Fran Cotton were keen to make the Divisional Championship into something big. Fran is a smart operator. A shrewd man. Intent on undermining the club scene which was veering further and further from his perceived requirements of the England national team. Cotton conceived of the competition as a way in which Twickenham could begin to grasp control of the players. It was a no-hoper from the beginning. English fans, like their Welsh counterparts, are generally urban dwellers. We support our cities, our towns, not some tenuous regionalisation. Doubtless had Twickenham won the battle, the four teams would have been given some ludicrous names to try and con the supporters . . . how stupid do they think we are?

Pretty stupid. At least in Wales. Swansea fans were going to flock into the Liberty Stadium to watch the Ospreys? A fine hunting bird Dylan Thomas doubtless admired looking out over the bay from his writing room in Laugharne. A shortage of poets and bird watchers put paid to that one. Then there's my first team, the Newport Gwent Dragons. Coal and steel. Used to be plenty of both in the valleys, but dragons? We east Wales kids reckoned they were more likely to be sighted spouting furious guttural Welsh in west Wales. As for the Blues and the Scarlets, there are a couple of names unlikely to stir the soul . . .

The world is yet to see a divisional, regional, franchise tournament proposed in France. Our French friends are not averse to madness in the realm of rugby but they do at least understand the sanctity of the clock tower. The locals come running on the chimes. Unites the citizens like nothing else. The camaraderie of the community. Winning is all. Especially on home soil. The mentality has turned the Top 14 into an at times astonishingly drab competition but there's no rugby tournament to touch it for vibrancy on the terraces. France still retains the communal attachment. This is just as well. The national team has struggled for the best part of the decade but the club game has lost none of its allure for all the failure of the French national team. The clubs are part of the problem, but a part the people put up with. Which makes me wonder . . . come August and your club is back playing. France suffer another series whitewash in South Africa? C'est la vie and a Gallic shoulder shrug . . . now think football. Every four years the male population of England readies itself for the long-awaited repetition of 1966. The immediate disappointment is abject but Manchester United are playing Arsenal and Liverpool meet Tottenham on the opening day of the season and few remember the national failure. Football has many faults but for all the financial madness isn't there a solace to be found in the fanaticism of the club fans? Week after week. Local loyalties. South of the Avon, Bristol City. North and it is Bristol Rovers. Hundreds coming down from Huddersfield to follow their lads. What should rugby emulate? The club game or the elite end international competition that once generated nearly all interest in union until the advent of professionalism and live club rugby? Ideally it's the balance between that's required. That's not what Moffett was after. A Welsh way of doing things was subjugated to the requirements of the international team. The undoubted problems faced by Wales at the turn of the century were all but irrelevant. Moffett had his template and he was going to do it his way. Come what may.

Too much has changed for the worse. The good to have come from his sweeping changes needed to be great. The improvements are dubious. At best. At the time of the first draft of this book in 2017 there was a tier two Premiership table including names like Newport, Neath, Bridgend, Swansea, Llanelli and Cardiff. A ring-fenced WRU Championship below it. Where Pontypool could not be promoted and where Tata Steel finished third. Am I getting conservative in my fifties or is this really too much slippage and sliding to handle? I was distracted by my immersion in the subject, taken briefly back in time by those Welsh rugby tables. Places from my past. Some clubs in the WRU League Two East. Hartridge – surely the same Hartridge where I lost my first ever game of rugby. I didn't have a clue they had a club. Abercarn. The first game of adult rugby I ever played. On a Sunday morning. My dad, sales manager at Thames Case, one of the many vice chairmen of the club. Proud of his fifteen-year-old boy. Starting out. Nantyglo; the name disappeared from memory until now. Coldest place Baize-leg first XV ever played. Windswept. Ice sheets. Somewhere near the heads of the valleys. A brutal Saturday morning . . . finally, Senghenydd. My first film role. Seventy-five years of the WRU celebration. The narrator, Richard Burton. The boy Barnes ran up what would now feel like Everest to old Stuart Barnes, a mere hill to the younger version back then. Camera trailed me. Artistically. The future of Wales. Later in the film I will swerve and step an entire team of white-clad men . . . no prizes for guessing the intimated enemy . . . all beaten and bamboozled in slow motion. The try. The entitled one. Anointed by the powers that be within the Welsh Rugby Union . . . a Sunday in Senghenydd . . . we all believed it was from places like Abercarn, Senghenydd, Hartridge (the mighty Torchie) and Nantyglo that Welsh rugby would thrive and forever flourish. From the roots. David Moffett and his fundamentalist top down ways ripped up the roots . . . in my eyes he is one of the worst villains to have visited Wales. Up there with Thatcher. Did she ever cross the Severn?

The title of this chapter is 'Villains'. It could have been 'Vandals'. Both in the plural. Having written 3,000 words on the impact of the man from waste management, it would be far too harsh to include idolised fly halves whose mechanised approach stripped the position of its poetry. Wrong to even mention not so sporting spin doctors for the hash they made of one of rugby's most famous teams on tour. I think the RFU remains worth a mention for its disgusting decision to ignore the international boycott and travel to South Africa in 1984. Ditto the All Black team which went there under the name of the New Zealand Cavaliers. Denis Thatcher, that former rugby referee and much welcomed guest on the rugby dinner circuit, had his South African business connections. His wife was a staunch defender of the apartheid regime . . . these people merit naming. Not so the violent players of my times. If they whacked me I probably deserved it. If my mates did something atrocious there was usually a reason. Even if there wasn't we would get pissed and forget about it afterwards. Some things though, some things should never be forgotten.

WORLD CUP, 1995

24 JUNE 1995 is a date I will never forget. Ellis Park, a bastion, no, call it a cathedral for Afrikaners, sends out a guttural roar which reverberates from one side of Johannesburg to the other. Nelson Mandela walks onto the pitch to greet the South Africans and New Zealanders who will contest the World Cup final. He's wearing a replica number six shirt, as worn by the white boy from Witbank, Francois Pienaar. The Springbok captain. The Springboks, a team historically synonymous with racism. The roar is unleashed. It echoes around Africa, let alone Ellis Park, gathering intensity all the time. Nelson Mandela, Nelson Mandela... 'Free Nelson Mandela, I'm begging you, I'm begging you.' Even British schoolkids revered Nelson Mandela. The hope of a continent if you were black, coloured or liberal. A world figure of genuine gravitas.

But he was also a terrorist, a man with blood on his hands, imprisoned on Robben Island. He was the most dangerous man in Africa if you thought like the average braai-barbecuing rum-drinking Afrikaners. Or Mrs Thatcher. But now he was the inspiration for South Africa, for mankind. Rugby administrators rushed to reinvent themselves. Players found a little liberal love for everyone living beneath the rainbow. As exercises in mass delusion go, Nelson pulled off one of the greatest tricks of all. It couldn't last. It didn't last. The end of poverty was a popular dream, corruption cut out its heart as it transmogrified from white to black. At least corruption has no colour barriers. Still, without Mandela, South Africa would have had a great deal more than the All Blacks with which to concern themselves. As it was, the nation united, perhaps for a first time that day, black and white, the oppressed cheering on the oppressors, the whites for once their team, Chester Williams as well.

Sporting legend has it the All Blacks were poisoned. The players who went out of the hotel to eat on the night in question say they didn't suffer the symptoms. The hotel maintains the All Blacks ate out against their advice and suffered the consequences. What I would like to know is who the world's conspiracy theorists think was behind this 'attack'? Did the South African rugby authorities invoke the spirit of *broederbond* in the bowels of the hotel kitchen or did the conspiracy go deeper? Did it go all the way to the heart of government then in Pretoria? If Mandela's men had once been prepared to kill to end apartheid, what's the big deal with New Zealand suffering a couple of days of misery and losing a game of rugby set against the cause of binding a nation together? To the All Blacks it was understandably quite some deal but compared to what South Africa had suffered, what it had been through . . . it was nothing. Or maybe New Zealand made it up. Couldn't take defeat. Crooked chef or poisonous PR man. You can choose whichever reality best suits your needs. You decide history.

I don't remember whether Mandela was on the field or not when the South African Airways plane flew from seemingly nowhere over the stadium. Blue sky, sun, the plane puncturing the heavens. For a split second we cowered in the press box. Unaware of what the next century had in store for America. This plane revealed its undercarriage and soared thankfully into the distance, the noise, the cheers and the vapour trails left behind. An afternoon turning into more than a rugby game, it was a nationalist rally. The SAA jumbo was a May Day moment in Moscow, a march past in North Korea, a nuclear bomb being tested, it was a display of state power. A real 'who do you think you're fucking with' pause for Kiwi thought; that is if they weren't thinking about the good fortune to be wearing all black as their guts griped and grumbled and the din grew ever greater.

Then the anthem, or rather anthems . . . the sweet harmonies of *Nkosi Sikilel iAfrika* . . . giving way to the booming Afrikaans *Die Stem*. Whatever you think about its history, it is one hell of an anthem, a rouser right up there with *La Marseillaise* and *Land Of My Fathers*, or as we English exiles once sang it, 'My Hen Had Fried Haddocks'. The press box awash with tears. Cynical men who made their money extracting unintended quotes cried. I had a brief blubber. I looked over to the part of the press box where the home journalists were standing proud and saw my crazy Huguenot friend in torrents of tears. In 1974 he had stood in Newlands, Cape Town, with the blacks and coloureds to cheer the Lions on. Twenty-one years on, the sins of South African rugby were forgiven, for at least this day. The slow realisation dawned, the impossible could come to pass, the unbeatable All Blacks would have to conquer a nation. No game has ever had more heft. This was not Tommie Smith and John Carlos in Mexico 1968 and the black power salute. This was spiritual healing . . . so it felt.

Wind the clock back a month to the first game, 25 May. A massive match, South Africa, the hosts making their first ever World Cup appearance after years in the sporting wilderness. Their opponents Australia, the defending world champions. The venue Cape Town, a beautiful rugged backdrop. One year after I had hung up my boots. One year after I had written of the sun that would 'never rise on their home grown fourth Reich'. One year on and I was ready to report and write on my first World Cup. None of that straining in training, no need to hide the odd hangover, just a flight schedule and a series of hire cars to send me careening around the country with my computer, pen and notebook. You know, I can't even remember how I filed in those early days. Was the world wide web up and running . . . from home I would fax my Monday columns to the *Daily Telegraph* . . . surely South Africa was connected to Canary Wharf by 1995? It was some trek for a pigeon, the bottom of Africa to those former East Indies docks . . . but an historical link. Looking for ley lines. My first tour alone, no tour manager to tell us what and where, no players taking their turn to number off the boys before the bus departs for the next destination. Alone, almost an adult. Terrible untruths told to my sports editor. The ANC connections (they were true, I met Mandela twice, once at a private party with the London literati set). Having turned my back on the 1984 tour of the Republic I was reaping the rewards for my youthful principles. I was trusted to take an early flight, touch down a week ahead of South Africa versus Australia. Find some angles. My crazy Huguenot friend was there to meet me at the airport . . . 'Close your eyes, Stuart, and open your mouth . . . trust me . . . Okay brother, now open your eyes and swallow, you are officially tripping in South Africa.' An Italian restaurant, a view of the ocean, dry white wine that sparkled in the Cape sun. A little too acid. Who would be a player when one could be a journalist? To hell with honour and the glory. Hotspur was already a fading memory when Shakespeare brought him to foolish chivalrous life. A warm breeze blowing through the Rainbow Nation. My promised exclusive could wait until the sun set on just 'another day in Africa, my friend'.

The sun inevitably went down over a rambling bar called The Shack. Black and white. Once the epicentre of the social scene in the liberal enclave that was District Six. An endless merging of drink and dope. A hippie haven. An escape from the escalating excitement that was the 1995 World Cup.

Flying into Cape Town, over the squalor of Gugulethu. Blacks were brutally shifted from beautiful Cape Town in the apartheid years. Majestic setting, sordid history. 'For sweetest things turn sourest by their deeds/Lilies that fester smell far worse than weeds.' Stunning Stellenbosch University was the birthplace of apartheid, the Western Cape incubator for one of this planet's most inhuman political systems. Now I see a giant poster of the Cape's coloured Springbok winger, Chester Williams, as the South African Airways plane steadies for its landing. As a child I saw a black centre, sometimes fly half I think, called Errol Tobias. He played for the South African Barbarians in Newport. A few caps for the Springboks but all too cosmetic a selection. The dice was loaded against anyone who wasn't white.

Spend a few hours in Soweto. When I toured South Africa one year earlier with England, when Nelson had woven a reverse spell that worked in England's favour in Pretoria, we visited the famed South Western Districts of Johannesburg. Television cameras were welcomed at the training session as they are not any other time. Newspaper photographers treated like royalty. Great photo opp. Some insurance company with their name plastered all around the scrublands converted to rugby field. For the day. Coaching the kids. Big smiles, cute pictures for the paper, great PR for the insurance company and a chance for us players to regale friends with the day we went and did our bit in Soweto. At the session end we gave away England training kit, a few balls and got on our bus to drive back to the luxury hotels in Sandton. Security everywhere. We were toys of politicians, smile for the camera kids, isn't life great. Enough to make a man as sick as an All Black – if you believe the rumours, that is. Sorry, another digression, more a confession, one to get off the chest. Where were we; Chester Williams?

More to the point, where was Chester Williams? Injury deprived South Africa of their left winger for the match against Australia and some of us columnists an opportunity to assess the Springbok wing, was he the real thing or a sop to the watching world? (He was the real thing.) I made my way to the press box in Newlands, heart beating with the prospect of watching this clash of rugby giants. Rugby is so much more enjoyable to watch when you don't have to formulate a column within a few minutes of the final whistle. I had a whole day to file . . . plenty of time for the pigeon . . . anyway, it is my first time in this particular press box. And I have nightmares about stadiums as I've admitted. But it is all right today.

Someone with a familiar look is dressed in a blazer and directs me to the press seating. God, do I know him? I am sure I have seen his face . . . yes, I know where . . . that billboard when I bounced into Africa on my SAA flight. Chester Williams. Damned if there were any other non-playing members of the Springboks smiling benignly and showing the press to their seats. Am I writing my way between fact and fiction here? Writing what I wanted to be true back in 1995 . . . that the change in South African rugby was literally only skin deep. I tell the tale to this day, not because I recall seeing Williams but because I recall recalling my shock when the thought hit me some time into the first half. Recollections, thoughts, facts? The warning signs were there when I wrote of my first encounter with the All Blacks. I fear fiction wins out. It is so seductive it transforms itself into fact. Well, I did study history at Oxford . . . South Africa beat the defending champions. No doubt about that. I bid farewell to The Shack and flew north to Durban, KwaZulu Natal and England's first match of the tournament. Argentina.

One day before the game and the first of many press conferences. Quotes as food. Jack feeds the press, always a tang. Ready processed stuff though, making their way to different newspapers but all coming out the same way. Little fresh material. We're content with repeating what a manager or players say, too little thinking as to the more interesting issue of what the words mean. Rowell is wary of me. A traitor, gone to the dark side. One year out of playing, the criticisms sting the more. Jack knew more about my inner workings than any other man but I could find my way around a few of his dark places. As for the match, I remember absolutely nothing other than the deluge. For the record England won 24–18. Rob Andrew kicked six penalties and dropped two goals.

Next up a flight to Johannesburg where the All Blacks would face Wales. That was four days away. There was time for me and my crazy Huguenot friend to get behind the wheel and hit the road. Nelson had made the journey from terrorist to national hero but here in Natal there was 'tension'. Chief Buthelazi was Zulu and Zulus were not enamoured of the Xhosa tribe who constituted the core of the ruling African National Congress. Consequently the Zulu region was regarded as dangerous. Now, as a craven fifty-something, I might stay in the Umhlanga Rocks Hotel and fill my face with addictive curries. The Indian influence on this Indian Ocean city was a culinary splendour. Then, early thirties and independent, no training, no team meetings, just a few deadlines . . . it was into the hire car and the inland hills. The South African press told us not to risk it, the local journalists begged us to stay with them in the hotel bar. We would never return. But my crazy Huguenot friend and I were immortal for a few weeks. To be afraid was to be racist. That was his view, I think he was right. He wanted to break down borders, black, white, coloured, ludicrous descriptions for human beings. 'Whatever you do, don't pick up any hitchers.'

We were driving through lands only seen on television by white men. Stanley Baker and Michael Caine. Bank holidays, *Men of Harlech, Zulu*. A teenager is waiting at a bus stop, sees us, sticks his thumb up . . . what the hell are two white men doing here . . . and we stop. He sits in the back, directs us a few more miles uphill, views of nothing but small Zulu holdings. Patchwork quilt fields. A magic pre-industrial age. His mother welcomes us. We drink beer on a rickety porch. A few too many. Hug and head back for Durban and its not so golden mile. It might have been more interesting to chronicle an escape from the dread hills, a dicing with death but we rolled double six, had a good day, hanging out with humans. As for golden mile, all that glisters is not . . . well you know the rest . . . beautiful beaches but a lot of white people were, and are even more so now, scared shitless.

Johannesburg. New Zealand 34 Wales 9. First glimpse of the All Blacks in the flesh, always a thrill for me, the spell not yet broken, the style of their game something to behold. Andrew Mehrtens a cheeky genius at fly half, Sean Fitzpatrick approaching legendary status at hooker . . . and Jonah. Wales did well to only lose by a quarter of a century. The lads from the land of my schoolboy friends' fathers were staying in a hotel called the Sunnyside in Parktown. It had a bar attached to it; ideal for the petrified white population of Johannesburg. Adrian Davies, a fly half, took a turn on piano, Robert Jones, he who split my skull with the Lions in 1993, admonished me for daring to venture from the hotel, the compound. Not far away was Bellevue, or Yeoville, no one seemed quite sure what the area was. But what everyone knew was Rockey and Raleigh Street were two of the city's most funky places. Black and white mixed, mingled, liberal . . . a good place for a coffee and a respite from the rugby. I would write a column in one of the many cafes. Jones shook his head and questioned my sanity. The security detail for each team took no risk. Behind each rock someone with a knife. Another half-remembered Robert Lowell poem . . . 'Central Park'? Somehow I ended up in a nightclub with the Welsh team after the All Blacks game. Determined to walk home from the club at three in the morning, I had the computer/laptop this time. I laughed, said any muggers would mistake it for a gun, stay well away. Maybe this was too macho. Either way I allowed the Welsh lads to bundle me into a minibus and retreat to the safety of Sunnyside.

My crazy Huguenot friend had left me to my own devices. He was staking out the Springboks. I made a solo trip to Rustenburg where Ivory Coast were playing Tonga. I was not the only member of her majesty's press in attendance at what was the lowest-profile game of the tournament, unless you happen to be either Ivorian or Tongan. The match was an excuse. Entrapment was the name of this afternoon's game. Pre-match, a now deceased sports writer stammers in disgust, spying the old South African flag hanging above the stands. I tell him it belongs to the Ivory Coast. I liked him, even though I was not as keen on the paper for which he wrote. Says me, writing for the *Daily Telegraph*. There was a natural bank, grassy, local guys drinking copious amounts of rum and Coke, rum and this, rum and that. What some might call white trash. I was accepted into their drinking ranks, welcomed into the fraternity of fans, even as I listened for the latent racism to break through. I accepted their largesse as I looked to shaft them. Retrospectively this was not my finest hour. The afternoon was to end in tragedy, real tragedy, not the overused sporting variety. Max Brito, a young Ivory Coast player, broke his neck. I had my bloody headline. From Rustenburg I drove to Pretoria. Loftus Versfeld, home to Northern Transvaal (now the Bulls). Where Nelson had inspired England against South Africa a year earlier. France versus Scotland . . . France won narrowly.

A week between the end of the pool stage and the quarter-finals. No TV commitments and only a couple of columns a week. Jazz in Melville at night, chasing round Jonah by day. The big man seemed bigger than the tournament but like the *Titanic* and the iceberg, New Zealand and South Africa were heading towards one another. I saw the Springboks win their quarter-final against Samoa. It was an ugly occasion. South Africa protested against the dangerous tackling of the Islanders, Samoa accused the Springboks of verbal racism. You could tell the politics of the rugby writers by the side they took; left liberals were with the little underdog, the hard right stood by the hosts. Instinct and belief had me firmly in the Samoan camp but some of the stuff they hit the South Africans with was frightening, sickening, beyond intimidation. I was able to imagine myself in the shoes of the savaged South Africans. Empathy can change a man's opinions. I guess Samoa were racially insulted and South Africa battered to the point of assault. This is the type of truth that comes packaged on the shelf. You simply take your pick.

Another truth. I didn't think for a second I could have dropped the goal Rob Andrew did to dramatically knock Australia out in Cape Town the next day. Had I not retired I would probably have been pushing as hard as I could for a place in the team. I reckoned our back play might have been slicker but Andrew's nerve that day (as it had been in Pretoria in 1994) was something to behold. I had a book published that year, *The Year of Living Dangerously*; on the cover was a shot of Rob Andrew striking that perfect kick with the 1991 winning fly half, Michael Lynagh, looking away.

There was nothing left to write about Jonah, so, in between the quarter-final win and England's date with New Zealand, I thought I'd ask England about the world's most famous rugby player. Specifically, Rob. It was a Tuesday, maybe a Wednesday, and England and Andrew had agreed to an hour's interview, Barnes on Andrew. 'What plans have you got to stop Lomu?' 'None, we'll just keep our system as it is, Tony [Underwood] will be all right.'

I was horrified. England had seen the man on television, not close up. I tried to warn them. Felt a little like a wildlife presenter stepping in to help the endangered animal when we all know nature is cruel and must be allowed to have her capricious way. But while I had no great love for England, the team was littered with mates and, above all, there was Jack Rowell in charge. I tried to tell Jack too. But I was already a hack, an irrelevance. Like I say, attendants at most, that's the media and that's how it should be. I didn't expect England to drop everything because I said so, yet the confidence they displayed in handling this never before seen force of nature was mind-numbing. I left the camp thinking them either arrogant after beating Australia or simply stupid. It wouldn't be the first time I thought the latter about England but a Rowell side?

Four Jonah tries later and England were destroyed, wide-eyed, 'where did that come from' horror on their faces. It was over, England were out and I was making my last flight from Cape Town to Johannesburg for the final. South Africa had beaten France twenty-four hours ahead of England's loss in controversial circumstances in Durban. The controversy would be heightened when Louis Luyt, the boss man of the South African union, presented the semi-final referee Derek Bevan with a watch for his performance that day. There was never a hint of anything untoward – by this I mean crooked – from the Welshman but this gesture humiliated him and reminded the world how hard done by France had been. Home pressure, Bevan cracked. A French try was disallowed. One of the best referees, one of his worst days. Homer.

Charlize Theron wasn't big, not back then. If she had been, the Hollywood heroine would, I am sure, have been up there with the Big Easy, Ernie Els, giving pointless press conferences in the days ahead of the final. The nation was preparing itself for New Zealand. Everyone was wishing them well. The day before the game I thought they could add Gary Player, Graeme Pollock and God into the list of celebrity well-wishers, even Desmond Tutu, it was going to make no difference. I watched the All Blacks' almost perfect final training session. It was brief. Maybe we now understand why. Later that day I watched the Springboks at an empty echoing Ellis Park, hands and heels, nerves almost visible. They didn't have a chance.

The truth is shrouded in myth. One day we will know the truth about the food poisoning but it will only be one side's truth, one side of the truth. What is incontestable is that South Africa came up with a plan to stop Lomu . . . that New Zealand – sick or not – should have utilised the tactical boot of Mehrtens and the dominant lineout work of Ian Jones more. Instead they threw the ball to their jolly giant too far from the try line and men like James Small pulled him down, lions and wildebeest. And we know Joel Stransky, the last fly half I ever played against (South Africa B in Kimberley) became a national hero with that drop goal. Kitch Christie, the Springbok coach, described him as 'the little Jew boy' in the post-match press conference. I have deleted the initial line, 'Joel didn't seem to care'. How did I know that? Why did I write it? Later that night I left my hire car in a traffic jam at the side of the road, bumper to boot to bumper on the exit road from Ellis Park; went off into the night with delirious South African men and some big hipped mamas, heading for the nearest shebeen. Black and white danced as one beneath the Rainbow Nation. There may never be another World Cup quite like South Africa, 1995, when the spirit of Mandela downed the giant.

XAVIER GARBAJOSA

WHO? WHAT? Most of all, why? Well, you astute readers will have spotted the 'X' in the name. Albeit it is Garbajosa's first name; I don't deny this is a bit of a con. We could have utilised the abominably overworked phrase, 'X factor'. Other than that, the options are pretty limited. X Men . . . I had a lot of time for Charles Xavier and his gang but this X has been hijacked. Stripped away from muscular mutants and factored into predominantly young people with well-defined yearning for televisual celebrity. The Saturday night superstar. All right. Times have changed. Our rugby heroes are not the strong silent types of yesteryear but let's give the players some credit. As for the former Toulouse and France winger and full back, yes he had a few shortcomings. Wasn't exactly the strongest or bravest. A French flower. Delicate. Divine. Beautiful in his playing days. So says my wife as she peers at a picture I am pondering. 'Who is he?' she gasps over my shoulder. 'He's the bloke who demonstrated all his side-stepping skills – to avoid having to throw himself in the path of Jonah Lomu in the 1999 World Cup semi-final

– that's who he is. What he is? A bit of a French coward . . .' I am cut off in my Brexit-sounding little England rant . . . 'I don't blame him for getting out of HIS way. You wouldn't want to spoil a face like that. Ruin all the fun he could have later in life.'

My wife has met a few of France's more famous rugby heart-throbs from the 1980s. Figured out a thing or two about their lust for life. Her logic, to many observers, is a sound one. Smarter than putting your body in a position where it is odds-on you will suffer a steamrolling as Jolly Jonah came at you in a way the sport had never seen. I mean 'never'. But rugby players? Representing their country? Fair France in this instance. Men who are supposed to throw caution to the four corners of Twickenham. Not do as he did . . . Above and beyond the call of duty. Fat chance. The French full back, a beautiful dyed blonde Adonis on 31 October 1999, eased a path to clear the giant's way to the line for the first try. Helpfully using both arms to push the black-shirted one amiably over. Early in the second half he watches from close range as Jonah shoves three fellow Frenchmen out of his ground-breaking path. Lomu touches down. Our X man dives on the behemoth. Patting him on the back in a display of congratulatory sportsmanship. Others might have regarded the gesture as cowardice. 'Sanity,' huffs Mrs B, and with only 'Y' and 'Z' as remaining chapters, who wants to come across the churl?

New Zealand were 24–10 ahead and stomping their way towards a World Cup final. France were being blitzed. Xavier was the unlucky one. The bloke who kept getting caught in Lomu's impossibly bright lights. Yet thirty-five miraculous minutes later those of a fraternal bent in the press box were hollering out *La Marseillaise*. Neutrality nowhere in sight. We had seen something exceptional. Had witnessed the greatest comeback in the World Cup. 'The biggest shock in the history of the World Cup,' according to that great around the corner kicker and commentator, John Taylor. Readers in La Rochelle, where the gorgeous one has achieved great things in his early years as a coach may be disappointed that one of their own is set to be filtered out of this chapter because, yes, he is no more than a very handsome conduit. He is a 'pathway' to a chapter where the subject is rugby union's great shocks.

Yet, even as I write this, another thought has dislodged what you will recognise as my rigidly structured previous game plan. As if I am a hollow-minded, hypothetical rugby manager. One who has ordered his hands to type certain words. Develop pre-conceived themes. The preparation has been excellent. Go out and write it, hands. There's a troublesome little fly half still in me, and he is causing trouble. Ignoring the boss. Trusting his instincts. Veering elsewhere and typing into life this thought that came upon me as suddenly as that SAA jumbo in the last chapter. Sod the structure. We have travelled from A to X with scarce a mention on the emotional peaks and troughs which play such a part in our glorious game.

Bravery and cowardice.

The peak. The trough. Terms, words, treated with a cartoon-like frivolity. 'Bravery' is much more than the sum of its reported parts. What appears brave can be the coward's way out. Its very antithesis. Let me try and explain what, to some of you, might initially seem a craven approach to the great game. The concept of 'bravery' is predominantly related to physical prowess. Especially in the United Kingdom. Perhaps it has something to do with the reverence in which the entire nation seemingly holds – and always has held – the armed forces. Have you got my point yet . . . we are good soldiers. Citizens, consumers. All proud of our soldiery. The courage of 'our brave boys'. You have heard the saying a thousand times. Sport and war, as Orwell, not a man for the west stand, saw the link between the two. HQ hosted the day's second-biggest sporting crowd on the planet on 29 April 2017. The Army against the Navy. Our brave boys drinking Twickenham dry. Not a good place for a pacifist to find himself (the biggest crowd was a world heavyweight boxing event at Wembley). Rugby players, in the main, are regarded as far braver than most sportsmen. Most humans. Consumers and citizens alike recognise the willingness to fall under the feet of eight men, sixteen sets of studs. Or more. One hundred and thirty stones. Or more. Recognise the guts to throw the body into the path of a colossus like the late Lomu. We understand the macho elements that constitute what we think it is to be brave.

Intelligence is underestimated and undervalued in most regions of the rugby world. Certainly by a substantial number of younger rugby fans. Born and bred on little bar the thunderous thump of the collision. Conversely, we are blind to the other sort of rugby bravery. Without witnessing the physical manifestations of it, we are blind to the virtue. Mental bravery. Talking about courage to make the brave decision. In 1999, France were nothing if not mentally brave. Men like Xavier Garbajosa might not have been in much of a hurry to lose their lovely looks, yet, to a man, they had the courage to run the ball from deep, from areas of the pitch where turnover ball against them would have proved terminal to their chances. It requires raw nerve to counter attack from deep against a team as good as that 1999 All Blacks vintage. France gave it a glorious go. They kept playing when a tightening of the game and an attempt to narrow the contest into a forward slog might have been the physically heroic way to play. Go down with all guns blazing. Take as many as you can with you. Darius Jedburgh, *Edge of Darkness*? Anyone? France, against all odds that Sunday afternoon, brought a different sort of bravery to Twickenham. The courage to run. Forgive Xavier his craven physical streak. Call it anything you want but remember he played his part in this resistance story of mental strength against the seemingly inevitable. The full back has fashioned a La Rochelle attack which plays in his image. Daring, dreamy, fabulously old-time French. The man is a hero.

Contrast him with Philippe Saint-André, the former French coach, and Patrice Lagisquet, the 'Bayonne Express' – men who made the gloomy conversion from flying wingers to the most risk-averse coaches. As head coach of Biarritz, Patrice presided over a gigantic squandering of a stylish club and French rugby talent. The man who ran the entire club? The hero and villain of chapter six, Serge Blanco.

Finally, the fly half's break from the initial writing plan comes to its conclusion . . . let me shout it from the top of the Gherkin. Anywhere high. There is nothing brave, nothing heroic, about running head first into the bloke standing in your way. Nothing smart about switching the brain into neutral. Allowing the defence an easy afternoon's work. The sport – at it best – is a rare combination of courage. Mental and physical. Something we have almost forgotten in the arms race to muscle up our new age professionals.

This is my final homage to our cowardly conduit with the hidden courage. Back to the game plan: the theme of the chapter . . . the great upsets. John Taylor pronounced France's 1999 victory the biggest shock in the history of the World Cup. Sixteen years later, Japan's rising sun eclipsed it, claiming rugby's most juddering shock of all. They beat the Springboks and stunned the world and the sport's literal giants. The South Africans cannot be accused of complacency. The side selected had 851 caps between them. The nation had a 1995 and a more recent 2007 World Cup triumph to their name. Japan had not won a World Cup match since 1991. Nearly 30,000 spectators packed into the Brighton Community Stadium. Few of them in expectation of a shock. More a nice day out in Brighton. Rugby as a giddy novelty.

That same afternoon I was working as a commentator for Irish television. High up in the then Millennium Stadium, praising a controlled display from Johnny Sexton. A comfortable, expected Irish win against Canada. Post-match, in the press box, in the bowels of the stadium, I was writing a run-of-the-mill match report for the next day's *Sunday Times*, one eye on the television monitor. Japan holding South Africa. Half an hour gone . . . interesting. The dam was bound to break. The only question was when . . . still worth an eye. Half-time and South Africa led by two points. Come full time they had lost the most sensational game of this or any other World Cup. By two points. A replacement with the not so Oriental name of Karne Hesketh, sprints diagonally. Right to left, into the left-hand corner of the football stadium – and into rugby history. The match is already in a molten-hot state of injury time. Twice, near the death, Michael Leitch, the Japan captain, has penalty kicks to tie the match. His kicker, Ayumu Goromaru, is in splendid form. The back row forward goes for broke. Eddie Jones, Japan's coach, admits he would have settled for the draw. But Japan had the mental courage to shoot for the moon. Hesketh's touchdown. The Apollo moment of 2015. The other Apollo, the winged messenger bringing bad news to South Africa.

Jones had prepared for this match. Month after month, minute after minute. Nothing else. He predicted a tougher game for the favourites than the world and the South Africans expected. The Eddie smile, make of it what you will. A promise. A threat. A joke? It was deadly serious. The eighty minutes needed to project him back into the big time and his future role as England supremo. Japan played their perfect game. Everything functioned. Japan didn't risk offloads. Didn't confront the overwhelming physical power of their opposition head on. They went to deck early. Support runners on and over the ball in a red and white cherry-blossomed flash. The smallest man in the competition, Fumiaki Tanaka, produced one of the greatest individual efforts of the tournament for his sixty-six minutes on the field at scrum half. Keeping the pace of the game at a helter-skelter full tilt. Japan wore them out. Rugby as guerrilla warfare. No sooner did the giant power know where the enemy was than it was gone. To another part of the pitch. Another skirmish where South Africa were numerically outnumbered. Hit and run. Japan kept running, the clock kept ticking. The game remained in the balance. Seventy minutes elapsed before I said to a Japanese journalist who had surely the worst job in the world for a Japanese rugby fan that day, I thought it was a 50/50 call. Seventy minutes for the evidence of my eyes to trickle into the disbelieving void of my brain. Fuck filing the Ireland–Canada game. There would be time. Hesketh scores. The Japanese contingent clap. Still polite. My chair topples to the ground behind me. I scream, surge into the air. Wildly unprofessional but this is sport as life. Blood-pumping stuff. This matters. No light entertainment there in Brighton.

Pre-game, Jones sounded more the pragmatist than the declared genius we, in the English press, were soon to anoint him. He said, 'We've got a little team, so we have to move the ball around and cause problems.' Japan never stopped moving. The problems never stopped coming for the South Africans as Jerome Garces finally blew time on rugby's greatest upset. The lightweight had outpointed the super heavyweight. Even England's embarrassing demise could not arrest the momentum the 2015 World Cup developed from that first Saturday in Brighton.

Union has not been overburdened with seismic shocks. Unless you claim that every New Zealand World Cup loss amounts to a shock. In 1991 the defending champions were odds-on favourites. The same way that Brazil are installed as favourites every time football holds its World Cup. Form is irrelevant for Brazil. They are simply Brazil. The All Blacks had – and have – that aura. Plus some. And unlike Brazil they were always one of the outstanding teams in the lead up to each tournament. My favourites every tournament bar 2003. Then I expected England to win. Finally got one right.

In England those of us of a certain age grew up with the thrill of the FA Cup. In my youth, when the leading clubs fielded their full teams, there was the palpable sense of shock in the air. It made third round Saturdays one of the great afternoons in a sporting child's year. Ronnie Radford pile-driving one from thirty-five yards – so I recall – against Newcastle for Hereford. Where the hell was Hereford? Cattle dealers, cider drinkers . . . what boy who watched Billy Bremner and his savage, soulless Leeds team lose a Wembley final to Sunderland will ever have to check Wikipedia for the name of Jim Montgomery, the heroic goalkeeper? This was romance, it brought a tear to my eye in the days when the FA Cup was more than a consolation for Premiership and European failure (I write this as a long-standing supporter of Arsenal). Until Japan, rugby union had nothing on the truly epic scale of shock. Why?

The answer is found in the contemplation of dimensions. A rugby pitch is generally something in the region of 120 metres long (ten metres for the average in-goal area) and most importantly, seventy metres wide. That is one hell of a width to defend, even with fifteen men. Contrast it with football. The width of the pitch is of great tactical importance (the narrower the field the easier it is for the inferior side to squeeze the superior one; the same basics apply in both codes), but what counts in the final summary is an area 7.32 metres wide and 2.44 metres high. The goal. Almost ninety per cent less territory to defend and one man dedicated to nothing but the protection of these posts and his net. A bad team might have a goalkeeper enjoying the greatest ninety minutes of his life. I recall Montgomery throwing himself around like it was yesterday; over forty years ago. At least I think I do . . . all the build-up play amounts to nothing if the keeper keeps making marvellous saves. And the strikers keep missing the target. Or firing straight at the protector of the posts. Occasionally these elements merge in an unholy alliance. The result is the defiance of both odds and logic. More often than not all the pressure eventually tells. But not five per cent as much as it does with rugby.

If it was merely a matter of defending those seventy metres from tries, this would still make a rugby rear-guard so much more difficult than is the case with its football equivalent. The hallmark of a defensive football team determined to contain the classier, more imaginative opponent? The foul. Think Italy when they win World Cups. Think Wimbledon when they beat Liverpool in an FA Cup final. The forever shrill whistle for the foul. It slows the superior side down, breaks down their flow . . . a few players are booked. So what? A problem for another day. Teams can be frustrated, hustled, hassled, out of their stride.

Rarely is this the case with rugby union. Rugby has its letter 'H' posts. The horizontal post is three metres off the ground, it is impossible to prevent passage of ball through posts once the kicked ball has cleared the maximum height of a forward trying to charge down. At 5.6 metres wide, the posts are a good bit narrower than football's but rugby lacks a tightrope walker tiptoeing along the crossbar, parrying the ball away. To utilise the parlance of football – we are talking open goals. Should a team concede a penalty within kicking range, the aggrieved party has an unopposed opportunity to kick three points. As the pressure mounts, the fouls multiply. Same in both games. But in football, the slowing down is advantageous to the more negative, the defensive team. Not so in rugby. The victims of cynicism can choose to accumulate points should their kicker be any good. Most are. Under a welter of pressure, the inferior team might not concede a try but they find themselves fifteen, eighteen, twenty-one points behind. The three-point penalties take their toll. In football there are endless 0–0s where the inferior team hangs on. More usually the pressure tells. A goal will come. It ratchets up the tension. It is all in the waiting. Rugby lacks this accumulation of tension. The three-point rugby penalties deflate the mood. Football is dramatic in a way rugby rarely is. Relish the staggering rugby shocks when they come along.

DUKE OF YORK

NO, NOT the current Duke of York. Good God . . . although nobody would deny links between rugby and the monarchy. In the glory years Will and Harry were a regular fixture in Twickenham's Royal Box, doing their bit for O2 sales. Television directors seemingly following the unspoken orders of the Establishment. An obsessive focus on the royals. And then there is Anne. The Princess Royal is patron of the Scottish Rugby Union; some title anyway. Always at Murrayfield, tartan on display. Her daughter, Zara, named after a fashionable women's clothing chain, betrayed Scotland by marrying Mike Tindall. But Andrew, isn't he big in the FA? I don't remember either him or Charlie leaping about through the course of a rugby game. And mum is one for the nags. With you all the way on that one, Lizzie. Maybe Andy and Charlie liked the game in their youth. I could be wrong. Anyway, I am with John McEnroe when it comes to that most sensitive of subjects, the British monarchy. In his autobiography the tennis great – or somebody else – puzzled over why gifted sportspeople should bow to royalty, the deference due to nothing but the good fortune of high birth. They bow and curtsey at Wimbledon, shake hands and nod at Twickenham.

So where were we? The Duke of York. I met an actor who played the Shakespearean part. Rather I was certain I did. As certain as seeing the All Blacks in 1973. Scroll down my mobile and there is the name. Duke of York. Added in the middle of the last decade. During the majestic cycle of Shakespeare's history plays. At the time my republican's idea of a droll personal joke. Now I see it as a bridge to this chapter's theme: sport and the arts. But my errant memory isn't through with me. Who the heck played the Duke of York? I can't write this chapter without crediting the name of the rugby-loving actor.

A few minutes rifling through my books is all it takes. Browsing isn't breaking the no-research rule . . . Nick Asbury. Nick wrote a lovely book that goes by the title of *Exit Pursued By A Badger*. Seeing his face on the cover triggered another memory, another whopping mental faux pas. He was never York. He was Somerset. A decade of him playing the 'wrong' Duke in my mind, acting in the red rose camp. An idiotic error. From 1972, or '73, to the first decade of a new millennium my mind keeps recreating this private world of Stuart Barnes. At complete variance with the rest of the world. The borders of my brain are crumbling. Never mind, we are not supposed to last forever. Forgive me Nick, you were never York, always Somerset. A decade or so on, the mistake on the mobile, 'The Duke of York' qualifies him to set the scene for the penultimate chapter of these pencilled sketches of mine.

It was definitely the Roundhouse, out Camden way, where Shakespeare's history plays had their London showing. A quiet beer in hand, thinking through the *Henry VI* I had just seen. *Part One* at a guess, but it really does not matter, not as far as this book goes. It might for Nick. An astonished voice from behind my back, 'Stuart Barnes!' It wasn't the snooty Prada accusation from nearly a quarter of a century ago, 'What are YOU doing here?' No, a tone of genuine enthusiasm . . . turned around, choked on my pint. How the hell does the Duke of Somerset know me? Nick is a rugby fan with a typical wide-eyed interest in England. Me? Something more than a passing interest in Shakespeare. He talked rugby, I talked Bard . . . he fancied tickets for an England autumn international, I couldn't get any for *Richard III* as the cycle of plays were drawing toward their epic end. I had seen seven of the eight and would have mugged someone for that elusive eighth and final ticket. We bartered. Financially, Nick had the best of the deal. Ex-players pay a lot of money for their guaranteed pair of Twickenham tickets. The Roundhouse tickets were considerably cheaper. But I saw something that a decade later remains one of the cultural highlights of my life . . . doubtful if Nick still recalls England versus Australia on some cold anonymous November day. Maybe he does. Not only do I get to one of the company's final *Richard III* productions but there is even a backstage invitation for a few drinks. This is how James Bond, or should I say Daniel Craig, must have felt when he found himself in the changing rooms of the Lions team after winning the 2013 series in Australia.

It is not quite as excitable in Camden. No cameras zooming in on the RSC cast post-show. Nick introduced me to Michael Boyd, the director of the history plays. I was at a loss for words; a rare occurrence for a commentator. What could a rugby broadcaster say to the director of the RSC? The England World Cup winners have their MBEs, knighthoods and their celebrity. Such trinkets will never be the lot of the majority who brought life to Shakespeare's version of English history. I'll tell another little tale from my days as a Shakespearean 'groupie'. It stunned me back then. Still does. Heading back to my flat in Chiswick. It must have been the Northern Line after a couple of post-play drinks. There's a face on the platform that looked familiar. Waiting for the same underground train. I can't place it, another Chester

Williams moment. Gawping like an idiot, who was he, of course, Henry IV! All I can tell you is the old king came across as plain as the rest of us, divested of his robe, crown and the presence of his extraordinary son, Prince Hal. Clive Wood was hunched, de-robed, dressed in jeans, jacket, shirt, waiting for the same train as commoners like me. Cheap digs in Hammersmith made the acting job just about profitable. There was me and the rest of the Sky crew – 'talent' is the televisual term – getting picked up from home and whisked to work in splendid luxury. The back seat to Twickenham or wherever, as if we were entitled to the very best treatment. No lines to learn. Same old stuff to spout.

How has theatre, the arts in general, come to play so secondary, tertiary a role to sport on the national stage? It has nothing to do with talent. The best actors can breathe life into words written over 400 years ago. They play their parts with something close to perfection. Certainly those history plays were as pitch perfect as anything I'll see for the rest of my life . . . Jonathan Slinger was magnificent. The leading light in the cycle of plays. He recently pitched up in a small non-commercial back theatre, the Ustinov, at Bath. He was superb but nobody waited backstage for his autograph. Why has sport so superseded the stage as an entertainment form? And what is it about sport that can ignite an actor's imagination whereas few rugby players appear interested in the theatre? I think back to a chat with Nick, he showed my wife his hand. It looked as if my old pantomime pal, Gareth Chilcott, had delivered a jovial stamp. But this injury occurred during rehearsals. The swelling made it hard to hold his sword through the elongated fight scenes. Not to mention play the piano which he then used to do for a second income at a jazz club in Chelsea, 606? That swollen hand. It hurt him like hell. He winced to hold a pint. The unfortunate result of a simulated scene. That is what theatre is, of course, a mocked-up version of life. All show. The conflicts at the RSC and the Roundhouse were only show. Agincourt, Falstaff and his scrapes, none of it really happens. All insubstantial. When the play ends, whatever the ability of the actors, the writer and the director, it takes quite an effort for the magic not to fall away in front of their eyes. Theatre is Prospero, broken staffs. To some, much that is needed in life is found in Shakespeare. Not the Bible or a nation's laws. But that is a minority. The majority will shrug their shoulders and look at the latest on their iPhone as they stream out of the theatre. It wasn't 'real', was 'only' pretence. With that, interest immediately reverts back to reality, the real world.

We find ourselves lost in the dilemma: what is real and what is not? The stage is definitely not 'real'. Through his characters' mouths, the greatest dramatist of them all tells us this often enough. If you take the great man at his word . . . yet what about sport? Isn't it only a game? Yet Orwell didn't describe Macbeth as a version of war minus the shooting. Sport, he despised, for its easy nationalism and sheer brutality. He is said to have resented it for the very reason a great deal of people love it. When trying to justify a preference for the attractive, intelligent team over any other . . . be they wearing a red rose on a white jersey or not, fans are often flabbergasted. 'But you are English, you even played for them.' 'Ah, but my love of rugby is greater than my love of England.' Eyes narrow at this woolly nonsense. Contempt and anger colliding. I like to see some style, something special. So many supporters care for nothing but the result. If their team prevails it has been a good game. Quality often has little to do with rugby union. The same can be said for any team sport. Winning is all. For players winning is all, certainly was in my Bath days.

What a contrast with the stage. A game of Test match rugby can be described as an epic, no matter how many unforced errors are committed. Mood matters. Can you imagine Kenneth Tynan watching a single game of rugby without being shocked at the mistakes made? Actors make a few but the good ones, in my admittedly limited knowledge, not many. They learn line after line, perfect their timing, even their capacity to wield swords and swoop all over the stage (the history plays had terrific fight scenes) while speaking. They understudy while performing lead parts, perhaps in another play. Daniel Carter's quality, even against the Lions in Wellington in 2005 was nowhere near the close-to-perfection performance of, say, Simon Russell Beale as Prospero at Stratford in 2017.

Yet here is a paradox to end them all. Drama lacks the sheer . . . what is the word . . . *drama* of sport. Actors are in complete control of their destiny. There is nobody to prevent them performing what they have endlessly rehearsed. Day after day. Nobody to punch them in the guts in the midst of a Danish soliloquy. What makes team sports special is the capacity to rise above the rubble to which even the least skilled opponents can reduce their superiors. There may not be that many shock results compared to football but the potential, the possibility, is the thrill of rugby. And the occasional reversal of the sporting order. Let's trip back in time to 1995. The day before the World Cup final again? Forgive the reiteration. I watched New Zealand produce the almost perfect, error-free half hour or so training session. Michael Boyd would have been proud of them. A few hours later the Springboks looked like those hilarious, idiotic mechanicals in *A Midsummer Night's Dream*. Come the final and the 'rude' South Africans went and disturbed that perceived sporting order of the rugby universe. Toppled the mighty All Blacks . . . there was also the Mandela factor . . . magic. No one saw it coming, Will would have made his *Midsummer Night's Dream* from this material, something magnificent of it. Yet the game itself was not great. Had it been anything other than the World Cup final it would have been swept, along with the dust of history, into rugby's forgotten annals.

It was in South Africa, many years later, that the genesis of this book took root. Lazy oaf that I am, it has been a long gestation period. The man who suggested these rugby ramblings was none other than Charles Dance. The English actor has the rugby bug. He didn't want to talk stage as we shared a meal in our Johannesburg hotel. A few tales were wheedled out of him but what's on tour . . . as the saying goes . . . mainly he thirsted for rumbustious rugby stories. Ireland too has its share of larger than life, rugby-loving actors. A missed opportunity to share a drink or thirty with the late, great Peter O'Toole in 2001 (anyone who saw him portray Jeffrey Barnard in Bath's Theatre Royal will testify to his capacity for stage greatness). Somebody was sponsoring a Sydney Harbour Cruise during that year's Lions tour. The same day Sky's co-commentator was struck down with a painful case of piles. Dear Dewi informed O'Toole, who proclaimed to all and sundry, 'Barnes has the Chalfonts . . .' His drinking mate, Richard Harris, was another film star who had a feel, or his own idealised feel, for the game. The two of them sat near me at a pre-Heineken Cup final lunch in Twickenham. Munster would later go on to lose to Northampton. Both of them mad for the Munster cause. Do men and women of the stage see the sport as 'the real thing'? The Man For All Seasons and his mate, A Man Called Horse, alive to the lack of stuntmen, here at Twickenham. When Pat Lam grimaced in agony, shoulder out, as he lifted the Heineken Cup, it wasn't a gripping display of method acting. The Samoan Saint was in a place where even the greatest actors would rather not go. A painful place, a privileged place. It isn't the perfection but the ability to see life played out in a mere eighty minutes that grips us so. It is not hard to see why, for all the stagecraft of Stratford, the world of theatre appreciates the reality of rugby union's dirtier form of drama.

A play can reach for the heights of perfection that rugby cannot contemplate but when the play begins the stage players know where the night is inevitably leading them. If the audience are unsure they can read the programme notes. Point them in the right direction. There's no use in reading a rugby programme. Nobody knows what is coming when the referee's whistle kicks the drama off. It's not perfection we pine for. More, excitement. After all these years of dismissing supporters for short-sighted support of 'their' team, I can finally see why the aesthetics of the game are of less interest than the end result. It does not make sport a superior form of entertainment to stage, just a different one. Orwell was right about the nutty notion of nationalism but why wouldn't a Bath boy want his team to play badly and win rather than play beautifully and lose? That's how I thought from 1973 to 1994.

Had this body and brain ever possessed an ounce of acting talent to take me past the dizzying heights of Dick Deadeye in the school Gilbert and Sullivan production (rugby training was the excuse to duck out of the part) I would have been destined for inevitable stage failure. Who does not admire the quest for perfection? Admire it from the circle and the stalls but to put yourself in such a position, so exposed beneath the spotlights, takes immense nerve. People like David Tennant must once have been afraid of failing. I too had that fear, but in rugby you can at least blur, if not hide it. We can huddle together and find solace in the right result. Nothing matters as long as the team wins. It's no coincidence that Eddie Jones began his England career focusing on performance. He understood in those first days before winning corrupted England that to bring individual greatness into the open this fear of failure has to be flattened. Maybe the definition between the great and the rest isn't just talent and a capacity to learn quickly. It is fearlessness when the abyss of failure opens up in front of you. Most of us tiptoe back from the brink and try to find a way to the other side without exposing, risking, everything. The great? They just close their eyes and leap; like Keanu Reaves in *The Matrix* . . . Greatness is not the perfect performance on the field. It is a state of mind. This, I suspect, is what seduces the likes of Harris, Dance, the late Richard Burton and O'Toole, not to mention the Duke of Somerset. Or York, as I thought.

There's little explanation required when it comes to relationships between sportsmen and businessmen. Each has something the other doesn't. And quite often they yearn for the missing quality. In his pomp, Fred the Shred, the much-derided Scottish banker, liked to surround himself with sportsmen and women, among them rugby players as revered as former Scotland and Lions captain, Gavin Hastings. It wasn't until the Shred's financial world came crashing down that Fred became a front-page news story. Well known before, yes, but essentially in the business world. Sport enables its superstars to transcend the limitations of their code. Rugby might well remain middle-class but everyone knew the big names of the England World Cup-winning side. Fame and glory.

Here's a personal example. Baize-leg school versus St Brendan's. Our adversary is a renowned Bristol rugby school. Playing for the Welsh side is Stuart Barnes. He will go on to have a small-scale international career. In the process he will become famous on a diminuendo scale. Once a building society manager. Against him that day is Bruce Craig. He will amass a chunky fortune from business whilst remaining utterly unknown outside his immediate circle of friends and rivals – until he buys Bath Football Club and makes them his own rugby club. It is not so much the eye of the tiger as the eye of the camera. Bruce eclipses George Ford, Anthony Watson, maybe even Sam Burgess in Bath's period of headline silliness . . . it took the purchase of a sporting institution to shed the anonymity and replace it with a larger-scale celebrity. Compared to football, the fame is, of course, nothing. That is sport bestowing celebrity on pretty much the ultimate scale. Football to rugby is as film to theatre.

Yet men like Craig have what so many of the world's rugby players want: money. Rugby players have fame. Glory. But few have the money. Has there ever lived a rugby player with money to match the owner of Bath? We dined together just the once, in the early days of his ownership. He was sounding out a few old Bath players. Smart thinking, keeping us onside. Or perhaps buying us out. In his first few years of ownership his box was always stuffed full of familiar faces – former players and fair enough. It's a good view and the wine is bound to be better than the stuff sold beneath the stands. As for me, I didn't know how to play it when I came face-to-face with this man made of money who once played against me. He generously proffered the wine list. Dining in the Bath Spa hotel. Expensive. Posh. Do I treat him like the rich man he is? Choose a wine beyond my glugging dreams, or act like I would with anyone else? Choose something in the middle-to-expensive range of wines? In the end I acted like a kid on his or her first seaside holiday. Tiptoed up to my waist in the water but not out of my depth. Get into three figures, a price range usually out of my bibulous depth . . . but not always . . . not when pissed and happy/miserable. Alas, this time the mighty Margaux remained untouched. As for what we talked about – there was a great deal of swaggering talk of using money, throwing it around. To make Bath not only the best team in England, but in Europe. Bruce Craig's money. The big talk all mine and cheap. A pleasant night. Singing for my supper. Singing about dreams and old cracked memories. We haven't dined out since. We have shared a drink and convivial conversation on a few occasions, but that's about it. Bruce isn't desperate for my company and I'm not for his. I've enough friends for my satisfaction. I am sure he too has.

Drop me away from the dosh and into the middle of the Cambridge Folk Festival and, whey, I'm as star-struck as the next sports fan. Or RSC groupie. 2017 and sitting on the buses that carry festival-goers from venue to campsite. Where I will make a drunken stage debut singing Dylan's *Like A Rolling Stone* late on the Sunday night. Pre my raging Dylan imitation there's the dawning realisation that the spotty-faced duo sitting opposite

me on the campsite-bound bus are Grey and Peach. Never heard
of them? Nor me until that evening. They played a sweet set of
tunes in the Club Tent, one an absolute beauty. And so a fifty-
four-year-old man hangs on the words of some lads barely out
of their teens. It's not the age. It's the talent. Not the fame. The
technique, not the potential for future greatness. No, the guts to
go for it in the moment. The Club Tent isn't even that big a stage.
Who gives a hoot for money, celebrity? But artistic talent . . . it's
the same at a reading, being sold someone else's books. I shared
a church with Richard Ford in Bath once. And a few hundred
others. Great American novelist . . . so many questions to ask.
So keen for him to nod at the perceptiveness of my question.
Instead sheer silence from the commentator – intimidated in the
presence of a writer touched with something exceptional.

There's a theme that occasionally slips into my newspaper
columns: the world of difference I perceive between sport as
business and business as sport. I am sure it has slipped into these
pages. The chapter entitled Professionalism. It's worth a second
thought. The former turns the game into a matter of gain, of
profit. Finance. Money. Business. The latter uses results on the
field as the arbiter of excellence. The rugby gods bless business as
sport. Yet more than anything, since hanging up the boots, I have
drifted in another direction. Sport as art. As something beautiful
on the eye. In my playing days, I couldn't spell – let alone explain
– aesthetics. No, it was win at all costs. The collective fear of
failure usurping the individual drive for excellence. Business is
more sport than art. The bottom line – even when it's 'business
as sport' – is result-driven. Profit and loss, win and lose. I played
my rugby with the mind of a businessman. Maybe on the
microphone, in print and via this rustic form of former fly half
philosophy I have been trying to atone for it ever since . . . that
world of difference between the two Dukes, Somerset and York.

ZIRAKASHVILI

DAVIT ZIRAKASHVILI. Is there a rugby fan who doesn't like what the Georgian from the Auvergne represents? It's that soft spot we share for prop forwards. It's the shape, the chunk. So many of them short and cuddly, round, roly-poly but pure poison when required. But, by and large – very large – these men are the characters of the changing room. Halfway towards a 'cwch' (what you Welsh readers know to be a hug) they will suddenly decide to crush you. For a laugh. Like all ex-players, I can't get enough of them, bruised ribs and all. Zirakashvili's career has been as traditional as they come. Yet even traditions can change to some degree, or evolve. The latest tradition (is that a contradiction, or do all traditions have to start somewhere?) as far as props are concerned grapples with the rugby-mad country of Georgia. Georgians playing in France. Rugby replacing wrestling as the national sport of Joe Stalin's country. Zirakashvili himself a former wrestler. A nugget. Uncompromising. All but impossible to put on the floor.

The most famous rugby player in Georgia's history is Mamuka

Gorgodze. The lock/back row forward is a giant within the Georgian international game. A mountainous man. Man of the Match against the All Blacks in the 2015 World Cup. His face when the announcement was made . . . the crag cracked . . . another under the spell of that old black magic. Yes, mention Georgian rugby and most mention Gorgodze. But the Clermont Auvergne prop has a stronger claim to being the greatest of the Georgians. No one else from this rugby outpost has played in five French Top 14 finals. In 2017 he played his inevitably indomitable part as Clermont wore Toulon down for a second triumph in recent times, a third in their history, I think . . . more than fifty caps for his country too.

In the 2016/17 season, the Z man made a mess of Jack McGrath, the Ireland loose head who later toured New Zealand with the Lions. That was the Champions Cup semi-final. In the final Saracens stopped him adding a European Champions Cup medal to his two French titles. But not before he shoved the Lions loose head prop, Mako Vunipola, around the park. In the French final he lasted seventy-eight of the eighty minutes. Normal props last no longer than the hour mark. It is a gruelling game for the big men. But this bear of a man – more black bear than big brown – kept going. Big heart, big man, great Georgian. Controversial country, small state with the giant neighbour. The put-in. Pressure. Oppression. Not just politics. Rugby too. There has been a growing call to include them either in an enlarged Seven Nations or as a replacement for the Italian team. Such talk is nonsense. It misses the point. Like I missed the kick at goal against Bath. Sloppy thinking. The debate not a matter of Italy being relegated and Georgia promoted. A clever political ruse put out a few years back by none other than Conor O'Shea, the man in charge of Italy.

The question is whether there should be an opportunity for the newer nations to rise. Georgia is another name for Growth.

Italy for New Privilege. Tough call to make on an Italian team that was barred from the Five Nations until its master craftsman of a fly half, Diego Dominguez, began to age. Italy entered the tournament five years later than ideal and struggled to be competitive. Why the hell is Italy going to roll over and drop down a tier with all the negative financial implications of playing in the virtually anonymous FIRA second tier championship? One good reason . . . of all the teams in the Six Nations they should be most aware of the frustration of being deprived the opportunity to prove their merit. To develop against higher class international opposition. Crafty Conor painted the discussion as an attack on Little Italy . . . what made them want to come and blow you away? Italy finished sixth. Georgia were expected to ride roughshod in the second tier. It didn't work out that way in 2017. Romania beat them. Germany beat Romania. Seismic shocks I unforgivably failed to include in the chapter on upsets.

How about sixth in the Six Nations versus first in the second tier? The worst of the Six Nations against the winners of the other tournament. The upstarts would have to beat the sixth of the six. Nothing more demoralising than a Georgian or Romanian team automatically replacing an England or France team who are fifty points better than the best of the rest. No one wants that. But a few of us cry out for fairness. Italy is only central to the discussion because they finish bottom of the table most years. No one has it in for Italy, certainly not the committee men who worship their Six Nations jollies. Rome trumps Tbilisi every time.

If Tbilisi is a harrowing thought, what about Bucharest? Once the Paris of the east. Communism and Nicolae Ceauşescu stripped Romania's capital city of its former charms. Would the committees and the broadcasters want to show live rugby from this eastern outpost of 'civilisation'? Bucharest . . . on tour with England Under 23s. Touching down for a game near the Russian border. Armed guards, hostile borders all too obvious.

A bookshop in Bucharest, me the great bibliophile (in my own deluded mind). Thinking Bucharest had their own literary family, like the Brontes. The Ceauşescu family; ignorance and dictatorial bliss. Years later, Bath are playing Steaua Bucharest. The Romanian army team. Romanians knocking late into the night on Bath's hotel doors. Selling caviar. We laugh, luxuriating westerners wallowing in our blissful ignorance. We beat them at the Recreation Ground. And we drink with them, deep into the small hours. A sense of sorrow emanating from them through the drink. They try to tell us about their lives. We say drunken goodbyes to our caviar-selling friends, the army team. Months later there's the uprising. The captain of their team dies at a roadblock. Fighting against the dictator's frenzied attempts to cling on to power. We try not to think. Play the game. Play up. Near as most of us ever came to great events. Most of us have probably forgotten the match, the man, the name (I did). Easier to forget than dive into the murk of memories that flounder and fail. Flawed, fantastic, fabricated memories. Battered brain cells. All sorts of rising, risible excuses. We were boys in a man's world, Neither curious, nor truly brave. When staff are wiping down the bar at the Recreation Ground after another match who is left to think, even fleetingly, of our fallen – if brief – friends? His name IS Florica Murariu. He died at a roadblock. Honour demanded his naming and a break with the fact-free feel of the book. The revolution began in Timisoara where I had played years earlier . . .

Rugby union failed Romania and Italy in the amateur age. Now World Rugby has chosen to address the discrepancy between the haves and the have nots. The signal for the governing body's determination to act was the 2017 law change which increased a player's required length of residency in another country from three to five years, lengthening the international eligibility process. It was seen as an attempt to stop the calamitous fall out of players from countries like Fiji to ones like France. Agustin Pichot is involved, World Rugby's Che Guevara. Power to the people and not just the giants who bestride the sport. The ex-Argentine scrum half is part of an unlikely tag team. Bill Beaumont, an old-fashioned English lock forward the other half. It actually was and is a well-intentioned decision to extend the three-year qualification period and make nation-hopping harder. The problem is . . . the problem is so much more than predatory behaviour on the part of the larger traditional rugby nations. The game has not escaped globalisation. Fiji was once a distant world from France. The Euro had no part to play in the Pacific Islands. In an idealised world we would get rid of the goddamned missionaries and let the place return to its enchanted island status. Until the rising sea level makes even seven-a-side rugby impossible.

Now Fiji finds itself bound to France, or at least a little rugby part of the country. On the island of Viti Levu, Clermont Auvergne have linked up with the Nadroga Rugby Union to build and staff a school. The quid pro quo is a production line of astounding natural Fijian rugby talent. In return for general education. A few years ago, Nadroga local lad, Napolioni Nalaga, tore teams to pieces in the bright yellow colours of Clermont. In the 2017 French final, a newcomer exploded on the scene. Alivereti Raka. Kicked the goals. Scored the try. Saw the mountain men to the French title. Another Fijian winger and Nadroga man, becoming almost as common as Georgian props. Raka left Fiji to join the Clermont Academy. The link between an island in the South Pacific and isolated Auvergne rugby island in the middle of France works well for little country and big rugby club. It is natural enough for them to throw in their lot with France. As a former Clermont Fijian, Noa Nakaitaci, has successfully done. The pressing issue is not nationality as much as personal priorities.

All the tinkering with the laws won't change the fact that men want to provide for their families. That is an eternal and universal truth . . . or as near as we will venture to any blurred formulation of truth in these rough pages. The professional rugby world is spinning on its axis. The mega money of the French and English clubs is altering the balance of these priorities. If a kid, picked up in Fiji, treated royally in the Auvergne, offered more money than Fiji has to give, decides to concentrate on club over country who can blame him? It is a sad reality that the individual might not perform at the highest level for his country. Never play to the absolute peak of his abilities. But compared to sending those cheques home to mum and dad, what is the ego of the professional sportsman? Who cannot understand the yearning for financial security? But we love international sport. In England it is a sacred duty to do your bit for Queen and country.

Only it's not. It is your duty to do what you think is right for you and those around you. Fans think they have an insight into the players but the players don't ask to look into the souls of the accountants and businessmen who treat an international at Twickenham as that sacred experience. It's the money and the glory, as much as the national emblem. When I played rugby, we did it for ourselves, for the glory of the game, for – in my case – the chance to eradicate (or at least face) my fear of failure. Now money is at least equally important. If you are an impoverished Fijian it is more important than the wearing of the national shirt. Why should sportsmen be any different to the rest of us? Rugby has been a profession for over two decades now. A bloody good job but still a job. Come a World Cup, the media get their proverbial knickers twisted when the Fijian stars twinkle in France rather than the world stage, indignation the seething order of the day.

But let's press the pause button and think for a second . . . who pays their salary? The club. Who looks after the player and his family? The club. Who will foot the financial bill for the player's recovery if injured on international duty . . . maybe there is insurance but who pays the insurance? The club. And who loses out when the player returns from say, a World Cup or Lions tour physically and psychologically in bits? You guessed it. The clubs are indeed a threat to the international game. A grave threat. The five-year rule of residency doesn't properly address the problem because the point is the money pot more than the colour of the international shirt. Even should the game's governing body dip into its financial war chest it still does not face up to club versus country. At the moment the international game holds most of the cards but in France and England, where clubs are the prime employers, matters may not stay this way. England may attempt to centrally contract their elite players in the manner of Ireland, Wales (to a lesser extent), Australia, Scotland and – most of all – New Zealand, but this will only transpire if the domestic game heads into a financial tailspin. At the moment that looks unlikely. Not impossible but unlikely. Our grossly unequal society has plenty of millionaires ready and willing to buy a club and satisfy their egos.

We haven't even touched upon South African rugby, from where so many players are moving to France. Not to play Six Nations rugby but to escape what they perceive as the accelerating demise of their country. You don't have to be a racist to recognise things are not going so well under the African National Congress and its alliance with traditional white business interests. Money, security, lifestyle . . . the planet is on the move as climate change and economic imperialism creates mayhem. The world's best are tilting the rugby-playing axis as professionalism and politics combine to rewrite the way a player sees his place under the sun. Men like CJ Stander would have quit South Africa with or without the so-called Irish 'player project' scheme. Still, for all the complications untouched by the club versus country debate, surely the five-year residency ruling is an improvement on the current three year period? Probably it is.

But. Big but . . . what is the greatest shock in the history of international rugby? One hundred per cent right. Brighton, the 2015 World Cup. Japan beating South Africa. The Japanese captain was a Kiwi who plays for the Chiefs, Michael Leith. Eddie Jones spent plenty of time pre-World Cup explaining to the Japanese powers that be it was no insult to squeeze a few players from Polynesia into the team. The native dynamism would enable Japan to add the necessary muscle to the micro management of Jones. Eddie has a Japanese mother; he is a smart man, knows about the delicacies of nationalism but he had to tell it as it was. As England coach he benefits from the Tongan frames of the Vunipola brothers. Everyone wants a slice of the island culture. Chris Boyd, head coach of the 2016 Super Rugby champions, the Hurricanes, now of Northampton, reckons the Fijians are the best athletes, the Tongans the most dynamic. Quite where it leaves the Samoans I am not too sure. But let's agree these three countries have added an exotic element to the sport a million times in excess of either their population or economy. Auckland is the biggest Polynesian city on the planet. Islanders will follow family for the economic opportunities available in New Zealand. Young Tongans born and raised in New Zealand have every bit as much right to represent the land of their upbringing as the land of their fathers. This bloodline nationalism bit can get scary. Jonah was a Tongan Kiwi, Michael Jones a Samoan Kiwi. Both of them were unquestionably great All Blacks. Neither of them, no one of Polynesian stock, should be expected to choose any of these admittedly wonderful three rugby islands ahead of the fame, glory and, yes, money, that comes with being an All Black.

The islanders have played a crucial part in the flourishing of international rugby, the flowering of the modern game.

Not the headline act. But without their unique Caliban/Ariel combination, there is no Prospero. No main plot and too few tempests. Quick recollections: 1999 and Stephen Bachop, then both an All Black and a Samoan international. There were two tiers of Test teams, second tier Samoa beating top tier Wales. Fiji whooping it up in the 2007 World Cup in Nantes. Again Wales the victims, before frightening the future winners South Africa in the quarter-final in Marseilles. Take a Tardis back to 1971 and Fiji beat the Barbarians, largely the Lions under another name, in Gosforth, Newcastle. A few months before the historic series win in New Zealand. Tonga, the first international team I ever saw. At Rodney Parade, against Newport. The Welsh team won but the exotic Tongans filled my imagination for months. Or am I romanticising?

Tonga beating France; the same France who will scare New Zealand in the 2011 World Cup final. Without the islanders, much of the magic is missing. Much of the madness too. Never mundane. Crowds love them for their brutal tackle techniques (or they did until the game's authorities eventually got wise to the danger of those straight arms, those swinging arms, those spear tackles). Who forgets the first time they faced Samoa? My only time. The Hong Kong Sevens. Never was hit so hard or late as that day. The crowd laughed, the crowd, in their fancy dress, cheering and swilling as the islanders bashed the rest of us around. Ouch . . . sevens is threatening to surpass fifteens as the sport's global game. It demands less concentration from the fans. Less variety and intellect from the players. Sevens requires less structure.

The venerable traditions of forward play can be forgotten. What takes ages – as France found in the 1920s and Italy are discovering now – to inculcate in fifteen-a-side rugby can be picked up overnight in sevens. Kenya, Portugal, unknown rugby nations make their mark while Fiji can be the best in the world.

Sevens grabbing the spotlight? Think Olympics. World Rugby is playing a dangerous game. Its panting desire to become a regular part of the sleazy corporate jolly opens the way for sevens to eclipse fifteens and the World Cup. A World Cup without a fully committed Island Three, without the best of USA and Canada, without any emerging nations, is a regression. There is so much more to global competitions than merely the final, the winners. It has to be a pageant. A celebration. Sport as life. The Olympics, with its ridiculously over-the-top opening and closing ceremonies, sells itself as such. Wrapped up in insidious advertising. Dumbing down in its quest for popularity, I despise sevens for making me feel the grouchy old man I didn't believe I could be. Women's fifteens are threatening to go under the tsunami of Olympic sevens. The priority for the women became the Games as fifteen-a-side contracts were axed until reluctantly reintroduced in the autumn of 2018. The obsessive focus on the Olympics. Fifteens usurped by the one-dimensional cousin. Women's rugby lacks the history and tradition to see off sevens. A threat, not an opportunity. Some see it as an opportunity. Who says fifteens should stay top dog? An old sport, an old world.

This book began with my musing on New Zealand. Where better for it to end than back in the country that has defined my rugby dreams. Kiwi dominance has been timeless but beneath the surface much is changing. The Lions versus the All Blacks was as much a matter of advertising and brands as it was rugby. We are entering a period where professionalism must either stick with its fenced-in elite or twist and attempt to make the game as global as it can possibly be. World Rugby's idea of an annual international competition with promotion and relegation is an interesting step. A play-off between the bottom-placed team in the Six Nations and the top European 'newcomer' would reflect even better on the moral health of union's privileged old guard. To show the sport has a side to it which places performance on the field and the development of the new rugby nations on a par with the money-grabbing. The greed. The unspoken awfulness that is the hidden baggage behind professional sport. Does World Rugby accept the growing threat of Anglo-French financial clout? Does it try to find a way to plug the economic gap between being a Clermont player and/or a fantastic Fijian international? Is the new proposal a stand against Fiji fading from the global game only to reappear ever more as the All Blacks of sevens?

Rugby union is at a tipping point. It could be on the brink of calamity as club and country stealthily arm themselves for the sport's civil war that has been brewing for more than twenty years, since the game went professional. We are entering the next phase of rugby's still embryonic professional life – the global season. Men with chequebooks are either saviours or murderers of this maddest and, I think, most magnificent of sports. Old club committee men in blazers stand for the integrity of tradition or the faded and irrelevant history of what was once the sport of blazers. Somewhere, tiptoeing between chequebook and ubiquitous blazer, there's a narrow cliff edge path rugby needs to find. The future is frightening, the future is exciting, no absolute right or wrong. Like normal everyday life. What were Dylan's lines in *Desolation Row*? 'Everybody shouting which side are you on?' After summoning forty-five years of these sketchy memories, the grey pockets of foggy recollection, lurking in the mists between the foolish demand for black or white – I really don't know. But feelings, not facts, was the point of this book, if it ever had one.